KU-364-266

THE GARDENS OF BRITAIN 5

GENERAL EDITOR: John Sales, Gardens Adviser, National Trust

To omit a single duty for the
cultivation of a polyanthus
were ridiculous as well as
criminal, but to pass by the
beauties lavished before us
without observing them is no
less ingratitude than stupidity.

Vicesimus Knox (1752–1821)

THE GARDENS OF BRITAIN 5

Yorkshire and Humberside

Kenneth Lemmon

In association with the Royal Horticultural Society

B.T. Batsford Ltd, *London*

First published 1978

ISBN 0 7134 1743 9

Filmset in 'Monophoto' Photina by
Servis Filmsetting Ltd, Manchester
Printed in Great Britain by
Redwood-Burn Ltd, Trowbridge and Esher
for the publishers B.T. Batsford Ltd
4 Fitzhardinge Street, London W1H 0AH

Contents

List of Illustrations

(between pages 112 and 113)

List of Colour Plates

(between pages 64 and 65)

List of Garden Plans

Foreword and Acknowledgements

It is important that the reader realizes that the gardens dealt with in this book are those open to the public at some time or other during the year. There are, obviously, other gardens in Yorkshire and Humberside which are not mentioned.

Although I have used the most up-to-date information available to me on opening times and other details, these do vary from time to time and from year to year. To be sure of visiting the gardens when they are open I would draw readers' attention to the following annual publications which are on sale generally at bookstalls and bookshops or can be got from the several charitable organizations. These are:

Historic Houses, Castles, and Gardens in Great Britain and Ireland (ABC Historical Publications).

Gardens of England and Wales Open to the Public (the well-known 'Yellow Book' of the National Gardens Scheme).

The British Red Cross Society Open Gardens Guide.

Gardens to Visit (The Gardeners' Sunday Organization).

I would like to thank all the owners of gardens and their gardeners who welcomed me, and to hope that I have done justice to their lovingly cared for pleasances.

My thanks must also go to my four 'chaffeurs' and companions on my many gardening visits, Mr James Marsden, of Leeds, Mr Bill Robson, of Ripon, who also took photographs for me, Mr Fred Stubbs, of Crook and Mr Peter Helmsley, of York, Mr John Harvey, and to my wife and my daughter, Mrs Dian Gruszowski, for invaluable clerical help.

For their most valuable and expert assistance with the climatic and geological details of the county I would also thank Mr J. Webber, Regional Soil Scientist, and Mr J.D. Tyldesley, Principal Regional Meteorological Officer, of the Ministry of Agriculture. For his invaluable assistance with indexing my grateful thanks must go to Mr Bill Elgie.

For permission to use plans and photographs my thanks are due to Bramham Park Settled Estates, Castle Howard Estate Ltd, Borough of North Wolds, Newby Hall Estate, Mr Bill Robson, City of Sheffield Recreation Department, the late Colonel Sir Leonard Ropner, Bt, M.C., T.D., D.C., Earl of Harewood Estate, Mr and Mrs Douglas Ward, Northern Horticultural Society, and York Minster Library.

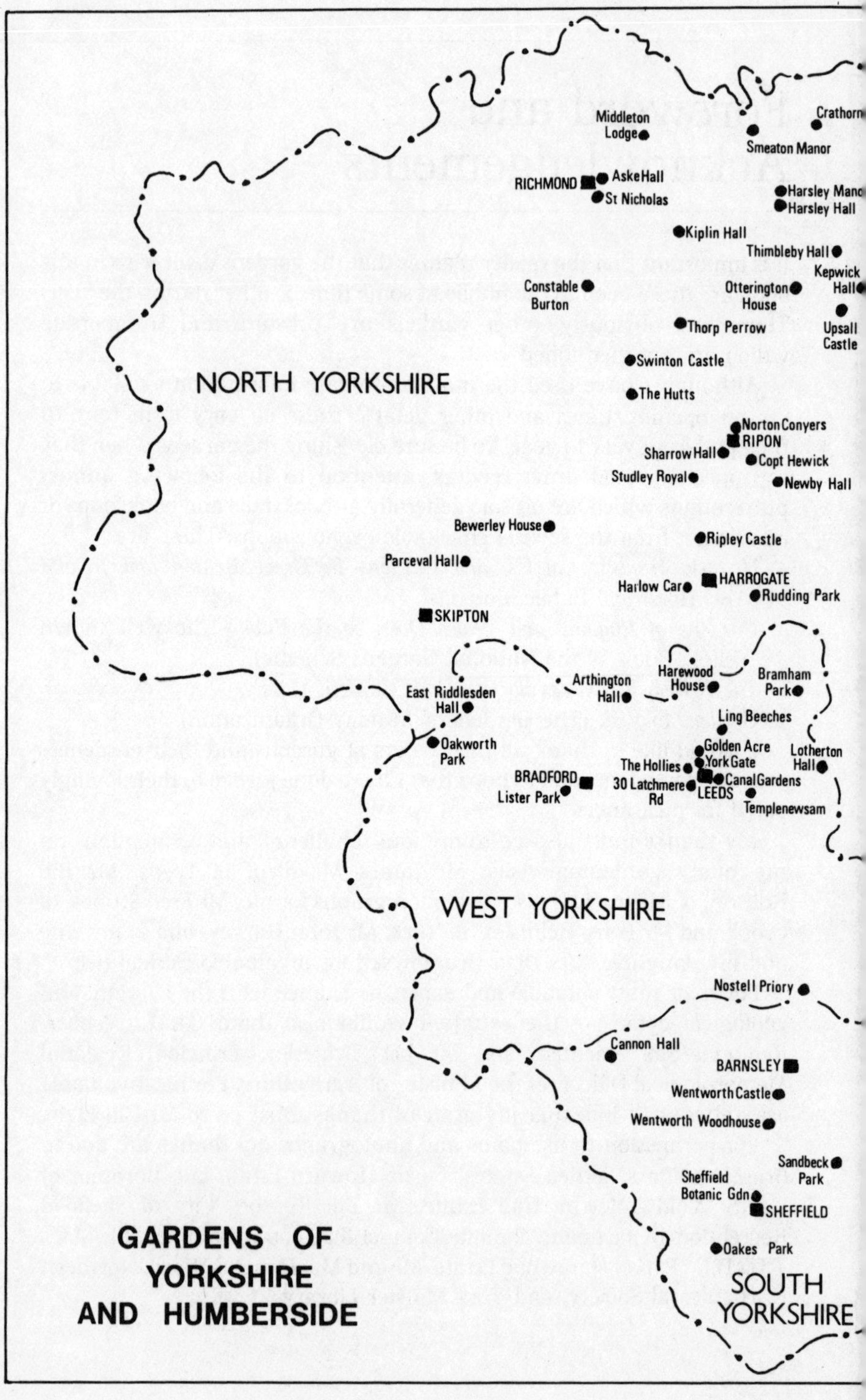

Middleton Lodge
Crathorn
Smeaton Manor
RICHMOND
Aske Hall
St Nicholas
Harsley Manc
Harsley Hall
Kiplin Hall
Thimbleby Hall
Kepwick Hall
Constable Burton
Otterington House
Upsall Castle
Thorp Perrow
Swinton Castle
NORTH YORKSHIRE
The Hutts
Norton Conyers
RIPON
Sharrow Hall
Copt Hewick
Studley Royal
Newby Hall
Bewerley House
Ripley Castle
Parceval Hall
HARROGATE
Harlow Car
Rudding Park
SKIPTON
Harewood House
Bramham Park
Arthington Hall
East Riddlesden Hall
Ling Beeches
Oakworth Park
Golden Acre
York Gate
The Hollies
Lotherton Hall
BRADFORD
30 Latchmere Rd
Canal Gardens
LEEDS
Lister Park
Templenewsam
WEST YORKSHIRE
Nostell Priory
Cannon Hall
BARNSLEY
Wentworth Castle
Wentworth Woodhouse
Sandbeck Park
Sheffield Botanic Gdn
SHEFFIELD
Oakes Park
SOUTH YORKSHIRE
GARDENS OF YORKSHIRE AND HUMBERSIDE

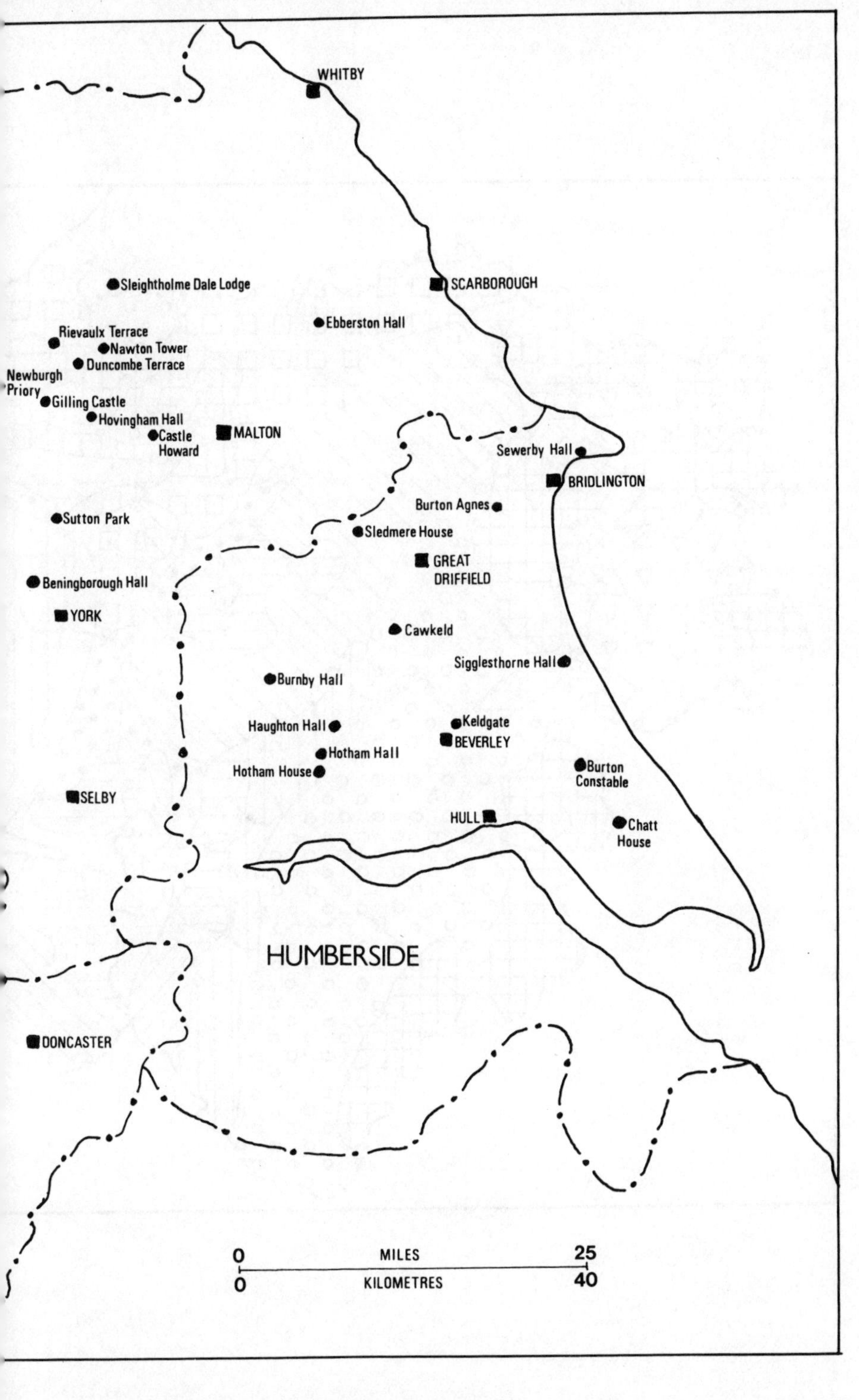
WHITBY
SCARBOROUGH
Sleightholme Dale Lodge
Ebberston Hall
Rievaulx Terrace
Nawton Tower
Duncombe Terrace
Newburgh Priory
Gilling Castle
Hovingham Hall
Castle Howard
MALTON
Sewerby Hall
BRIDLINGTON
Burton Agnes
Sutton Park
Sledmere House
GREAT DRIFFIELD
Beningborough Hall
YORK
Cawkeld
Sigglesthorne Hall
Burnby Hall
Haughton Hall
Keldgate
BEVERLEY
Hotham Hall
Hotham House
Burton Constable
SELBY
HULL
Chatt House
HUMBERSIDE
DONCASTER
0 MILES 25
0 KILOMETRES 40

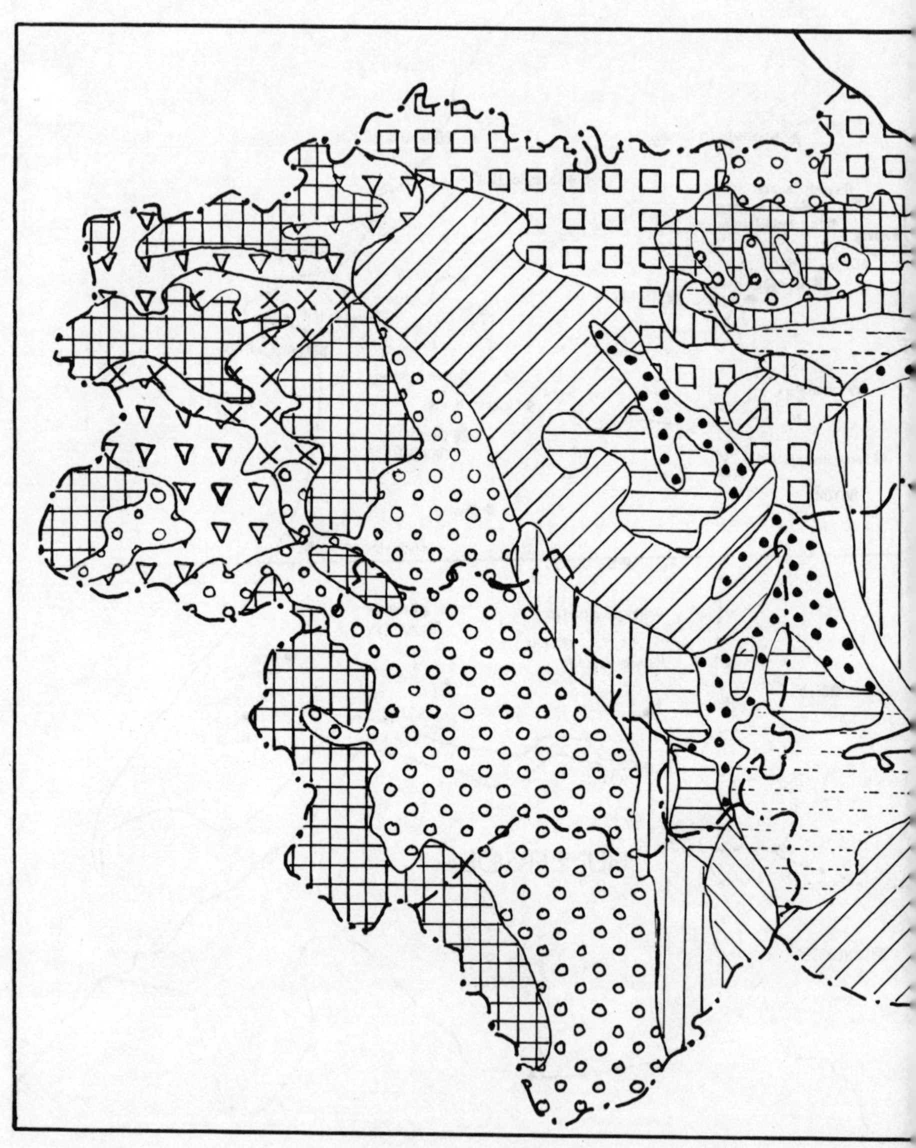

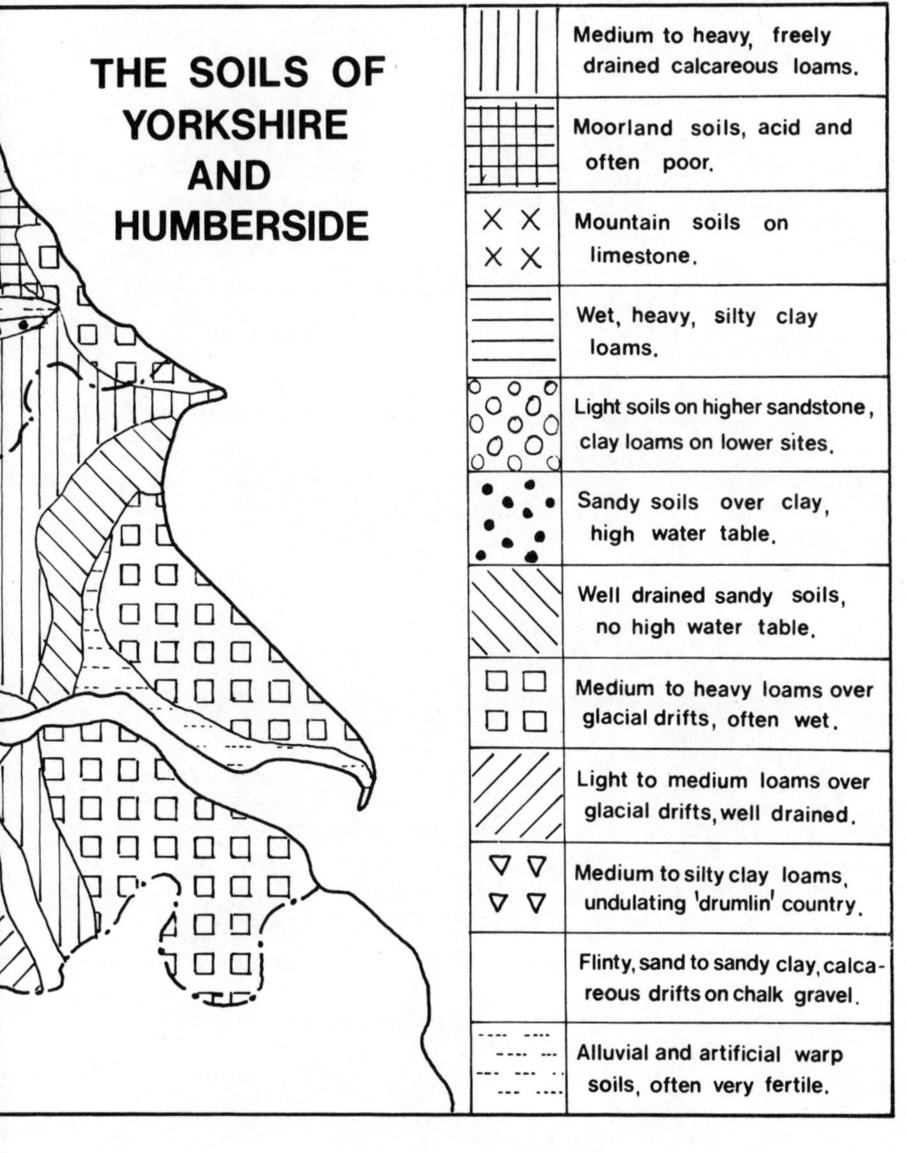
THE SOILS OF
YORKSHIRE
AND
HUMBERSIDE
Medium to heavy, freely drained calcareous loams.
Moorland soils, acid and often poor.
Mountain soils on limestone.
Wet, heavy, silty clay loams.
Light soils on higher sandstone, clay loams on lower sites.
Sandy soils over clay, high water table.
Well drained sandy soils, no high water table.
Medium to heavy loams over glacial drifts, often wet.
Light to medium loams over glacial drifts, well drained.
Medium to silty clay loams, undulating 'drumlin' country.
Flinty, sand to sandy clay, calcareous drifts on chalk gravel.
Alluvial and artificial warp soils, often very fertile.

A County Garden Survey Past and Present

Yorkshire with its three ridings – the thirdings or thridings of the Anglo-Saxons – is no longer that age-old entity so beloved by its natives, for it was taken from us by the philistines of Whitehall and is now defined as West Yorkshire, North Yorkshire, South Yorkshire and Humberside, the last taking in part of Lincolnshire, West Yorkshire losing part to Lancashire and North Yorkshire losing some territory to Cleveland.

It is still, however, the largest county in England and contains as great a variety of landscapes, soils, climates, geological differences, urban and rural scenes, as can be found anywhere in the country, comprising as it does wild moorland, rough Pennine heights, the infinite variety of the coastline, the long low Plain of York, the monotonous levels of the warp lands wrenched from marsh and sea and the geological glacier- and water-formed valleys and dales; and its teeming centres of population bearing all the scars of the Industrial Revolution. Yorkshire's scenic qualities may well be adduced from the fact that of the ten National Parks in the country the county embraces two, the Yorkshire Dales National Park 176,000 ha (680 sq miles), and the North Yorkshire Moors Park, 143,000 ha (553 sq miles), and includes also 17,400 ha (67 sq miles) of the Peak District National Park.

Climate, Geology and Soils

Climate

Climatically Yorkshire has wide variations, as one would expect from the contours, bearing in mind that temperatures decrease with height and rainfall increases. Indeed the rainfall range is very variable, from up to 1,780 mm (70 in.) a year on the Pennines down to between 610 and 690 mm (24 to 27 in) in the Plain of York and Holderness.

The county can conveniently be divided into four regions according to annual average rainfall; the Pennine country with an average of 1,780 mm (70 in.), the North Yorkshire Moors, 910 mm (36 in.), the Vale of York, 640 mm (25 in.) and the east coast, 660 mm (26 in.). Because of the conformation there are sometimes quite startling differences in rainfall between adjacent areas, so that, for example, while on the Pennine moors values of 1,780 mm (70 in.) are recorded, in the Aire Valley just below figures of 1,140 and 890 mm (45 and 35 in.) are recorded for townships like Haworth on the lower slopes and Bingley in the valley. Harrogate at 146 m (479 ft) records a yearly average of 790 mm (31 in.), Sheffield at 136 m (450 ft) records 1,020 mm (40 in.). The North Yorkshire Wolds figure exceeds 760 mm (30 in.), while the Howardian Hills, not much further north, record just below 760 mm (30 in.) on their crests. The Plain of York, the chief arable area of the county, has the lowest rainfall. October is normally the wettest month, with December not far behind, and April usually the driest.

On the lower ground of North Yorkshire (the old East Riding) snow, which is very variable from year to year, can be expected to lie from 17 to 20 days, while in the Ouse Valley 10 days is an average, increasing to 50 and more days in the high Pennines. The likelihood of snow lying increases by one day for each 15 m (50 ft) altitude above 60 m (200 ft) so that there are villages in the high Pennines and on the crests of the Wolds which may be cut off for days or weeks in winter by high drifting.

The threshold temperature which dictates the growing season, accepted as around 42°F. (6°C.) recorded in the standard screen, makes three weeks difference in the growing season between the county and the south of England and another three weeks difference between low and high ground within the county, so that spring is later and winter earlier, though, as will be realized, the earliness or lateness of the seasons does depend, not only on microclimates (which can work so much to the advantage of the gardener be they artificially contrived or natural) but also on aspect, soil texture and drainage, general exposure and the distance of the area from the coast, with the proviso that spring will be delayed about one day for each 9 m (30 ft) above sea level. Indeed a south-facing slope may have a growing season longer by 20 days than a level site in the same locality, while a north-facing slope can lose a gardener 20 days.

In sunshine hours the Yorkshire region is not so fortunate as southern England, York and Oxford values being 1342 and 1501 hours respectively, a difference of 159 hours. Yet Spurn Head enjoys a yearly average of 1481 and hence the number of Dutch glasshouse vegetable growers on Humberside. Winter light is generally poorer in the north than in the south.

Geology and soils

The soils of the county are very varied, a reflection of the range of rocks and drift deposits from which they are derived.

Thin well-drained calcareous soils occur on the Wolds, a curving ridge of chalk running from Flamborough Head on the coast to within a mile or so of the River Humber near Brough. Soils with similar characteristics but derived from magnesian limestone occur in a narrow belt running from Wetherby in the north to Worksop, while small areas are found along the northern edge of the Vale of Pickering. The mountain limestones of the Craven area give medium to silty clay loams, but except where they are very shallow the surface soils are often somewhat acid.

Between the Wolds and the sea, and over most of the Vale of York, north of York itself, the soils are derived from drifts left behind when the glaciers melted some 10–20,000 years ago. The soils vary from the freely drained sandy loams of the Thirsk area to clay loams in Cleveland, and include some of the best land in the country. Further south in the Vale of York and in the Vale of Pickering we have the remains of a shallow lake, often giving clay soils, but with sands deposited over the clay in many areas, producing the sandy soils with high water tables which are of such great agricultural value. Along the lower reaches of the Aire, Don, Ouse and Trent, as well as along the Humber to Spurn Point, there are warp soils. These are deposited by water ranging from sandy loam to silty clay loam in texture, usually well supplied with lime and giving fertile potato and sugar beet land.

To the west of the magnesian limestone we have the Pennines and their foothills. The foothills, including the lower reaches of the valleys of the Tees, Swale, Ure, Nidd and Wharfe, are mostly medium to heavy loams on mixed glacial deposits. Further south in the valleys of the Aire, Calder and Don, the soils are mainly heavy in texture over coal measures.

The high Pennines, with the exception of the limestone areas of Craven, have acid and often wet moorland soils, becoming peaty on the hilltops. The soils vary in texture, depending on whether the underlying rocks are shale, giving poorly drained clay loams, or sandstone, which gives sandy loams, often with better drainage.

The North Yorkshire Moors also often have acid soils, but these are frequently drier and heather-clad because of the lower rainfall and more porous grits from which they are mainly derived. Glacial drifts on the lower slopes give more fertile loams.

Yorkshire's Diversity

Helping to civilize the rugged Pennine and moorland scene, bringing variety to the uniformity of its levels and adding a cosmetic touch to the uncompromising, bleak ugliness of much of its industrial face, are Yorkshire's gardens – those torn from the moorlands, those taming its once wild valleys, those adding the grace of woodland and copse to rolling hill and vale, those where the putting down of Palladian and Italianate vanities on the landscape have created an elysium and those gardens bringing the beauty of flowers and greenery to its dark, satanic mill towns.

Here we must pause a moment in this introduction to the pleasures of Yorkshire gardens to define our terms. Gardens, in any context, must embrace the noble, dignified, far-ranging landscapes where the art concealing art of a Vanbrugh, a Kent, a Brown or a Repton has taken over mediocre features of land and turned them into scenes of 'natural' beauty. In these settings, such as Castle Howard, Harewood, Ripley and Studley Royal, the whole aim, the conception of the 'garden' was to form a perfect lord's eye view from the piano nobile windows of the big house of rolling landscape satisfying the aesthetic ideals of the time. So it is that *Gardens of Yorkshire and Humberside* will, nay must, include those seemingly interminable vistas down tree-lined avenues, over woodland and parkland to classical or Gothic architectural features at some vista end, and over wide, quiet water to the hemming edge of trees. Here the ancient meaning of a garden as a yard or enclosure loses all validity, yet these garden landscapes are creations of genius, blending nature to beauty, bringing an unseen and unsuspected orderliness to the landscape, creating that supreme eighteenth-century artistic export, the *jardin anglais*.

There are too, of course, the formal gardens, the gardens of flower beds, of roses and rhododendrons, of trees (the arboreta), and there are the informal rural and urban cottage gardens. We hope all these will take their place naturally and appropriately among the landscapes of the stately homes.

The County's Gardening History

Yorkshire, I have found, is always a surprise to gardeners from the south, who tend to equate our gardens with the former West Riding, its giant conurbations of population and the bewildering air- and earth-polluting variety of its industry. Yet the county as a whole has a long and honourable history of gardens and gardeners.

In written records we go back to Richard Shanne (1561–1627), of Methley, who left us one of the earliest plant lists. His gardening is recorded as early as 1573, his plant list being dated 1615. Shanne was a herbalist and in his orchards and garden he grew most of the old cottage garden flowers we know today, sweet williams, hollyhocks, primroses, snowdrops, golden rod, columbines, but it was said of him that his 'chefest delite was in plantinge all manner of herbes and trees and [he] had growing in his gardinge a great number of rare and strange plants, there was not allmost anie herbe growinge but he knowes the severall names thereof and the natural opperation of the same'.

I have a great fondness for William Lawson, that grand old Yorkshireman who, after 48 years of practical gardening, laid down his spade to write the first book on northern gardening and the first-ever garden book for women gardeners. His *New Orchard and Garden* (1615) and *Countrie Housewife's Garden* (1617) published together as they were, are called by that fine writer on horticultural subjects Eleanour Sinclair Rohde, one of the classics of English garden literature. Lawson himself she called 'the Isaac Walton' of garden writers. His writing is so warm and so dedicated to the simple delights of the garden, his love of the soil, of his fruit trees and plants, his joy in the singing of the birds and the humming of the bees that the reader seems to be with him in the garden. Lawson is also notable as being the first writer to give full details and a plan of the terraced Elizabethan garden.

The Rev. Walter Stonehouse, of Darfield near Barnsley in South Yorkshire, left a plant list, along with drawings of his rectory garden, dated 1640, and the list is the most complete English horticultural record of this early period. From 1640 to 1644 he kept a record of his gardening in which he gave some 866 different kinds of plants. Many of these were, it is agreed, of botanical interest only and many were brought in from the wild, but in his list were 14 species from Virginia, 5 from Guinea and 4 from New Zealand, including walnuts and maize, the earliest recorded from that part of the world. One might well wonder what has happened to our climate since those far-off times, for Parson Stonehouse could boast of peaches, apricots and pomegranates covering his west and north walls and a vine on his house wall. His 'best garden' was decorated with Elizabethan knots, and a long saffron garth brought revenue from the saffron crocus, then sold at £1 a pound for use in dyeing.

The Rev. William Mason (1725–97), a native of Hull and for many years a Yorkshire clergyman, has his place in garden history for his long poem 'The English Garden' (1772–81).

One of Yorkshire's most famous gardening sons was Thomas Johnson, the botanist, born at Selby, North Yorkshire, who died in 1664 of wounds he had suffered serving in the Civil War as a soldier in the Royalist cause. It is often claimed that Gerard's *Herbal* owed its long lived popularity and credence to Johnson's excellent editing and revision of 1633. He became an apothecary running a shop in Snow Hill, London, where he exhibited the first bananas ever to be seen in England, while his 'Flora of Kent' was one of the first of the English floras.

A great military figure in our history, General John Lambert, one of

Cromwell's generals, who was born at Carlton, near Shipton, in 1619, devoted his life after soldiering to gardening and at Wimbledon House, which he bought in 1651, had one of the finest collections in the country of tulips and gillyflowers. Later in Guernsey his collection of bulbous flowers was rare for the time.

It always gives me the greatest pleasure to boast that the oldest botanic garden in this country, the Oxford Botanic Gardens, established in 1621, was the result of a gift of £5,000 from a Yorkshireman, Henry Danvers, first Earl of Danby, a title taken from his North Yorkshire home. The estate of the Rectory of Kirkdale, also in North Yorkshire, at Lord Danby's death in 1644 was left for the upkeep of the garden.

Well known in garden history is the seventeenth-century garden of radiating tree avenues of Squire Kirke, of Cookridge Hall, Leeds, now alas a mass of housing estates. Here, on a hilltop woodland of 50 ha (120 acres), he laid out a 900 m (3,000 ft) long broad walk half-way along which was an oval clearing from which radiated 12 further broad walks each 6 m (20 ft) wide, 65 intersections in the walks giving long and beautiful views over the hills and moors of Baildon, Ilkley, Morley, the far West Riding Pennines and the Plain of York to the Wolds and the Hambleton Hills.

Although nothing is now known of the seventeenth-century gardens at Nun Appleton House, near York, they were the inspiration of one of the most famous poems in the language, 'The Garden' by Andrew Marvell, who was in the early 1650s tutor to Mary Fairfax, daughter of Lord Fairfax, the famous Parliamentary soldier who owned Nun Appleton. You may remember those oft-quoted lines from Marvell's poem:

Stumbling on melons, as I pass,
Insnar'd with flow'rs, I fall on grass.

Of the educated and distinguished coterie of seventeenth- and eighteenth-century botanists and gardeners whose interest and love of plants so greatly enriched our store of garden treasures and knowledge about them, the county can claim some distinguished sons. One of these is Dr Richard Richardson, a student of Oxford and Leiden universities who at his home, North Bierley Hall, Bradford, from 1663 to his death in 1741 was renowned for having one of the finest collections of native and foreign plants in the country. His correspondence embraced about every eighteenth-century naturalist of note in Europe. In the garden of Bierley Hall he planted in 1707 the first Cedar of Lebanon in the north of England, and one of the finest in the country; the stump is still there. It was a gift from Sir Hans Sloane. His grounds were famous for a miniature Stonehenge, now in a fallen state, a giant cave grotto, and one of the earliest flued-wall hothouses.

Another of those natural history 'scientists' of the eighteenth century was the Yorkshire Quaker Dr John Fothergill, who was born in 1712 at the tiny isolated hamlet of Carr End in Wensleydale and was apprenticed to Bartlett, a Bradford apothecary. In 1762, having built up a successful and lucrative London practice, he abandoned medicine to devote the rest of his life to plant study and to collecting plants from all parts of the world. Sir Joseph Banks considered that Fothergill's garden at Upton, West Ham, London, contained more scarce and valuable plants than any other garden in Europe. The tea tree (then *Camellia sinensis*) first flowered in England in this garden in 1774. The glasshouses held upwards of 3,400 species of exotics and in the open garden nearly 3,000 species of flowers and shrubs 'vied with the natives of Asia and Africa'. This Yorkshire doctor turned plantsman was one of the earliest growers of alpine plants and possibly the first to employ a collector in the Swiss Alps. He had agents (plant-hunters) in China, Hindustan, the East and West Indies, Siberia, North America and Mexico; in partnership with Sir Joseph Banks and Dr Pitcairn he commissioned William Brass to collect in West Africa; and through the Quaker gardener Peter Collinson he employed both John and William Bartram, pioneer plant collectors of North America.

Another Yorkshireman who stands out among this celebrated band of eighteenth-century naturalists and botanists and gardeners is Richard Anthony Salisbury (né Markham) born in Leeds in 1761. He too was among the founders of the Horticultural Society, and he was the Society's first Secretary proper. In his garden at Chapel Allerton, Leeds, which is not traceable today, he grew a fine and varied collection of plants both in the open and in his greenhouses, including plants from the Cape, Australia, the Falkland Isles and Honduras, and 154 different species of plants from the East Indies, which botanists came from all parts of the country to see. His other garden, which he moved to from Leeds in 1800, was the famous one of Philip Miller at Mill Hill, just outside London. His writings on horticulture form part of the canon of the early transactions of the Horticultural Society.

Following men like Salisbury in his enthusiasm and dedication to botanical study and his devotion to gardening and plants was the Rev. William Herbert, who gardened at Spofforth, near Harrogate, where he was rector from 1814 to 1840. His delight and pleasure was in bulbous plants, unusual crocus species, crinums and the amaryllis family, on which he wrote the standard work, *The Amaryllidaceae* (1837), graced with 48 of his own drawings, now a rare book and a costly one if ever it comes up for sale at the book auctions. He was a pioneer at Spofforth in the hybridization of plants, writing an important paper on 'Hybridization among Vegetables' in the RHS *Journal* for 1847. Dr Herbert, later Dean of Manchester, is claimed as being the first to hybridize rhododendrons.

There are a few more names which cannot be omitted from any list of Yorkshire botanists, gardeners and plant-hunters. George Caley, son of a Cravendale, Yorkshire, horse-dealer (1770–1829) was one of the first collectors sent out by Sir Joseph Banks to Australia. He travelled on the first ship to take convict women to Botany Bay, sent many plants home and did much travelling in the then unexplored hinterland of what is now Sydney. Henry Shaw, of Sheffield, emigrated to America, made a fortune selling knives and turned to gardening, leaving his garden and greenhouses with a legacy to form the now well known Missouri Botanical Gardens.

Finally, we must never forget that when Sir Henry Goodrich, in Rouen in 1707, tasted an apple he liked, he sent the pips home and established the famous Ribston Pippin, called after the family home, Ribston Hall, near Wetherby. The tree flourished, famous in horticultural history for its great age, until 1835 when it was blown down in a gale. A shoot from the old tree survived, however, until it too was blown down in 1928.

The Professionals

Yorkshire, like Scotland, has always bred skilled professional gardeners, among them William Mudd, of Bedale, North Yorkshire, who became one of the early curators of the Oxford Botanic Gardens, and George Nicholson, who was curator at Kew from 1886 to 1902 and published the eight volume *Illustrated Dictionary of Gardening*, still a well thumbed work.

James Theodore Bent (1852–97) of Baildon, West Yorkshire, was a plant-hunter for Kew in Arabia Felix, in Nubia and Socotra. An early curator of the Royal Botanical Society's gardens in Regent's Park, London, was Daniel Cooper (1817(?)–42) of Leeds, who also wrote *Flora Metropolitana* (1836).

If only for his enthusiastic and colourful travel books, Reginald Farrer must be known to many. Farrer, who was born at Clapham in the midst of the limestone fells in 1880, was a noted alpinist and plant-hunter in China and Burma, sending us many favourite plants including *Viburnum farreri (fragrans)*, *Rosa farreri* and *Clematis macropetala*. His books *The English Rock Garden*, *On The Eaves of the World* and *The Rainbow Bridge* are classics of their genre.

The Backhouse family, of the famous Victorian nurseries at York, were well to the fore in bringing rock and alpine gardening to this country. James Backhouse as a Quaker missionary in 1831 travelled in Australia, Mauritius and South Africa, sending his plants and seeds home to his brother and partner Thomas who, in 1816, had taken over the ancient nursery business of Telford. Later James visited Norway, penetrating almost to the Arctic Circle.

Richard Spruce (1817–93), who was born on the Castle Howard estate, near York, was one of the most respected and notable of the botanists and travellers in South America and the Amazon. His detailed and meticulous work on the rubber yielding genera *Hevea* and the *Cinchona* (the source of quinine) over 15 years did much to bring a scientific application to the culture of such economic and important crops.

We conclude this list of Yorkshire gardeners and botanists with the name of William Bateson of Whitby, a noted biologist who brought the applications of Mendel's laws of heredity into the practical work of plant breeding in England, and whose work, from 1920 to his death, as the first director of the John Innes Horticultural Institute (the creators later of the much used J.I. composts) was a leading factor and inspiration in the work on improved breeding methods for both plants and animals.

And one wonders how the subsequent career of Sir Joseph Banks, that creator of Kew and archetypal figure of plant-hunting history, might have gone without his round-the-world experiences on *Endeavour* with Captain James Cook, circumnavigator and cartographer extraordinary, who was born at the village of Marton in Yorkshire and learned his seafaring trade at Whitby.

Yorkshire and the Trade

Most readers of garden history, having come across so many mentions of the southern-based nurseries of London and Wise, James Lee, Thomas Fairchild, James Gordon, Colville, and Loddiges in the seventeenth, eighteenth and early nineteenth centuries, might well have reached the conclusion that all nursery stock was raised in London or the London area. Thanks to the painstaking researches of John Harvey, whose book *Early Nurserymen* bears testimony to his labours, we now know that there were many nurseries almost as influential and extensive in the north and quite a few in Yorkshire, with the ancient city of York being a principal centre. The oldest was that of the Telford family, established on the site of the old monks' garden of the Dominican friary there and recorded as early as 1666. John and George Telford are notable for producing, in 1755, what seems to be the first catalogue of nursery stock to be priced throughout, and for supplying young forest trees and hardy shrubs to many of the landed gentry of the north who in the eighteenth century were creating their great gardens. Known for his splendid vegetables was Thomas Rigg (1746–1835), whose nursery at York Mr Harvey describes as 'having achieved national fame as the source of the best seed of early York Cabbage'. In North Yorkshire, in 1760, Christopher Thompson began a nursery at Pickhill, between Thirsk and Bedale, where he supplied forest and orchard trees, shrubs and flower seeds until around 1849.

At Pontefract, hard by the ancient castle, another famous family nursery was established by John Perfect very early in the 1700s. Perfect's nursery supplied forest and ornamental trees, shrubs, roses, (13 kinds) and orchard stock; by a bill of 1717 it can be seen that the nursery was supplying John Aislabie with many of the trees for his plantings at Studley Royal.

Barnes and Callender, who are recorded as having a shop in Park Row, Leeds, in 1717, were supplying sweet pea seeds to Edwin Lascelles at Harewood House in 1782. Thomas Barnes later (1758–9) published *A New Method of Propagating Fruit Trees and Flowering Shrubs*.

William Pontey (*fl.* 1782–1831), who had quite an extensive nursery at Kirkheaton, Huddersfield, was an expert on trees, being described by a contemporary as 'the Evelyn of the nineteenth century' and published *The Profitable Planter* (1800), *The Forest Pruner* (1805) and *The Rural Improver* (1823).

At Handsworth in Sheffield a nursery founded by John Littlewood before 1779 became notable for its raising of rhododendrons and hollies after Fisher, Holmes and Co. had taken over on Littlewood's death in 1825. According to Mr Harvey they were among the first to receive *Fuchsia magellanica globosa*, one of the first hardy fuchsias. They were known also for their fine collection of rhododendrons including the popular 'Handsworth White' and 'H. Scarlet', as well as a good variegated holly which goes under the nursery name. It was said of them that many of the cemeteries of America were planted with shrubs from Handsworth.

John Barratt, of Wakefield, who started out in 1796 as a market gardener and the owner of a florist's shop in the city, later branched out into the growing of forest and fruit trees and greenhouse plants in pots. His son William in 1833 was reputed to be carrying the largest collection of fuchsias in the trade and also had on offer 170 varieties of pansies and many calceolarias. He was reporting in 1834 on his experience of growing *Erythrina crista-galli* in the open and he bred one of the earliest of the improved strains of *Ribes sanguineum*, known then as *R. coccinea*.

A figure of some note in the Victorian northern carnation fancy was Benjamin Ely, of Rothwell near Leeds, who from his nursery grounds sold carnations to the then hundreds of specialist florists, his 'Dr Horner' picotee being sold at 7*s*.6*d*. for two in 1869.

Orchids have been bred and sold in Yorkshire for well over 100 years at the Crag Wood Nurseries of Mansell and Hatcher, at Apperley Bridge near Leeds. Although no exact date has been given for the start of the nurseries, which are so unusually situated on the steep slope of a wooded hillside overlooking the valley of the Aire, it is known that J.W. Moore Ltd were selling orchids there in the 1890s. But Lady Amherst in her *A History of Gardening in England* states that one of the earliest orchids ever to reach this country was grown on this site. It was the species orchid from China, *Phaius grandiflora*, sent by Dr Fothergill in 1778 to his niece Mrs Hind, at Apperley Bridge, Yorkshire, where it flourished in her stove house (i.e., heated glasshouse).

Historic Gardens

Although the county with its northern climate might seem an inhospitable setting for the making of great gardens, down the centuries owners and garden designers have moved villages, levelled hills, made 'mountains', excavated great lakes, planted woodlands and stately avenues, to bring seemliness and adornment to this county of the broad acres.

Thus the historic gardens in Yorkshire are many and varied, from the early topiary work at Wrestle Castle in Humberside, mentioned by John Leland in his *Itinerary* of 1534–45, to the creation some 20 years ago of probably the last large-scale garden, the trial and ornamental gardens of the Northern Horticultural Society at Harlow Car, Harrogate.

But let us first look at Leland's garden survey of the county in those early days. At Wrestle Castle he wrote of 'a mounte opere topiaro writhen about in degrees like turnings of cokilshells to come to the top without payne', his description of topiary worked low hedges edging the path of a spiral walk to the top of a mound in the orchard there. At Ulleskelf on the Wharfe near York, the King's Antiquary cited, on prebendary land 'at Uskelle village about a mile from Tewton, is a goodly orchard with walks opere topiaro', and of the De la Pole mansion at Hull, Leland wrote, 'lyke a palace with a goodly orchard and garden at large, enclosed with brike'.

Some of the greatest landscape conceptions, many unique, such as the formal Italianate water gardens of Ebberston Hall near Scarborough, the classical elysium of Castle Howard, the canals and pools of Studley Royal, the 'Versailles' of Bramham Park, the ruined Gothic castle of Wentworth Castle grounds and the terraces and vistas of Duncombe and Rievaulx, were among the earliest of their kind in the country.

Almost all the great names in gardening history, architects, landscape designers and just garden makers have set their individual seal on Yorkshire gardening, so that examples of the work, genius and character of Bridgeman, Switzer, London, Vanbrugh, Lord Burlington, Kent, Van Nost, Hawksmoor, Campbell, Payne, Brown and Repton may be seen and appreciated.

It should be remembered that although Kent's work was largely outside the county both he and his life-long patron Lord Burlington were of Yorkshire stock. Kent was born at Bridlington and apprenticed to a Hull carriage painter before going on to greater things. Even his first professional experience of painting and architecture in Italy was made possible by the patronage and financial aid of a group of Yorkshire landed gentry headed by Thomas Wentworth of South Yorkshire. Kent's 'father in the arts' was Richard Boyle, third Earl of Burlington and the scion of a notable East Riding landowning family and Lord Lieutenant of this riding. Nor must we forget that Lancelot ('Capability') Brown's first real experience of garden design came while he worked under Kent at Stowe.

Conclusions

In their gardening Yorkshiremen are fortunate in that their roses last longer and have enhanced colourings in the northern climate, and that the great family of primulas from Eastern lands finds Yorkshire conditions very much to its taste, so that stream- and lake-sides in the county's gardens, large and small, are bright in their season with the flambeaux of candelabra primulas. Trees, including conifers, grow well, as witnessed by such woodland estates as Harewood, Thorp Perrow, Hovingham and the blanketing of many of the vales and hills of the North Yorkshire Moors with varieties of the *coniferae*, including Sitka and Norway Spruce, Corsican Pine, Japanese and European Larch, the Scots and Lodgepole Pines, Douglas Fir, Western Red Cedar, Lawson's Cypress and Western Hemlock. Rhododendrons in the acid peat soils of reclaimed moorland or ancient dried-up lake floors are happy and show it by their profuse flowering in so many county gardens. The tiny ground-snuggling inhabitants of the mountainous regions of the world transplant well to the many alpine and rock gardens and heather burgeons on the wet acid soils.

In conclusion it would be true to say that the many beautiful and varied gardens in Yorkshire and Humberside provide the garden lover with an almost complete picture of the English garden from cottage to castle and through its many superb landscapes, of the artistic and aesthetic evolution of the *jardin anglais*.

Humberside

Gardening on the Flat Lands

Burnby Hall Garden

Stewart's Burnby Hall Gardens and Museum Trust

On outskirts of Pocklington 21 km (13 miles) E of York on B1247. Open April to September Monday to Friday 10 am–7 pm, Saturdays and Sundays 2–7 pm. Free car park; teas available in grounds; dogs allowed. An unusual water garden created by the late Major P.M. Stewart, a great world traveller, who gave the garden and his collection of exotic fish, game and ethnic objects to Pocklington on his death in 1962; this is now housed in a museum in the garden, open Easter to end of May Saturdays and Sundays 2–5 pm, May Bank Holiday to end of August every day. Situated 35 m (120 ft) above sea level on post-glacial sands subject to severe drying out. Sheltered to S and E. Average annual rainfall 640 mm (25 in.). Staff of two.

Burnby Hall has one of the largest collections of water lilies in Europe – some 5,000 plants in 60 different varieties, which may be seen in bloom from May until October, the main display being from late June until mid-September. Early plantings totalled some 90 species of *Nymphaea*, of which 30 would not stand up to the Yorkshire climate, leaving those that grow and flower well, a good pointer for northern choice.

From two ploughed fields Major Stewart constructed in 1904 two large ponds, at first for his own private fishing and swimming; in 1935 they were converted to the planting of lilies. The two ponds, the upper one of 0.6 ha (1½ acres), 180 m (600 ft) long and 60 m (200 ft) at its widest, the lower one 0.2 ha (½ acre) and 3 m (10 ft) below the upper one, 100 m (330 ft) long and 30 m (90 ft) at its widest, are connected by a stream 60 m (200 ft) long running through a rockery where small cascades break the gentle flow. Each pond contains an oval island planted with water-loving marginals. The pathways round the ponds are undulating, in places giving long views to the Yorkshire Wolds, and are planted with a varied collection of shrubs and trees – the Indian Horse Chestnut, *Aesculus indica*, a *Ginkgo biloba*, brooms, tamarisks, dogwoods – and a generous planting of 58 differing varieties of bog and waterside plants. Here can be seen *Acorus calamus*, the yellow flowering Sweet Flag, many species of *Aponogeton*, including *A. distachyus*, the Water Hawthorn, *Alisma plantago-aquatica*, the Water Plantain, a variety of single and double *Caltha*, the Marsh Marigold, a host or irises and musks, *Myosotis palustris*, the Water Forget-me-not, Arum Lilies, a tremendous number of species of *Primula*, rushes (*Scirpus*), all manner of ornamental grasses and hostas. In the water are hundreds of golden carp, orf and shubunkins tame enough to come to the surface for titbits, while moor hens and dabchicks are swimming around, and kingfishers are diving for the fireflies and smaller fish.

The lilies in all their waxed petalled, sumptious splendour range in colour from pure white through all shades of red, pink, crimson to deep yellow. There are nupheas and nymphaeas too numerous to mention by name, but do go and see them when '500 bloom every day in July', as Major Stewart used to say. There are many of the species and even more of the hybrids. It can truthfully be said that the planting leaves unrepresented very few of those to be found in an up-to-date catalogue of water lilies, so that at Burnby we have an illustrated, living catalogue of the genus.

Burton Agnes Hall

Marcus Wickham-Boynton Esq

In the village of Burton Agnes, 10 km (6 miles) SW of Bridlington on A166 Bridlington-Driffield road. Open May to 15 October every afternoon except Saturday. Light refreshments available; dogs allowed on lead. Elizabethan house open: antique furniture, carved ceilings, Oriental china and the largest private collection in the north of England of French Impressionist and modern paintings. A restrained but pleasant formal garden with woodland walks, situated 55 m (180 ft) above sea level on light chalky soil. Average annual rainfall 640 mm (25 in.).

Entered under the arch of a handsome early Jacobean gatehouse (dated 1610), the wide drive running through the forecourt is edged with a long line of ball-shaped yews. At least a hundred can be counted on the south and east side of the hall, a dignified and aesthetically satisfying approach to the main south front and its graceful red brick relieved by stone plinths, mullions, quoins and carved decorative work. This forecourt is a relic of the contemporary formal gardens swept away by Brown in the eighteenth century. Midway the drive is cut by two sidewalks lined with cut yews, one to the right leading to a path by the kitchen garden wall where taller square-cut yews form the backcloth.

To the east of the house looking over the flat pastoral farmlands there is again a large expanse of lawn lined with cut yews and ending in a vista-terminating fountain where tall angular cut yews form the background to a group of statuary and a lily and fish pool on two levels, kept fresh by water from a central Neptune and from the feet of the figures of a gardener and his wife. There are contemporary bronze statues on these lawns.

To take the eye to the west of the lawn a path leads through a woodland avenue to the countryside beyond, up several stone steps to where a filigree ironwork circular temple stands. To either side of this walk are woodland paths where under the beech, oak and sycamore has been planted interesting ground cover: *Iris foetidissima*, hostas, daffodils, bergenias, *Alchemilla, Epimedium, Polygonum, Brunnera, Vinca*, astilbes and ferns.

In pleasing contrast to the quiet serenity of clipped yew and green lawns the borders to the woodland screen have been planted with a mixture of flowering shrubs and herbaceous material – Cotton Lavender, the graceful low-growing *Genista lydia*, the purple leaved berberis, sweet smelling, early blooming *Viburnum* × *carlcephalum*, the evergreen large leafed *V.* × *rhydophylloides*, lilacs, *Escallonia, Euonymus*, lavender, *Cornus alba* 'Sibirica', *Senecio*, delphiniums, *Skimmia, Acer pseudoplatanus* 'Brilliantissimum', *Philadelphus* and *Cistus*, both red *C.* × *purpureus* and white *C. albus* 'Elma', which do well in this chalky soil. A central seat alcove is backed by gold pyramidal conifers and hydrangeas, breaking the line of the border. To the left bright green foliaged *Griselinia littoralis, Pyracantha* and the rose 'Grootendorst' form the background.

From the top of the south front garden we find our way into the extensive walled enclosure neatly lined out with vegetables and fruit, but see first, running down from the entrance, a long blue herbaceous border in which delphiniums, irises and geraniums predominate among *Helenium*, asphodel, veronicas, *Euphorbia polychroma* (*epithymoides*), multicoloured lupins and fine red *Cistus*. The wall at the entrance, next to the long greenhouses, is filled with two floriferous climbing roses, 'Casino' and 'Golden Showers'.

Burton Constable

J. Chichester Constable Esq

At Burton Constable, 11 km (7 miles) NE of Hull on A165. Open from Spring Bank Holiday to end of September, Tuesdays, Wednesdays, Thursdays, Saturdays, Sundays and Bank Holidays 12–6 pm. Teas and meals available. Elizabethan house of 1570 open, with interior decoration by Robert Adam, Wyatt and Lightoller. 80 ha (200 acre) parkland estate and formal landscape, situated 20 m (66 ft) above sea level on medium loam. Average annual rainfall 610 mm (24 in.).

The landscape to this fine Elizabethan house is by Brown, and there is correspondence with Brown on this. His plans (1774) for the south courtyard and the grounds, for Mr William Constable, were carried out with the existing ha-ha for the front lawns, and Brown's characteristic clumping and screening are still to be seen. The 1.6 ha (4 acres) of lawns and gardens round the house are simple in layout to emphasize the brick and stone patterning of mullions and transoms, the battlemented towers and the overall symmetry.

To the front of the house the extensive lawns, terminated by the ha-ha, are divided by a wide gravelled walk between tall and ancient clipped yews, leading the eye up a gently sloping avenue of greensward to the far statue of a stag on a stone plinth. Crumbling classical statuary dots the lawns and their perimeters.

A long walk extending from the house front, edged with roses in the border and on the back of the courtyard wall, leads to the 1780 orangery. This is a most pleasing building, seven-bayed with arched windows, a curved roof and a parapet decorated with urns and statues. The path by the front of the orangery leads directly into the large courtyard at the side of the house, where the long brick wall provides shelter for a herbaceous border full of tall *Rudbeckia, Echinops, Eryngium* and *Phlox*.

The 9 ha (22 acres) of lakes used for boating and fishing are not visible from the house.

There are other diversions at Burton Constable as well as the garden – a model railway, aviaries, a farm machinery and miniature figure museum, and a children's playground.

Cawkeld

Mr and Mrs B. Flint

At Cawkeld, Kilnwick, lying off A164 Beverley-Driffield road. Open occasionally for charity. An unusual farmhouse garden, situated some 15m (50ft) above sea level on clayey soil over limestone. Average annual rainfall 640mm (25in.). Staff of one with help.

Unusual to find in this flat, featureless 'East Riding' countryside is this lovely old brick-built farmhouse framed by strikingly coloured beds of large flowered begonias, large ornamental pond and undulating lawns. Lawns and rose beds fan out from the gravel paths around the house and its small paved sitting-out places. From one of these on the east side of the house is seen the roughly oval pond, fed by natural springs, with a central island of grass and habited by wildfowl.

Woodland, underplanted with rhododendrons and with graceful willows at its edge, screens the pond and shelters the garden from the east. A path through this woodland shines with the gold of daffodils in spring and by it the pond runs in a series of cascades into a wild piece of scrub woodland, small ponds and water courses, the haunt of many moisture-loving wild flowers in their seasons.

There is a pergola arch covered in *Clematis montana* over the path leading from the house down the gently sloping lawns to the kitchen, ornamental gardens and an orchard where two large tubs filled with fiery red salvia somehow complement the strident screech of peacocks nearby.

Following this path towards the edge of the pond a small shrubbery edged with *Buddleia alternifolia*, that 'waterfall of blue' as Farrer called it, provides both a screen and a 'pocket' for a quiet lawn, flower beds and a seat.

Chatt House

Mr and Mrs Tom Harrison

At Burton Pidsea to N of B1362 Hedon-Withernsea road. Open occasionally for charity or by appointment. Dogs allowed on lead. This charming pleasance of some 1.4 ha ($3\frac{1}{2}$ acres) on the flat lands of Holderness was landscaped in 1959 by the late George Taylor, landscape gardener and well known contributor to *Country Life*. Situated 8 m (25 ft) above sea level on alluvial soil over boulder clay. Average annual rainfall 610 mm (24 in.). Staff of two and occasional help.

On the rich lands of Holderness, in the middle of the Spurn Peninsula, Chatt House garden is full of interesting plantings and features, a most successful essay in the art of landscaping a completely flat area.

In the area of the old kitchen garden, surrounded by warm red brick walling, is a bathing pool, and all around the walls are aglow with the roses 'Nevada', 'Frühlingsmorgen', 'Frühlingsgold', 'Penelope', 'Perle d'Or', *Rosa chinensis*, 'Albertine', 'Elmshorn', *R. moyesii* 'Geranium', 'Fritz Nobis', *R. rubrifolia* and 'Daisy Hill', all making a beautiful picture in their varying colours and forms. To front this clash of colour and to give a cooler, more sober effect, the borders around are planted with the greys, blues and light greens of *Senecio*, bergenias, rue and *Rhus*.

Separating the bathing pool lawn from the rest of the garden is a brick-pillared and wooden roofed pergola covered with vines (the small grapes are used for wine). Intertwined with the splendid foliage and hanging fruit of the vine are honeysuckles, clematis and the more vigorous climbing roses such as 'Mermaid', 'Etoile de Hollande', 'Caroline Testout', 'Paul's Scarlet' and 'Albertine' and large leafed ivy.

The view from the pergola is through the iron grill of a gate to the countryside beyond, and housewards to a stone-flagged low-walled patio by French windows. The scene here is impressively curtained by the wall-hugging 9 m (30 ft) high giant foliage of an *Aristolochia*, grown from seed, which bears its 'Dutchman's Pipe' flowers each year in profusion. There are wisterias, *Clematis* in variety, *Ribes speciosum* and, growing happily in beds in the paving, *Phygelius capensis*, the Cape Figwort.

The lawn cut through by the pergola is bounded by a formally clipped yew hedge through an opening in which more lawns are reached, cut off from a view of the house by another yew hedge, apsidal in shape. The design here has been skilfully arranged to give, over the planned heights of the hedges and pergola, an ascending view of the rose filled 'kitchen garden' wall. At the rear of the second yew hedge and apse the lawns were planted some 18 years ago with a careful selection of specimen trees – the pyramidal hornbeam *Carpinus betulus* 'Fastigiata', *Cercidiphyllum japonicum* with its almost circular leaves for autumn colour and, curious to see in their young stage after having seen them more often in their gigantic maturity, young Wellingtonias some 1.8–2.1 m (6–7 ft) high. *Cedrus atlantica glauca* is growing away very well indeed, as is a *Metasequoia glyptostroboides*.

The lawn by these trees leads to two ponds divided by stepping stones, one almost round, the other square, the banks of which in spring are smothered in colour from a generous planting of bulbs and polyanthus. Pond-side planting is with the yellow flag iris and the dark blue *Iris sibirica*.

A conifer hedge separates a tennis court from the lawns and from view, a raised gravel path by its side being planted with *Phlomis*, lilies, many roses including 'Maiden's Blush', *R. willmottiae*, the spectacular thorned *R. omeiensis pteracantha* and, giving contrast in colour and height, *Thuja plicata* 'Aurea'. On the far side of the tennis court another border backed by a beech hedge, again serving to restrict any overall picture, flaunts the giant silver leafed thistle *Onopordon acanthium* and tall cream flowered *Phlomis*.

Overlooking this area is a small paved semicircular garden carpeted with thymes and containing a bed of the newer dwarf irises in a colourful selection. The pineapple-scented broom *Cytisus battandieri* and a young *Ginkgo biloba* act as sentinel features.

Seen from the windows at the front of the house and at the rear of the beech hedged tennis court is a formal yew hedged lawn with the apse forming a green setting for a piece of modern metal statuary. Four cherries have been planted at the other side of the apse to blossom over the hedge top in spring, with most pleasing effect.

Hotham Hall

Mr and Mrs G.R. Odey

In the same valley as Hotham House and quite near A1034 Market Weighton-South Cave road. Open occasionally for charity during the year. A small formal garden and parkland, situated 30 m (100 ft) above sea level. Average annual rainfall 610 mm (24 in.). Staff of one.

This garden is notable for magnificent specimens of the Copper Beech. Screened by a thick yew hedge, the front lawn to the house is interestingly filled with herbaceous island beds planted with an eye to colour to be seen from the windows. Beyond is a large sunken lily tank rimmed with hostas, iris, bulbs and hebes. Adjacent is a tastefully planted gold, grey and silver garden in which the effect comes from hebes, Cotton Lavender, *Senecio, Elaeagnus*, golden foliaged marjoram, *Chamaecyparis lawsoniana* 'Stewartii' and the golden Mock Orange. To the right of this garden, appropriately under a Weeping Ash, is the resting place of the household pets, the dogs and cats of the family, each with its tiny memorial plaque.

Beyond the yew hedge to the left of the lily tank is a secluded swimming pool with a rustic dressing room at the far end, with *Agapanthus* and green foliaged plants in tubs on the patio paving. Landscaped some 200 years ago, the neutral beck to the east of the garden was formed into a series of ponds.

Hotham House

Colonel and Mrs J.B. Upton

Off A1034 Weighton-South Cave road 1.6 km (1 mile) to W. Open occasionally for charity, when tea is served. Parkland and 1.6 ha (4 acres) of formal garden, situated 30 m (100 ft) above sea level on shallow chalky soil. Average annual rainfall 610 mm (24 in.). Staff of two.

Another surprising garden nestling in the folds of the Wolds country. A formal yew hedge, bounding on one side a raised lawn to the west of the house, is full of the fiery red flowered *Tropaeolum speciosum*. This lawn centred by a small stone statuette is bedded out with begonias in the summer and a shrubbery contains a variety of flowering shrubs with Floribunda roses and lilies in front interspersed with tulips and dahlias in season. The far side of the lawn is edged by the kitchen garden wall on which grow tall spreading climbing roses, clematis, the Winter Jasmine *Jasminum nudiflorum*, tamarisk, *Berberis* and quince. In a corner by the house is an immense pendant Golden Yew. Steps down to a lower lawn are made of three giant millstones. There is a large border of the rose 'Peace' connecting the lower bedded lawn with the upper, which is retained by a dry-stone wall in which grow aubrieta, yellow alyssum, stonecrops and houseleeks, giving a splash of colour in the spring. At right angles to the border of 'Peace' roses is a long bed of six varieties of Floribunda roses. Early in the year aconites, snowdrops and crocuses cover large areas of the ground under the trees which grow so well at Hotham. It is evident that the chalky soil suits many trees which are magnificent and of huge proportions, particularly Copper Beeches, clothed to the ground. Growing in the mixed planting to the front of the house are the Evergreen Oak, the Swamp Cypress, Weeping Ash, lime, the common beech and sycamore.

The house entrance wall is clothed in Firethorn, Virginia Creeper, *Euonymus* and *Garrya elliptica* and to the east of the entrance is one of the many ancient *Robinia pseudoacacia*.

From the south front there is a fine prospect into typical Wolds country over two large lakes divided by a waterfall and a carriage-wide bridge. Between the house and the water there is a rock garden where, among all manner of alpine and rockery garden plants, miniature roses, irises, heathers and rock roses in all shades, shrubs give height and contrast – *Viburnum plicatum, Juniperus horizontalis, Buddleia, Phlomis, Potentilla, Senecio* and *Colutea*, the Bladder Senna.

A mixed border picks up the line of the lakeside with shrub roses, Mock Orange, white *rugosa* roses, *Stachys, Geum* and *Phlox*. By a path leading from the lawn and the stream which feeds the lake are more trees, fine sycamores, elms, *Liquidambar styraciflua*, Scots Pine and an iris border. Under the trees near the house and in the light woodland near the lake daffodils grow in profusion.

Houghton Hall

Lord and Lady Manton

At Sancton, 3 km (2 miles) S of Market Weighton on Market Weighton-Cliffe-North Cave road. Garden and house open occasionally for charity. Landscape garden with some 2 ha (5 acres) of ornamental grounds, situated 35 m (120 ft) above sea level on light soil. Average annual rainfall 610 mm (24 in.).

The landscape garden here is attributed to Thomas White in 1768 to match up with the finely proportioned brick-built house of 1760. A long tree lined drive leads to the house front conspicuous for topiary worked yews on the gravel by the walls.

To the garden side of the house the extensive view is over two lakes some 5 ha (14 acres) in extent with a footbridge over a waterfall to rising tree studded parkland in which fine oaks are prominent. The rear lawn runs to a ha-ha between yew hedges, to the left being a croquet lawn and to the right a long walk with a Copper Beech hedge to the kitchen garden wall border filled with a satisfying variety of roses, flowering shrubs and flowers.

The trees here, as at nearby Hotham, are large and flourishing, comprising oaks, limes, chestnuts, Copper Beech and walnut. Despite the light soil and the suspicion of limestone not very far under the soil, rhododendrons grow well here.

Keldgate Manor, Beverley

Mr and Mrs J.W. Odey

In Beverley on Keldgate, within two minutes of Beverley Minster. Open occasionally for charity. A cathedral close garden of some 2 ha (5 acres), situated 15 m (50 ft) above sea level on light loam over limestone. Average annual rainfall 640 mm (25 in.). Staff of one.

Almost wholly behind high walls, this garden has all the secluded charm of a cloister separated narrowly, but completely, from the bustle of the surrounding town.

A pleasant courtyard from the main street leads through a narrow passageway to an oasis of green with commanding views from the lawns of the soaring towers of Beverley Minster. The way in is past two tonsured yews on to two large lawns divided by rose beds and terminated by a rose filled wooden pergola.

On one side of the roses is a low brick-walled croquet and putting green and on the other a stretch of green centred on a raised, stone edged formal lily pond fed by a bronze fountain statuette.

By the side of this lawn and running from the well stocked conservatory attached to the house under a high brick wall, where yuccas and hydrangeas are a feature, is a long woodland glade. Here are many tree sized yews and an ancient mulberry, the walk being terminated by a large rounded yew. There are pear trees on the house wall. The kitchen garden, off the path by the croquet lawn, has a range of glass.

Sigglesthorpe Hall

Mr and Mrs J.E. Townend

Off B1244 Hornsea-Beverley road, 5 km (3 miles) SW of Hornsea. Open occasionally for charity. Landscaped and well wooded garden of some 3 ha (8 acres), situated 15 m (50 ft) above sea level on well drained sandy loam and clay. Average annual rainfall 640 mm (25 in.). Staff of one and occasional help.

A nicely varied small landscaped garden notable for fine trees. At the far side of the house from the entrance drive a rustic summerhouse on a raised terrace looks over a sunken lawn walled on the right with rough mellowed brickwork, a patchwork of colour in the spring when the various *Aubrieta* and *Alyssum* make a hanging curtain.

In the flanking woodland to the left are fine Copper Beeches, a pleasingly symmetrical ancient oak, a laburnum arcade and a small pool surrounded by a collection of species and hybrid rhododendrons. The glade is filled early in the year with a carpet of snowdrops, aconites, crocuses and daffodils.

Beyond the sunken lawn at the terminal fence of the garden the view extends over low-lying country towards Hull.

The way back to the house lawn is through more woodland, well planted for effect with specimen trees of golden and blue conifers, a very large *Acer negundo*, a high, thick-boled Indian Bean Tree, *Catalpa bignonioides*, and *Pinus cembra*, the Arolla Pine, notable for its deep blue cones. A clearing in the glade reveals a stone-built wellhead with overhead ornamental ironwork decoration. A Wellingtonia rears its massive head above the rest of the tree canopy and within view of the house front is a very large, old and gnarled Cut-leaved Beech whose leaf cover and branches reach to the ground.

A south-facing border to be seen from the house is backed by cherries, oaks and a far spreading Cedar of Lebanon.

The kitchen garden, handy to the service entrance of the hall, is walled on three sides and on the fourth are hedging and a large, spreading, high-growing Sweet Bay.

Sewerby Hall

Borough of North Wolds

At Sewerby, Bridlington, 3 km (2 miles) NE from town centre. Open daily throughout the year. Meals available in garden May to September; dogs allowed on lead. Estate of 20 ha (50 acres) on the clifftops with views over the sea, walled and ornamental gardens sheltered by trees, situated 15 m (40 ft) above sea level on clayey, chalky soils. Average annual rainfall 690 mm (27 in.).

The hall and its gardens are on the edge of the town in which William Kent, the 'father' of English landscaping was born. There has been a house on this site since Saxon times. The Yorkshire families of Greame and Yarburgh were connected with Sewerby from the late seventeenth century until it was sold to the then Bridlington Corporation in 1934. It is to Mr Yarburgh, who came into ownership of the house in 1841, that we largely owe the present layout and much of the tree planting.

To the front of the hall a Victorian balustrade has the figures of Ceres and Flora effectively silhouetted against the sea and this divides the smaller tree studded lawn from the extensive sweep of greenery stretching to the clifftop and over it to the swell of the North Sea and the curve of Bridlington Bay. To the right is the chimera+*Laburnocytisus adamii* with its three different flower colours and, giving shelter from the sea breezes, there are fine stands of Copper Beech and *Acer negundo*.

Going past the front of the house and turning left, we come to the formal garden with a great lawn dominated by a planting of giant Monkey Puzzle trees, *Araucaria araucana*, some of the earliest introductions in the country, placed on either side of a wide walk backed spectacularly by two large and magnificently weeping birches *Betula pendula* 'Youngii', the whole area being well screened by a belt of trees. The bedding gives a subtropical effect with its uses of the Dwarf Fan Palm, *Chamaerops humilis*, Pampas Grass, tall yuccas, the Foxtail Lily (*Eremurus spp.*), abutilons and *Fatsia japonica*.

Trees are a fascinating feature of Sewerby, with its plantings of *Eucalyptus*, Red, Sweet and Horse Chestnuts, Holm, Cork and English Oaks, walnuts, many tree-size yews and a fine collection of conifers. Under the trees, in season, can be enjoyed thousands of snowdrops and aconites followed by daffodils, violets, anemones and bluebells which, in turn, give way to *Fritillaria meleagris*, Martagon Lilies, red and white campions, blue campanula, wild monkshood, the tiny *Cyclamen hederifolium* (*neapolitanum*) and graceful foxgloves among which are wild ferns to give greenery and contrast.

A walk under the arch of Monkey Puzzles reaches a raised terrace and 'temple' from where we can look back on the garden and the colourful, formal Victorian bedding of a central basin and the beds around it over which a statue of Pandora keeps close watch. The right-hand side of the lawn, laid out in the form of a rockery outcrop, has a more open appearance. To get to it from the terrace we walk under a green and tantalizing arch where so closely have a large beech and an equally large yew been allowed to grow into each other that it is difficult not to think that the yew is sporting beech foliage and the beech, yew. The path side to the open parkland here is colourfully and interestingly planted with a variety of ornamental trees, Golden Irish Yews, *Ginkgo biloba*, walnuts, the Dawn Redwood, *Metasequoia glyptostroboides*, the Cotton Tree, *Hoheria lyallii*, a small grove of Holm Oak and a copse of fine beech.

But this is only one aspect of Sewerby, for through the tree belt on the other, northern, side of the formal garden is a narrow path to the walled garden where on the wall by the entrance gate is a well grown *Ribes speciosum*, its fuchsia-like flowers being borne in profusion. Through high walls we walk into the Old English garden laid out with topiary

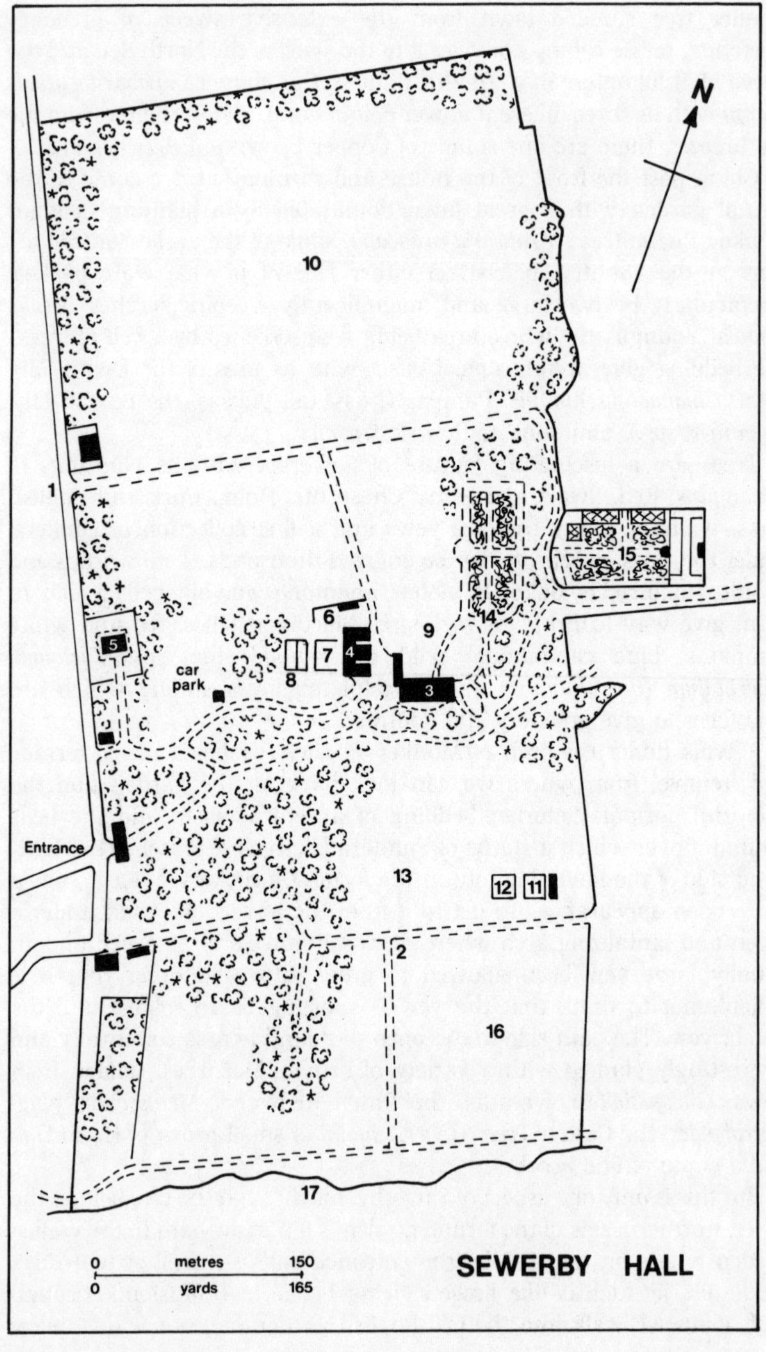
N
10
1
15
14
6
9
5
7
4
car
park
8
3
Entrance
13
12
11
2
16
17
0
metres
150
0
yards
165
SEWERBY HALL

worked yew hedges, box edged paths and geometrically shaped enclosures planted with herbaceous plants in cottage garden variety. The central fishpond is watched over by the leaden figure of a copy of Verrocchio's *Boy with a Fish*. The time-weathered walls provide shelter for many flowering shrubs – *Garrya elliptica, Cistus* in variety, *Buddleia*, jasmines, the New Zealand Daisy Bush, *Olearia haastii*, the Carolina Allspice, *Calycanthus floridus*, the Golden Bush, *Cassinia fulvida*, the Mexican Orange, *Choisya ternata, Drimys winteri*, variegated ivies and the waving plumes of Pampas Grass.

On the far side of the garden are the greenhouses following a Georgian layout where, along these northern walls, fruit trees are espaliered and fan trained. The greenhouse is a riot of colour overhung with *Bougainvillea* and a large trailing *Hoya carnosa*. A gateway at the far end of this garden leads the way to the rose garden, another high walled pleasance with box edged geometrically shaped beds filling in the large enclosed area between the gravel paths, eye-searing in summer with the bounty of roses. In the beds and on the walls are seen a grand variety of the rose tribe including the Hybrid Musk 'Felicia', the 'Austrian Copper' *R. foetida* 'Bicolor', the old Hybrid Perpetual 'Gloire de Ducher', Gallica roses including the striped red and white 'Versicolor', the Red Moss 'Henri Martin', *R. rubrifolia*, forms of *rugosa*, 'Canary Bird' and among the old roses some of the modern shrubs 'Frühlingsmorgen' and 'Frühlingsgold'.

On the far wall a strong linear pattern comes from the clever planting of six conical Lawson's Cypresses. If we go along the path by these conifers to an iron gate we enter a narrow walled walk leading us back to the main entrance. This warm south-facing enclosure provides the right conditions for sun-loving shrubs such as the quite tender *Pittosporum tenuifolium* and its variegated form *P.t.* 'Variegatum', *Olearia* in variety, including *O. macrodonta, O. nummularifolia, O. traversii* and *O. forsteri, Aralia*, the New Zealand hebes *H. hectori, H. hulkeana, H. salicifolia* and *H. traversii, Cistus* again, relishing the

---

1. Leys House Entrance
2. Cliff Entrance
3. Sewerby Hall
4. Old Stables
5. Sewerby Church
6. Zoo
7. Archery
8. Children's Playground
9. Putting Course
10. Golf Course
11. Bowling Green
12. Croquet Lawn
13. Putting Green
14. Large Formal Gardens
15. Old English Garden
16. Cricket Ground
17. Cliffs

shelter; as well as many species of *Viburnum, Buddleia* and other flowering shrubs.

There is still the parkland to see, with its herd of Formosan Sika deer, a zoo and an aviary, as well as the house with its Amy Johnson collection.

Sledmere House

Sir Richard Sykes, Bt

At Sledmere on York-Bridlington road, 13 km (8 miles) NW of Driffield at junction of B1251 and B1253. House and garden open regularly May to October excepting Mondays and Fridays. For hours see current issue of *Historic Houses, Castles and Gardens.* Car park; teas available in grounds. Georgian house, started in 1751 completed in 1788, with magnificent ceilings and decorative plasterwork by Joseph Rose, who did so much work for the Adam brothers, and notable for the great library said to be modelled on the Roman Baths of Diocletian, the Chinese bedroom and an unusual Turkish room. An exemplary Brownian landscape, gardens and parkland of 60 ha (150 acres), Italian and rose gardens, situated 122 m (400 ft) above sea level on shallow, chalky Wolds soil. Average annual rainfall 660 m (26 in.). Staff of four.

Sledmere house and village, sitting neatly in its enfolding hills and woodlands, is a monument to the work of Sir Christopher Sykes (1749–1801) in bringing under the plough this once primitive, wild land (wolves roamed here until well into the seventeenth century), and making 'this bleak and barren country . . . the most productive and best cultivated district in the County of York'.

It was he and 'Capability' Brown – whose original plan of the layout, dated 1777 and covering the whole of the 800 ha (2,000 acre) estate, can be seen in the library – who moved the old village and rebuilt it in its present form where family monuments, the Sledmere Stud stables and village housing are worth more than a passing glance.

On our way to the garden side of the house past the cupola-capped stables we cross a lawn backed by sombre groves of tall yews hedged in by *Prunus cerasifera* 'Pissardii', the Purple-leaved Plum and, facing south against a high wall, a long and colourful herbaceous border. There are climbing roses on the walls and on posts overlooking lawns with a view of the parish church through a fine stand of massive chestnuts which Sir Richard puts at at least 200 to 250 years old. Nearby are tall and stately cedars and a large shining-boled Copper Beech, both of which do very well on this chalky soil.

An Italian garden, which was built in 1911, is the classical feature to the north-west of the house. The stucco walls of the three-sided square are topped with stone urns while statuary and busts, eighteenth-century copies of Greek and Roman originals, stand out from the greenery on the walls of climbing roses, honeysuckles and wisteria, with bedding roses and herbaceous plants at their feet. The view from the lawn is over the extensive paved area and a circular fountain pool to a two-columned niche containing a bronze statue.

The south-east front of the house has views over the typical Brownian landscape with lawns sweeping right up to the house foundations. Large Copper Beeches rim this lawn to the right. The view to the front, over an ornamental pool with a fountain (a later addition) is of characteristic rolling landscape clumped and dotted with fine trees, beech, elm and oak predominating, to the far distance where Brown's signature, the enclosing belt of woodland, brings the eye to a restful halt.

Going left from the house terrace there is a path through thick woodland to the kitchen garden area where, outside the walls, is an unusual informally shaped rose garden and tree and flowering shrub walk where Wellingtonias make the background. There are cherries, laburnums and lilacs, cordon apples, magnolias and weigelas to make massed colour in the spring. By the wall side there are old roses such as 'Penelope', *R.* × *cantabrigiensis, R. rubrifolia,* the Hybrid Musk 'Felicia', a deep red, highly scented rose, old and nameless, and sweet smelling briars. In the ornamental beds are a colourful mixture of Hybrid Teas and Floribundas, an intimate garden scene in this otherwise open landscaped garden.

North Yorkshire

County of Superb Landscapes and Long Vistas

Aske Hall

Lord Zetland

Off B6274 Richmond-Gilling road. Open occasionally for charity. A well wooded landscaped estate, situated 130m (430ft) above sea level on light soil over limestone. Average annual rainfall 760mm (30in.). Staff of four.

The hall looks across terraced lawns and tree-studded parkland to a picturesque lake and the far Cleveland Hills. To the west the lawns to the side of the house are distinguished by good specimen trees, cedar, Wellingtonias, a Weeping Oak, *Quercus robur* 'Pendula', beeches, Sweet Chestnuts and limes.

There is a 2.8ha (7 acre) walled kitchen garden carrying fruit, flowers and vegetables in a good state of cultivation. An avenue of *Sorbus aucuparia* outside the garden wall leads off into thick woodland of Scots Pine and deciduous plantings underplanted with rhododendrons, mainly *R. ponticum*. Several paths in this woodland lead to a most ambitious 'Gothic' folly, the Aske Temple, with turrets, arcaded ground floor, a raised platform entrance and a turreted central dining room and viewing balcony. Garden historians credit Brown with the building as he was known to have done some work at Aske. From the raised front of the folly a downhill grassed avenue, tree and rhododendron edged, leads back to the rear drive.

Beningbrough Hall

National Trust

Three miles W of Shipton, 13km (8 miles) NW of York, leaving A19 York-Thirsk road at Shipton, well signposted. Garden and house closed for repairs during 1978, open in 1979, for details of which see National Trust literature. Teas available; no dogs. House and gardens given to the Trust in 1958 by the Treasury from the estate of the late Countess of Chesterfield. House built in 1716 for John Bourchier, period paintings and furniture.

Garden and woodlands of 2.4 ha (6 acres) in parkland, situated 15 m (50 ft) above sea level on mainly alluvial silt. Average annual rainfall 640 mm (25 in.). Staff of one.

The formal garden, one of geometrically patterned parterres, on the south front, as shown in an old print of *c.*1720, was replaced later in the century by lawns, specimen trees and a long ha-ha to give views over the water meadows to the sweeping course of the River Ouse, a short distance away. The house is approached through a short double lime tree avenue to a grass and gravelled courtyard with one outstanding green feature, a large tree-like *Viburnum rhytidophyllum* in the right-hand corner of the house front.

Surviving from the older styled garden, to the east and west of the south front entrance are two small formal paved and bordered enclosures bounded by clipped and recessed yew hedges. In the east garden a pool and fountain are the central features and by an early stone-pillared summerhouse in the corner on the nearby wall, growing very well for so far north, is a double yellow Banksian rose. The box topiary work of domes and birds is cut low so as not to be seen from the outside walk. The small beds in the paving are being filled with pastel shaded flowers.

In the west formal garden the planting is one of contrasting colours, heady reds, oranges and deep yellows. An old, gnarled thorn is against the wall and a sundial is in the centre of the paving and small flower beds.

From the south terrace the lawn slopes gently upwards to its most prominent feature, a vastly spreading Portugal Laurel, *Prunus lusitanica*, some 23 m (75 ft) across and 4 m (14 ft) high. Looking over the level parkland to the river are Brownian clumps of oak, lime, beech, including Copper Beech and willow. A Cedar of Lebanon and a tree holly mark the western boundary of the lawn, the holly playing host to that rather rare evergreen, twisting climber from China, *Holboellia coriacea*. In front of the house is a long border of the old English Lavender, *Lavandula spica*, and climbing through the ornamental ironwork of the steps at each side of the front entrance are two *Jasminum officinale*.

Going left from the south front entrance and passing the formal garden the visitor comes to a long border backed by a high, once flued wall, facing south. This fine shrub and herbaceous garden, designed and planted within the last ten years or so and undergoing more planting during 1978, has much to show. The roses, both climbers and shrub, are an eclectic collection including that deepest dyed of old roses

'Tuscany Superb', 'Gruss an Aachen' of 1909 vintage, pale apricot pink and of the flat old rose shape and the Hybrid Musks 'Penelope', 'Vanity', 'Skyrocket' ('Wilhelm'), 'Prosperity', and 'Cornelia'. Then there are *Rosa rubrifolia* with its coloured foliage and stems, the Scotch Rose, *R. pimpinellifolia* (*spinosissima*), 'Nevada', with large white flowers, 'Mme Grégoire Staechelin', the single blush pink *R. macrantha* and the more modern 'Golden Wings', 'Scarlet Fire', 'Frensham' and 'City of Belfast'. Taking full advantage of the wall is a large spreading wisteria and a bevy of *Clematis*, both species and the large flowered hybrids, 'Abundance', 'Minuet', 'Perle d'Azur', 'Gipsy Queen', 'Sir Garnet Wolseley' and 'Huldine'. Among the herbaceous plants and other shrubs to give variety of form and height as well as colour to the border are *Hemerocallis* 'Kwanso Flore Pleno', a selection of shrubby *Potentilla, Buddleia* 'Royal Red', *Cotinus coggygria* 'Notcutt's Variety', *Hypericum* 'Hidcote', *Paeonia* 'Lady Alex Duff', *Ceanothus* 'Topaz', *Iris pallida* 'Dalmatica', *Echinops ritro*, the Mount Etna Broom, *Genista aetnensis*, and, for later blooming, the Spanish Broom, *Spartium junceum, Acanthus mollis, Philadelphus insignis* and 'Belle Etoile', *Caryopteris clandonensis*. A short border at right angles to this border is a pleasing example of colourful planting with underplanting for ground cover of *Bergenia crassifolia, Symphytum grandiflorum* 'Hidcote Pink', and *Iris foetidissima citrina*. Punctuating this are two trees, a large Bay and the Mount Fuji Cherry, *Prunus* 'Shirotae'.

The long border leads us to the long brick wall of the 0.4 ha (1 acre) kitchen garden where, through a decorative ironwork gate, we see the now grassed-over space where vegetables were once grown, but do spare another look at the centre walk arched and avenued by meticulously espaliered and trained pears of many different varieties for 'walls' and 'arcading', a most pleasing conceit. Outside there is a double border hedged in on one side by box and on the other by the kitchen garden wall where Hybrid Musk roses are very much in evidence among herbaceous geraniums, stachys, veronicas and campanulas.

A path by the far kitchen garden wall leads past climbers in a narrow border, several *Jasminum officinale* and *J. beesianum*, the later flowering clematis *C. flammula, Pyracantha, Vitis* 'Brant', a climbing 'Iceberg' rose, a fig, a spreading *Rosa moyesii* and *Choisya ternata*, the Mexican Orange.

This path leads to the so called American Garden where during the nineteenth century 0.4 ha (1 acre) or so of the garden to the east side of the house was developed with conifers and meandering paths. This is now being redeveloped with North American plantings, more in keeping with the name, such as *Kalmia latifolia, Taxodium distichum,*

Magnolia tripetala and *M. acuminata, Sassafras albidum*, an aromatic tree, *Ilex aquifolium* 'Laurifolia Aurea', *Rhododendron arborescens* and *R. calendulaceum*. Remaining from the original planting are a *Cedrus atlantica*, some tree yews, a large *Magnolia* × *soulangiana*, a walnut, oaks, some old *Rhododendron ponticum* and old cherries.

As we retrace our steps to the front of the house, passing more original oaks and a mulberry, the lawn proper ends with a screen of *Robinia pseudoacacia* and near the house on the east side on a wall are two large climbing roses, 'Turner's Crimson Rambler' and one of the varieties of 'Canary Bird'.

Going right across the terrace to the west side there is attached to the house a well maintained conservatory, which it is hoped to fill with an interesting selection of Victorian pot plants and climbers.

Beyond the conservatory are more borders, flanked by an L-shaped wall which gives warmth and shelter to an interesting collection including the not often seen rose 'Blairii No. 2'. Another Mount Etna Broom appreciates the shelter, as does a large bush of the early flowering, sweet smelling *Sarcococca confusa*, the holly-leaved *Berberis calliantha* and the dark red, waxen petalled *Paeonia delavayi*. There is an old fashioned Victorian *Aucuba japonica* 'Crotonifolia' and the not often seen *Tovara virginiana filiformis*, one of the *Polygonum* family. Here also are *Hoheria glabrata, Mahonia pinnata* with early flowering rich yellow racemes, hostas, geraniums and *Cotoneaster glaucophyllus*, handsome throughout the year for foliage, flowers and berries.

Beyond this border is a small, wooded area known as the wilderness, of hollies, yews, two tall limes, a walnut, snowberries, more oaks, with bamboos and laurel filling in. A winding path through here leads to the laundry house and yard. Here in the house can be seen the torture chamber of Victorian washerwomen, with its great wheels to turn the wooden washing 'machine' or to shake the great wooden trough of clothes backwards and forwards, and the giant clothes racks, so heavy that windlasses are needed to raise them.

On the long, north-facing wall of the yard are being planted trained Morello Cherries and *Hedera canariensis* 'Variegata', fronted by *Euphorbia robbiae, Mahonia aquifolium* and for pretty ground cover, the wild alpine strawberry *Fragaria vesca semperflorens*. On the west wall are being planted the climbing rose 'Albéric Barbier' and *Hedera colchica*, the border being filled with the architecturally foliaged Cardoon, hostas, *Geranium macrorrhizum*, and *Iris foetidissima citrina*.

Bewerley House

Mr and Mrs A. Sigston Thompson

To left off B6265 Pateley Bridge-Grassington road, about 1.6km (1 mile) above Pateley Bridge in Upper Nidderdale. Open occasionally for charity, when tea is served. A plantsman's garden of 2.4ha (6 acres), sloping S, situated some 150m (500ft) above sea level, on acid soil over millstone grit, with excellent drainage. Average annual rainfall 940mm (37in.). Staff of one and occasional help.

This hillside garden when the owners came 30 years ago consisted of the two present flower beds in front of the terrace, an impenetrable Victorian shrubbery, the remains of a rock garden planted in the 1930s by the one-time nursery firm of Backhouse of York and one or two fine parkland trees.

The house was originally the agent's house for Bewerley Hall. The hall itself was demolished in 1925 and the site, with one of the original towers remaining, now forms the top lawn. This explains the entrance to the garden through the big archway, which was originally one of the minor entrances to the estate.

Mr Thompson's interest in plants is catholic – he describes himself as a plantsman rather than a gardener and explains that this is the reason why the garden has no organized plan. He would define his principal interests, as reflected in the garden, as trees and shrubs, particularly *Rhododendron, Meconopsis,* shrub roses and rose species; but any plant of interest finds a welcome here.

Entering through the archway, the terrace and house lawn are on the left and the shrubbery on the right. Immediately on the right is a *Magnolia campbellii mollicomata* which was planted 30 years ago and flowered for the first time five years ago; since then it has flowered well every spring, except when the flowers are cut by late frost. Away to the right is the clearing containing many rhododendrons, *R. fictolacteum* 'Kingdon Ward Form' and *R. macabeanum* being large leafed species happy in this shelter, along with *Meconopsis spp.*, lilies, *Nomocharis spp.* and other plants which relish the shade.

Continuing up the garden, steps to the right lead to the top lawn, the site of Bewerley Hall. The views from here to the hills and dales all around are delightful and extensive. The New Zealand Lobster Claw,

Clianthus puniceus, grows and flowers in the studio verandah here so long as winters are mild, as does the prolific peach 'Peregrine'. Climbing roses, old and new, cover the walls, and 'Kiftsgate' clothes the remaining tower of the old hall.

The banks of this lawn were the site of the rock garden constructed in the 1930s for the then owners. All that remains of this today are the so-called 'dwarf' conifers included in the original planting. Now they are a splendid sight – *Picea abies* 'Clanbrassiliana', as fine a specimen as one could want, *Juniperus chinensis* 'Aurea', Young's Golden Juniper, a golden column 4.5 m (15 ft) high, and a dozen others besides.

Beyond this lawn are two pools connected by an artificial stream, and the rock outcrop surrounding the upper pond with scree and alpine plants.

Beyond all this again is the more recently planted part of the garden, leading down to the stream with an open area of grass planted with trees and shrubs, solitary or in groups, sheltered on the west by a double screen of *Thuja plicata* and on the east by Scots and Austrian Pines. Returning towards the house on the lower level there are long borders which are slowly being converted into shrub borders to ease maintenance; this is also the part where old fashioned and shrub roses are concentrated. They grow in the grass, which is not the happiest place for them, but nevertheless they give good results. Lilies, both species and hybrids, are tucked in every possible space, as also are hydrangeas, again both species and hybrids, which are of special interest to the owners.

Plants growing well in this high Dales garden (subject always to the risk of the flowers being cut by frost) which one might not expect to find are, besides rhododendrons in quantity, *Magnolia* (many species), *Camellia* (planted clear of morning sun), the Chilean Fire Bush *Embothrium coccineum* (*lanceolatum*), *Cornus kousa*, and its *chinensis* form, *Cornus mas*, *Crinodendron hokeranum* of the crimson lantern flowers and *Desfontainia spinosa*, late summer flowering with its scarlet tubular flowers.

Walls are used extensively for plants. A nurseryman once said: 'You cannot see anything of Mr Thompson's house except for a few windows, it is all covered with plants.' The same goes for many other walls which the garden is fortunate to have.

The gardening is carried on under difficulties as the garden is used as a 'home' by pheasants, wood pigeons, collared doves, rabbits, and Mr Thompson's own guinea fowl which wander free – not to mention the dogs.

The Bewerley chestnuts are worth seeing; they are the sweet

variety, *Castanea sativa*, and there are three of them, very old. Two are past their prime, but the third is a magnificent specimen and in hot summers provides nuts of a size worth eating.

Many of the rhododendrons about the garden are the owner's own seedlings from crosses made in the 1950s. While Mr Thompson agrees there is nothing world-shattering, there are a lot of very pleasing specimens.

Castle Howard

Castle Howard Estates Ltd

Off A64 York-Scarborough road 8 km (5 miles) SW of Malton, signposted 'Castle Howard'. Garden open Easter Sunday to first Sunday in October daily 12–6.30 pm. The castle, a treasure house of art, sculpture and furniture, is also open. Meals available; dogs on lead allowed, but not in house. Estate of 400 ha (1,000 acres), ornamental gardens of 18 ha (45 acres), situated 86 m (281 ft) above sea level on light to medium soil, slightly acid. Average annual rainfall 690 mm (27 in.). Staff of six full time, three part time.

Castle Howard, set in the soft rolling Howardian Hills, is a sublime landscape, 'the noblest in the world fenced by half the horizon', as Horace Walpole put it, and it has gardens and plantings to match both its unique architectural landscape features and Vanbrugh's opulence and grandeur.

The castle and its setting (built 1700–26) were designed by the soldier-playwright Sir John Vanbrugh, whose first attempt at architecture and landscaping it was, assisted by Nicholas Hawksmoor.

The approach from the York-Scarborough road is by a beech and lime north-south avenue, running as straight as an arrow up hill and down dale for 8 km (5 miles). The venerable limes near the house are of the original planting of 1709.

The outerworks or bastions prepare the visitor for the magnificence ahead. First there is the southernmost Carrmire Gate, with its heavily pedimented arch, stone pyramid ornaments and fortified walls, ending in two round fortified towers. Then follows the Pyramid Gate topped by a massive pyramid in stone, flanked on either side by a bastioned wall with its 11 different fortress towers reminding us of Vanbrugh's military background. The gateway focuses the eye on the 30 m (100 ft) obelisk which marks the turning from the north-south avenue to the house and commemorates in its inscription the creation of this epic elysium by Charles, third Earl of Carlisle.

How to start the perambulation? Well, from the cark park by the stable block we can glance through the beautifully wrought ironwork of the Victoria Gate down the 230 m (750 ft) long broad walk, lined on the one side by ancient and noble beeches and on the other by the massive garden wall. The broad walk is reached by walking through the tree avenue where a fine collection of *Clematis* on the wall and a venerable collection of shrub roses are the particular interest, especially a very old Ayrshire rose, one of the few left in the country, which is some 9 m (30 ft) long by 3.5 m (12 ft) through and around 205 m (8–9 ft) high. In the wall here is the famed Satyr Gate with its gigantic grinning heads. The turning by the end of the wall sets the feet on the edge of the twin lime avenue, leading the eye to a classical statuary piece at the far end. Under the trees in spring are cool swathes of primroses, followed by forget-me-nots and wild saxifrage. At this time clouds of daffodils meet the eye at every turn.

Some half-way along the wall skirting the lime avenue is another finely patterned ironwork gate which in 1978 will allow the visitor into the revitalized rose garden, an artistic and satisfying piece of period reconstruction, the geometrically shaped beds and wooden *treillage* work of pyramids and square arbours echoing the formality of Vanbrugh's own stone pyramids and castellated fortifications, and fast becoming covered by climbing roses. Here one of the finest collections of old shrub roses is being assembled, where some of the oldest known and most picturesquely named will not only make a riot of colour but will also provide a backward glance into the history of the rose, with plantings of the groups of *pimpinellifolia* (*spinossisima*), *rugosa, alba,* Damask, *centifolia, gallica, wichuraiana,* Moss, Musk, Noisette and the old Hybrid Perpetuals.

On the south-facing walls around such species and cultivars of *Clematis* as *C. lanuginosa* 'Henryi', *C. chrysocoma, C. viticella* 'Ascotiensis' and *C. armandii* are intermingled with the old climbing roses our great-great-grandmothers knew. The tender shrubs *Campsis grandiflora, Buddleia × weyerana, Cytisus battandieri* and *Solanum crispum* serve to provide contrast in form and foliage.

Leaving the rose-garden, having admired the inside 'face' of the Satyr Gate and the neat appropriateness of the garden house, the way is across the lime avenue where, to the west of the house, the grass slope to the right is dominated by a giant Cedar of Lebanon, and to the left is a large square lawn centred by a larger than life-size figure of a boar on a huge pedestal. From the house terrace the view is over the parterre garden, between two great Renaissance vases full of flowers at all times of the year, and a notable sight is the pride of some 20 peacocks. In the centre of this formal garden is the Atlas Fountain brought here by Nesfield from the 1851 Exhibition. On either side of the greensward are old stands of conifers including many cedars and, at the far end on the right-hand side, a most beautifully round-headed and many-trunked beech, matched on the other side by a huge Copper Beech. At the far end of the fountain garden a turn right brings into view a most unusual statue of one of the muses on a tall pedestal, the whole pedestal carved in bas-relief with a highly romantic elysian landscape of high waterfalls, caves, grottoes, shepherds with their flocks, trees, mountains and pastures.

A walk away from the house down the grass slope to the left brings us to the South Lake 2.6 ha (6½ acres), so skilfully placed as to reflect in its waters the grandeur of the castle and also the long ropes of a multiple planting of old bright yellow leaved willows. At the far end of this rush edged water a stepped, sloping cascade leads the eye down the water to Temple Rush, a smaller lake which runs into the New River under the graciously arched 'Roman Bridge' and away to the Mausoleum, that great classical rotunda by Hawksmoor, which completely dominates the far landscape.

From the South Lake level to the foot of the cataract a steep path leads down to the new bog garden awash with the vivid colourings of *Primula denticulata*, a large mixed bed of candelabra species of *Primula* and *Meconopsis*, backed by massive clumps of the Giant Prickly Rhubarb, *Gunnera manicata*, the shiny yellow spathes of *Lysichitum americanum*, alders and the Swamp Cypress, *Taxodium distichum*. In Temple Hole, still by the waterside, a new shrub and tree garden has been planted under the old birches and tall yews: ten different species of the 'Snowy Mesphilus' *Amelanchier*, with white flowers in spring and vivid autumn colour, azaleas, magnolias, and a most comprehensive collection of newly planted *Sorbus spp.* and *Betula spp.*, in the hope, of both Mr George Howard and Mr James Russell, of keeping the many species in existence and growing in natural surroundings. From the river level the path slopes upwards among *Enkianthus spp.* Here in spring the banks aglow with daffodils are further splashed with the primaries of rhododendrons and azaleas, particularly the round-headed fiery red *R.* 'Elizabeth', the creamy *R.* 'Augustine' and the strawberry coloured *R.* 'Raoul Millais'.

The climbing path now comes to the statue terrace, a straight grassed walk with sloping sides swathed in heathers, where now the Temple of the Four Winds is seen for the first time, terminating the terrace; 'as beautiful as anything in Europe', according to Sacheverell Sitwell, it was Vanbrugh's last inspirational work at Castle Howard, created 1724–6. From the steps of the temple pedestal the ha-ha and wall marking the boundary of Ray Wood can be followed, and a better view gained of the Pyramid, which houses a large bust of Lord William Howard.

Ray Wood's 27ha (66 acres) was the eighteenth-century battleground of London and Wise versus Switzer, when Switzer won the day on behalf of informal wild woodland and waterworks as against the London and Wise plans for strict formality. It is here that some of the most exciting planting at Castle Howard is now taking place. For in this mixed oak, beech, birch and chestnut woodland new winding woodland walks will lead among a vast variety of rhododendrons that Mr James Russell, the well known nurseryman who now lives on the estate, brought with him from the south. Not content with just a rhododendron wood, Mr Russell has planted a large variety of trees and shrubs – *Picea, Abies, Acer, Carpinus, Liquidambar, Photinia, Prunus, Stewartia, Styrax, Magnolia, Arbutus, Halesia, Nothofagus* and *Cercidiphyllum* – with the idea, apart from the beauty and the fascination of seeing such a wealth of sylviculture, of safeguarding many species and varieties which might disappear altogether as nurserymen concentrate on the popular and well known in their breeding and sales. A cherry walk has been planted by the side of the wood above the statue walk. On this green promenade, which was once the village street of Henderskelfe, a village wiped out to make the landscape, there are views over the lake back to the magnificence of the house façade o'ertopped by its great dome, the first of such a size ever to be placed on a domestic building. An unusual green and white variegated oak, *Quercus robur* 'Variegata', is by the terrace side near the colonnade border in which

---

1. House
2. Stables
3. Obelisk
4. Gate House
5. Market Garden
6. Satyr Gate
7. Pyramid
8. Rose Garden
9. Boar Lawn
10. Fountain & Formal Garden
11. Colonnade Border
12. South Lake
13. Temple Hole
14. Temple Rush
15. New Bridge
16. Temple of The Four Winds
17. Mausoleum
18. Ray Wood
19. Great Lake

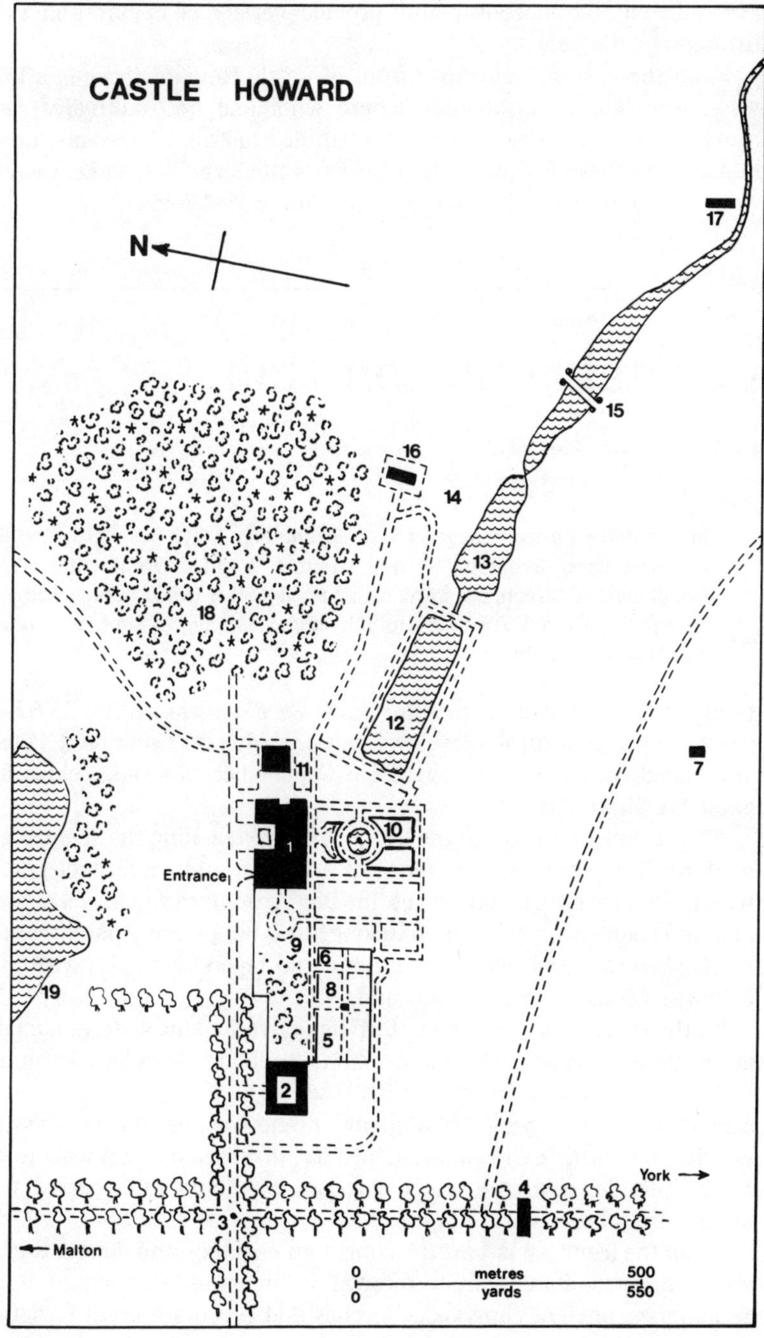
CASTLE HOWARD
N
17
15
16
14
13
18
12
7
11
10
1
Entrance
9
6
8
19
5
2
York
4
3
Malton
0 metres 500
0 yards 550

100 different herbaceous plants provide variety of colour and form throughout the year.

From the east and entrance front of Castle Howard there is a long view over rolling countryside where woodland and cultivated land provide a chequered picture, the red pantiled roofs of villages and farms making splashes of colour. Right below is the large East Lake, heavily wooded around its edges and mirroring the wide Wolds sky.

Constable Burton Hall

C.W. Wyvill Esq

In Constable Burton village in Wensleydale, on A684 5 km (3 miles) E of Leyburn. Open frequently during summer months. Ornamental walled woodland and streamside gardens, situated 150 m (500 ft) above sea level on light sandy soil. Average annual rainfall 810 mm (32 in.). Staff of one and occasional help.

From the front lawns of this fine John Carr mansion (built 1762–8) there are peaceful rural views over cattle grazing on rising land, copsed and belted with mature heavy-boled Copper Beeches, oaks, elms, and giant Wellingtonias.

On the entrance drive to the left, just before reaching the stepped and platformed entrance to the house, is a stream and small pool garden where *Gentiana acaulis*, saxifrages, the Bog Arum *Lysichitum americanum* and drifts of heather grow in an incongruous but pleasing patchwork. A *Cercidiphyllum japonicum*, Silver Birches and Japanese maples with their coloured foliage form a background.

To the right a path runs by a steep bank overlooking a stream, a lake, an ornamental rustic bridge and a small bubbling cascade. A retaining wall for the house lawn into which rose beds are cut, on the left-hand side of this path, provides a genial home for the spring alyssum, aubrieta and other early alpines which like good drainage. A walk to our right leads down to the water through woodland interspersed with laburnums, cherries and maples.

From the front lawn, past the courtyard entrance and offices, there is an inviting woodland walk to the walled kitchen garden where, under Scots Pines, ancient elms, oaks, birches and beeches a great variety of

1 Harsley Hall, North Yorkshire: a green oasis of lawn set off by the impressive arch of Yew and mounded spring blooms

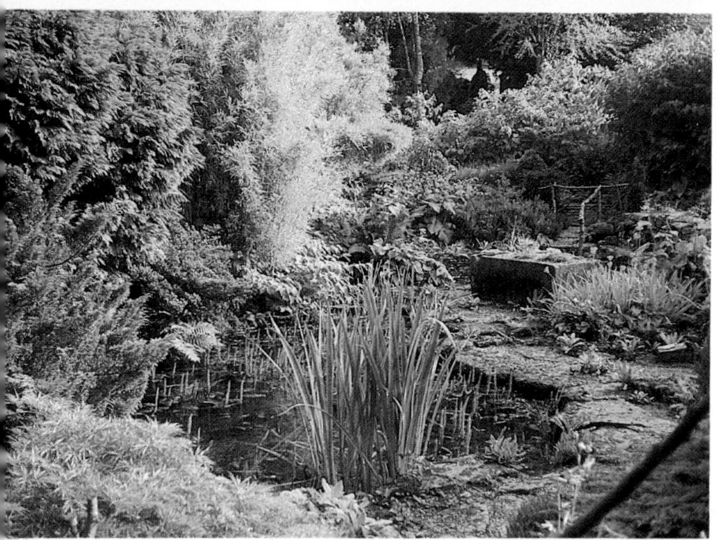

2 Newburgh Priory, North Yorkshire: a colourful corner of the Wild Water Garden where many springs trickle down the hillside as the setting for a wide variety of trees, shrubs, bamboos, marginal aquatic plants and alpine screes and troughs

3 Lister Park, Bradford, West Yorkshire: a hark back to the halcyon days of Victorian country house gardening and their troops of gardeners – Victorian bedding-out

4 York Gate, West Yorkshire: a beautifully laid-out herb garden, full of interest and fragrance and sheltered by high hedges of Yew. Spirals and balls of Box add to the sympathy of the garden picture

5 Burnby Hall, Humberside: the Upper Water, one of the two lakes planted with one of the largest collections of water lilies in the country

6 Newby Hall, North Yorkshire: the long border, probably the most impressive in the country, running from the south front of the house to the River Ure

7 Temple Newsame. Leeds: a highly colourful part of the rhododendron walk where over the years a large collection of hybrid rhododendrons and azaleas have been planted to line a long, winding, downhill walk to the rose garden and greenhouses

8 Harlow Car Gardens, North Yorkshire: the limestone rock garden – in distinct contrast to the sandstone one nearby – reflecting the flora of Yorkshire's limestone fells. The fastigiate and rounded conifer forms provide pleasing height contrasts

crab apples and cherries have been planted to give, in spring, a colourful pink and white ceiling to the woodland floor, itself, in that early part of the year, carpeted with a host of many coloured wild flowers. Large drifts of *Cyclamen hederifolium* (*neapolitanum*) and spotted orchids mingle with wood anemones, bluebells, cowslips, primroses, daffodils and forget-me-nots. On the right, as the wall of the kitchen garden comes into view, there is a 'magic casements' view down a precipitous wooded bank to the stream and the lower woodland walk by whose meandering way there is a return to the house. The kitchen garden is large and beyond the care of the labour at hand, but the old flued wall and offices are of eighteenth-century provenance and a splendid Sweet Bay flourishes in their shelter.

Copt Hewick

Mr and Mrs Robin Compton

Turn left off A1 for Ripon at Dishforth roundabout (junction with A168); after 3 km (2 miles) turn left and 180 m (600 ft) ahead are the white entrance gates. Open for charity occasionally during year. No dogs. Ornamental and walled gardens of 1 ha (2½ acres), situated 50 m (160 ft) above sea level on medium loam with clay subsoil and a neutral pH. Sheltered by trees to N and W. Average annual rainfall 760 mm (30 in.). Staff of one and occasional help.

A Victorian garden with unusual and tender plants not often attempted in the harsh northern climate and a charming iron-framed conservatory still used as it should be for sitting out and afternoon tea, and furnished with basket-wear on a coloured tile floor exotically surrounded by plants in pots and hanging baskets.

But let us start our garden walk immediately west of the house, near the conservatory, where a delightful small grey and silver garden has beds, divided by paths of brick and stone paving, holding among other plants *Artemisia, Dianthus, Senecio* and *Hebe pinguifolia* 'Pagei'. To the north of this pretty little sun-trap garden there is a curving wall covered with the tender, for this part of the world, *Clematis armandii*, the hydrangea-like *Schizophragma integrifolium*, *Xanthoceras sorbifolium*, comparatively rare in the north, and another plant needing a sheltered position, the many-flowered *Abutilon vitifolium, Hebe* 'Mrs E. Tennant', *Clematis alpina, C. macropetalla* and the less often seen cowslip-scented *C. rehderana.* Climbing roses add to the wall's tapestry along here, 'Lady Hillingdon' and 'Mme Grégoire Staechelin' being prominent.

The south flank of this garden is formed by the old conservatory, furnished appropriately for its date with lemons and oranges in large tubs and with other tropical and subtropical plants among which are seen the climbing *Mandevilla suavolens, Hoya carnosa, Stephanotis floribunda, Jasminum polyanthum* and hanging baskets of *Columnea gloriosa*

A gravel path leads through a wild garden on the left and a border on the right to an iron gate, the entrance to a spacious old world brick-walled rose and shrub garden, with a lily and fish pond in the centre of the lawn. The roses on the mellow brick walls include such old favourites as 'Mermaid', 'Leverkusen', 'Dr W. Van Fleet', the very old *R. laevigata* (1759) and *R. soulieana* (1896). The shrub roses in the beds in the lawn have been chosen for colour and foliage form and with an eye to rose history, for here we find 'William Lobb', *R. centifolia* 'Muscosa', which was grown before 1750, 'Ferdinand Pichard', the 100 year old 'Gloire des Mousseux', 'Great Maiden's Blush' (of before 1738), 'Conrad F. Meyer', the highly fragrant 'Fritz Nobis', 'Commandant Beaurepaire' (introduced in 1874) and the striped Moss 'Oêillet Panachée'.

To give contrast and variety, interspersed among the roses is a fine and, for the north, rare selection of trees and shrubs, among them being that native of Chile *Azara lanceolata, Callicarpa bodinieri giraldii*, with unusual lilac coloured fruits, the Snowdrop Tree *Halesia carolina*, the Strawberry Tree *Arbutus unedo*, the tricolour foliaged *Actinidia kolomikta* and *A. chinensis*. Two less common honeysuckles, the rich coppery yellow flowered *Lonicera × tellmanniana* and the very showy golden yellow flowered *L. tragophylla* show the eclectic taste of the planter.

The large lawn to the south-west of the house has old oaks and limes standing on the edge of the ha-ha fence and in the lawn are an old walnut tree as well as two Handkerchief Trees, *Davidia involucrata*. Directly in front of the house the circular drive of gravel surrounded by a Victorian stonework balustrade is neatly studded with four mop-headed *Robinia pseudoacacia* 'Inermis' and tall yuccas.

Carefully planted for maximum shelter in the tree-sheltered beds leading to the big lawn are more Copt Hewick treasures, the Chilean Fire Bush *Embothrium coccineum lanceolatum* 'Norquinco Valley', two more shrub rose escapees from the rose garden proper, 'Fritz Nobis' and

'Canary Bird', the silvery silky leafed *Convolvulus cneorum*, the red and black fruiting *Viburnum henryi*, and *Cistus*, not a lover of northern cold, is well represented by *C.* × *corbariensis, C. populifolius, C. laurifolius* and *C.* × *aguilari*.

Encouraged by the shelter of walls and trees provided at Copt Hewick, the flowers of *Eucryphia* × *intermedia* crowd the branches and *Magnolia campbellii mollicomata*, with water lily flowers, the rare highly scented *M.* × *watsonii*, the lilac pink flowered 'Leonard Messel' and the slow to flower *M. kobus* all flower well. Also in this bed and relishing the protection offered is a variety of other shrubs – *Cornus kousa chinensis, Colutea orientalis*, Bladder Senna, with copper coloured flowers, *Leptospermum scoparium*, the New Zealand Tea Tree, *Viburnum plicatum* 'Lanarth' and *Prunus serrula*, for its polished mahogany red-brown bark.

Another bed on the left of the high wall provides congenial conditions for the rarely planted original single white *Rosa banksiae*; the small bluish-white pea-flowered *Sophora viciifolia*; the *Daphne odora* 'Aureomarginata'; camellias; the not often seen Climbing Gazania, *Mutisia oligodon*, with heads of salmon pink flowers through the summer; the evergreen *Drimys* here seen in *D. lanceolata* (*aromatica*) rather than the more common *D. winteri* and the dwarf Russian Almond, *Prunus tenella gesslerana*.

The end bed by the wall contains the prolific autumn berrying *Viburnum betulifolium* and Lacecap-hydrangea-like *Viburnum furcatum*. To complete this real plantsman's garden – after all the owner is the son of the late Major Compton of nearby Newby Hall – there is a new interest coming to fruition, a walled, cobbled garden, planted at the time of writing with irises and yellow wallflowers, but there is no doubt much more to come.

Crathorne Hall

Lord Crathorne

On A19 S of Yarm. Open occasionally for charity. Paved, formal and woodland gardens, situated 85 m (280 ft) above sea level on light chalky soil. Average rainfall 640 mm (27 in.). Staff of one and occasional help.

The beauty of Lord Crathorne's house and garden is its commanding position above the steep valley of the River Leven and its well wooded hillside following the river's course. The 1 ha (2½ acres) of kitchen garden still retains some of its former splendour in its greenhouse range and its espaliered apples in the orchard. Oaks, chestnuts and conifer woodland screen the house at the rear and a woodland and yew hedged walk takes the visitor to the pleasant open south-facing front garden and its views to the Cleveland Hills. From the top path of the house lawn the river can be seen through the trees, its tortuous course broken by a fast-running weir and a ford. From this path winding downhill to the river level another path goes through cherries behind a screen of oaks and shrub roses. The top path to the left leads down an imposing flight of stone steps to light woodland, planted with oaks, sycamores and round shaped Golden Yews, which in spring is densely carpeted with primroses, daffodils, bluebells and later with a grand scattering of spotted orchids.

Below the nursery wing of the house is a sunken paved garden with a lily pool on the corners of which stand four bronze cherubs. From a central fountain bronze frogs spout streams of water. Formal beds in the paving are filled with dahlias and roses, while on the outer sloping borders the old fashioned flowers, Sweet Williams, sweet smelling stocks and Rock Roses are in keeping.

On the house walls are a fine old 'Albertine' rose, the climbing *Hydrangea petiolaris* and quince. From the daisy spangled lawn by the entrance courtyard at the rear of the house a Red Chestnut avenue leads from the house up the drive to the main road.

Duncombe Park

Trustees of Duncombe Park

Rievaulx Terrace

National Trust

Duncombe Park is in North Yorkshire Moors country 1.6 km (1 mile) W of Helmsley off A170 road to Thirsk. Gardens and terrace open May to September Wednesdays 10 am–4 pm. Teas in Helmsley. Situated 110 m (350 ft) above sea level on freely draining soil (light brash over limestone). Average annual rainfall 640 mm (25 in.).

It is the terrace at Duncombe which is its glory and the garden's *raison d'être* and this, combined with that at nearby Rievaulx (see below), prompted the late Christopher Hussey, doyen of landscape historians, to comment: 'perhaps the most spectacularly beautiful among English landscape conceptions of the eighteenth century'.

Created by Thomas Brown Duncombe, who took over the estate in 1711 and died in 1725, Duncombe Terrace, a crisply mown lawn, sweeps for almost 1 km (½ mile) in a gently concave curve on a ridge above the valley of the Rye. On its outer edge as well as on the inner the terrace is bounded by woodland.

A level lawn surface 90 m (300 ft) square extends eastwards from the house, now in use as a school, to an imposing figure of Father Time watching a sundial (ascribed to Van Nost), placed not quite centrally on the inner terrace rim. To the left the velvety grass leads to a dignified classical domed and open Ionic rotunda which has all the marks of Vanbrugh's similar one at Stowe. To the right the lawned walk takes the visitor to a wooded promontory where, on a circular turfed emplacement, stands a closed, circular Tuscan temple. Looking down the escarpment on the way, through rides cut in the woodland are seen delightful vignette views of the Rye in its wooded valley. From the rotunda at the other end of the terrace there are charming views of the red pantiled roofs of Helmsley.

Below the rotunda and holding up the end of the terrace is a serpentining ha-ha, notable in that it preceded Bridgeman's at Stowe and is one of the earliest recorded in gardening history.

There are walks from the Tuscan temple turning west along another escarpment and north-west of the temple through a 'secret garden' woodland walk to a temple and an old conservatory or orangery. To the west of the temple in Terrace Bank Wood is the tallest lime in Great Britain at 47m (154ft) and in the same wood the tallest ash at 45m (148ft). Vanbrugh, Bridgeman and Switzer are given by the historians as possible consultants for the layout.

Rievaulx Terrace

Off B1257 Helmsley-Stokesley road 4km (2½ miles) NW of Helmsley. Open April to October Tuesday to Saturday and Bank Holiday Mondays 10am–6pm, Sundays 1–6pm or sunset. Teas in Helmsley; dogs allowed. Situated 175m (575ft) above sea level. Average annual rainfall 690mm (27in.).

This noble winding terrace, created by the third Duncombe in 1754, 40 years after that at Duncombe Park, is a landmark in the eighteenth-century ideal of the picturesque, realizing as it does in an entirely new aspect the idealistic vision of Poussin, Claude and Salvator Rosa, those continental artists whose works were so influential in supplanting formalism in the eighteenth-century English garden.

Again the terrace sweeps in a great curve along a high wooded escarpment with classical temples at each terminal point, but for the first time an architectural vista was to be seen and this 'with moving variation' as Arthur Young described it in his *Six Months Tour of the North* (1770–71). Through drives cut in the almost precipitous descending woodland the noble majesty of the romantically sited Cistercian Rievaulx Abbey is seen in changing perspective and views or again, as Arthur Young so aptly put it: 'You look through a waving break in the shrubby wood, which grows upon the edge of a precipice, down immediately upon a large ruined abbey, in the midst, to appearance, of a small but beautiful valley, scattered trees appearing elegantly among the ruins, too elegantly picturesque to admit of description. It is a bird's eye landscape; a casual glance at a little paradise, which seems as it were in another region.' Miraculously the view is the same today.

This picturesque almost 1km (½ mile) long terrace is, however, quite different in concept from the Duncombe Terrace of 40 years before, for the break from formality had taken place in the theory of landscape design. No longer do the straight edges of the Duncombe lawns prevail; here both on the precipice edge and on the other side there is to be seen a wavy line of trees, and no longer is the eye led from one temple to the other but a gentle, moving picture of classicism and romanticism is revealed slowly as the walker proceeds along the shorn lawn, which, to give a feeling of informality, varies from 55 to 110m (180–360ft) in width.

It we start the terrace perambulation at the gracious Ionic temple, Palladian in style, with steps leading to a columned portico, inside we come upon Thomas Duncombe the third's magnificent banqueting house. The ceiling and coving bear mythical scenes by the Italian artist Guiseppe Mattia Borgnis (1758–61), seemingly as fresh today as the day they were painted. Under these ennobling frescoes is the mid-eighteenth-century furniture made for the temple, together with contemporary additions – 12 mahogany dining chairs, a pair of superb gilt settees (part of a set designed by William Kent), surrounded by other equally sumptuous pieces including two pairs of carved pine terms supporting brass candlesticks, a pair of George II eagle consoles, Siena topped tables and elegant pier glasses. The table is set as for a Duncombe family meal with a Charleston Worcester dinner service.

Now we walk along the terrace, not missing one of the 13 bird's eye views of the abbey and noticing about half-way along in flanking walls, a pair of rusticated gate piers, for this was the entrance when the family came to visit by horse and carriage from Duncombe. Seen only as we round the curving terrace, a circular Tuscan temple comes into view and from its raised platform we are able to look into the 'paradise' of the Rye valley – the abbey, a romantic pack-horse bridge crossing the river – and over moorland ridge and vale to the distant blue haze of the Cleveland Hills.

Through the windows of the Tuscan temple we can admire the richly worked, highly coloured plasterwork, the painted roundel with a winged female deity in the dome, the curved casing of the door and windows and its central feature which an early eighteenth-century Italian octagonal table partly hides, a thirteenth-century tesselated pavement, said to have come from the abbey in the valley below.

If only the tremendous conception of Thomas Duncome the third had materialized we should have had a five km (three mile) terrace leading from the Duncombe Terrace to the Rievaulx Terrace high above the valley with tremendous views over the Plain of York, but alas it was not to be, though the finding of a heap of dressed stone in the valley beneath gave a possible clue as to how near the plan came to fruition.

Ebberston Hall

Mr and Mrs de Wend Fenton

On edge of North Yorkshire Moors on A170 Pickering-Scarborough road 11 km (7 miles) E of Pickering. Open by appointment. Situated 30 m (100 ft) above sea level. Average annual rainfall 640 mm (25 in.).

This historic garden, now alas in a sad state of decay, is for the genuine garden archaeologist and lover of garden history who can view the landscape with imagination.

Built on the rim of the Vale of Pickering with extensive views over open country to the far Wolds, this Colen Campbell casino, or Summer Pavilion, built in 1718 for William Thompson, Member of Parliament for Scarborough and Master of the Mint, was the setting for one of the first outstanding formal landscaped gardens of the eighteenth century. In miniature, as it were, it was in the Italian Renaissance Villa Lante style. For here, running up a gently sloping wooded valley behind the casino, were ornamental waterworks based on a formal canal 360 m (1,200 ft) long. A collecting basin at the head of the water enclosed an island on which a tall pyramid surmounted by a statue of Mercury, based on that of Giovanni da Bologna, was the feature. A low cascade brought the water into the canal proper and then by further cascades into three formal pools, finally disappearing over a final cascade just under the loggia of the house. In other days the water was led underground to two more ornamental pools in front of the house.

Paintings attributed to Balthazar Nebot, *c.*1730, and now in the possession of Lord Hotham, whose ancestors were former owners, show the landscape in its original conception. Christopher Hussey thinks that Switzer was probably responsible for the creation and design of the waterworks.

Today the last pool and its cascade can still be seen, as they were meant to be, from the loggia of the house. Two other pools are still there but silted up, and the long course of the canal in the valley between thick woodland climbs gently to the head of the dale and the natural spring which was the source of the 'hydraulics', though the canals and island are lost in thick undergrowth and bog.

Fortunately too 'the exquisite Palladian casino' with its rusticated masonry, balustraded roof-line and pedimented doorway, approached by a flight of stone steps, is still to be seen, as is one of the two original flanking pavilions, once linked by a curving wall to the house, so that enough remains for the discerning visitor to visualize the beauty and extent of the house and its landscape in its original form.

Gilling Castle

Trustees of Ampleforth College

At Gilling East, 28 km (18 miles) N of York on B1363 York-Helmsley road. Open July to September daily, except Sundays, 11 am–5 pm. A spectacular terraced garden sheltered by wooded hillsides, situated 67 m (220 ft) above sea level on light loam over boulder clay. Average annual rainfall 760 mm (30 in.).

Going up the gently sloping tree lined drive, from the road above the village, the visitor comes unexpectedly on the fine old Elizabethan castle of which the splendid Great Chamber and Hall are open every day of the year except Sundays. Even then the dignified courtyard does not prepare us for the south-facing garden side where four narrow terraces plunge down the steep hillside from the wide lawn at the top to the green vale far beneath. The steeply rising heavily wooded hillside curving away on both sides into the distance of the North Yorkshire Moors forms a great backdrop to this dramatic picture.

The top lawned terrace, which skirts the castle's lovely old stonework, is yew hedged to the south and west, while the terrace wall is bounded by a narrow bed of red roses. In the angle of the old wall is a healthy fig. To the north a fine long view between hemming masses of woodland gives on to the far countryside with, here and there, red roofed farm-houses peeping through the greenery. In the corner, up stone steps through a balustraded wall, is a small paved garden with a central circular lily pool.

Down steep steps is the second terrace where the sun beating down on the high brick retaining wall gives shelter and warmth to trained peaches. Tall hollyhocks in front help to screen the tracery of branches. The terrace is bisected by a gravel path centred on a circular raised bed filled with roses and a tiny bronze statuette on a raised plinth. In the far wall border grow fuchsias, roses and, rather uncommonly, many standard trained *Hydrangea paniculata.* At the north end of this terrace some boldly castellated and rounded yews terminate the vista.

The third terrace is a narrow strip of lawn, its back wall graced by honeysuckles, trained figs, pears and apples. Low-growing roses give colour in the long border against the retaining wall.

Another steep stairway leads to the final terrace where the natural slope of the land to the foot of the valley has been used to advantage to make a mixed garden of flowers and vegetables. From the 4.5 m (15 ft) high retaining wall wide green paths lead through two large herbaceous borders and the vegetable garden is at the lowest point, lying snugly out of the winds. Under the wall at the far end of this last terrace is a neat range of lean-to greenhouses filled with a variety of indoor plants. The wide borders on one side are filled with a range of colourful annuals – rudbeckias, chrysanthemums, larkspurs and salpiglossis among monkshoods, carnations and campanulas. On the other side the planting is cottage garden style with shrubs among the flowers, roses, hypericums, paeonies and buddleias. Here we find Michaelmas Daisies, heleniums, Sea Lavender, pelargoniums and a long bed of *Aquilegia.* A tall, spreading Cedar of Lebanon terminates the view at the lowest level before the lush green pasture starts to climb steeply to the rim of the woodland frieze.

Stone steps from the west end of this terrace lead up a rough winding path through massed rhododendrons to a small amphitheatre of a garden with a small central lily pool beset with astilbes and ferns – a quiet, flat oasis in this plunging downhill garden.

Harlow Car Gardens

Northern Horticultural Society

At Harrogate, 2.5 km (1½ miles) from town centre on B6162 Otley road, entrance in Crag Lane. Open all the year round 9 am–dusk. Free car park; teas available at Harrogate or nearby Harrogate Arms Hotel. Ornamental and trial gardens of some 24 ha (60 acres), situated 140 m (460 ft) above sea level on a south-west-facing slope on extremely heavy loam (between 4.8 and 5.6 pH) over millstone grit. Average annual rainfall 690 mm (27 in.). Staff of eight.

This is one of the country's most recently created 'great' gardens, for it was only in 1948 that the Society started on its task of making a 'northern Wisley', between the botanic gardens of Kew and Wisley in the south and Edinburgh in the north. Now it comprises trial grounds for roses, kniphofias, delphiniums, annuals, perennials; it has a model vegetable and fruit garden, wild woodlands (the remains of the ancient Forest of Galtres), most pleasingly designed sandstone and limestone rock and scree gardens, streamside garden, lily pools, peat garden, raised beds for alpines and a foliage garden. There is also a comprehensive collection of hellebores, hostas and bergenias, old fashioned roses and a new garden for Australian *Hebe* and *Eucalyptus*.

The avowed aim of its directors has always been to make Harlow Car a 'gardeners' garden' and to collect and label there as many plants as possible, the primary object having always been the collecting of the plants of each genus which are of the greatest garden value. For this same reason plants of one family are not necessarily planted together, as they might be in a botanic garden, but, so far as is possible, planted out in the most practical and eye-satisfying places in the overall ornamental scheme.

Because the soil is on the acid side, the garden is favourable to the planting of rhododendrons and to the other main ericaceous plants, so that there are some 200 different rhododendron species and over 250 named hybrids in the sheltering woodlands.

In the recently landscaped Tarn Meadows, where massive man-made outcroppings of the natural sandstone keep watch over a rock pool and a closely planted streamside, one of the largest collections of heathers has been brought together, so that at any time of the year there is always something colourful and interesting to see, skilful planting of the newer coloured foliage heathers having made this part of the garden a revelation for those who tend to equate heathers with wild moorland.

A walk round Harlow Car is very much dictated by the individual gardener's interests but, having entered the recently erected stone gatehouse, one way is by way of the herbaceous and shrub planted broad walk, with a long vista down and over the stream in the valley and up into the woodlands to a glimpse of Doric columns, once the façade of the Spa Rooms at Harrogate.

Only a little way down the broad walk is the first cross-path to the left, leading to the old heath garden and lily pool. Here, closely ensconced in a broad planting of azaleas, dwarf conifers and heathers in huge drifts, is the Forrest form of *Rhododendron racemosum*, the outstandingly blue foliaged *Picea pungens* 'Koster' and, despite the elevation and the windswept nature of the site, there is a prolifically blooming Chilean Fire Bush *Embothrium coccineum* (*lanceolatum*) 'Norquinco Valley'. Continuing along the lawns below the Tarn Meadow planting of heathers the new rose garden (created 1972) comes into view entered through island beds of shrubs, one forming in its plantings a chronological history of the rose. In autumn one of the best views of the glorious foliage colour the garden is noted for can be had from the large summerhouse by the long row of climbing roses.

Returning from the rose garden downhill, along the course of the upper stream falling in gentle cascades (notice the new Tarn Meadow pool, its island filled with water-loving plants), the upper outlying beds of the sandstone rock garden are reached. Here a series of interconnecting paths, following the several courses of the stream running through it, allow the visitor to see at close quarters the quite bewildering variety of 'rockery' plants. These include many dwarf rhododendrons, *Ceanothus prostratus*, many saxifrages, Asiatic species of *Primula*, big drifts of *Gentiana sino-ornata* and *G. acaulis*, miniature narcissus and species tulips. The plateau-like rock garden, cut by various stream courses, ends in two long 'tails' of scree where those tiny alpines needing sharp drainage and stony soil do so well – *Raoulia glabra*, helichrysums, *Hypericum nummularium*, *Pimelea prostrata*, *Linaria alpina*, *Hutchinsia alpina*, *Arenaria tetraquetra* and *Teucrium*.

From the screes a stone bridge, festooned with honeysuckles, leads across the main stream, ablaze in its season with the bright shouting colours of massed astilbes and Asiatic primulas, the golden yellow of the American Bog Arum *Lysichitum americanum*, the giant leafed, tall stemmed *Gunnera manicata*, the musks hugging the water's edge and, casting their green veils over the picture, Weeping Willows and the conifer-like foliage of the Swamp Cypress, *Taxodium distichum*. The path above the stream and by the edge of the woodland is planted with the Siberica group of iris in blue and white, *Meconopsis*, Kalmia, *Pieris* and spring bulbs.

Not far away from the bridge is the newly rebuilt and refurbished peat garden, terraced and tiered under a most skilful and artistically created 'natural' outcrop of massive sandstone rocks. In the peat garden, where the paths are pine-needled, grows a host of candelabra primulas, including the Harlow Car Hybrids, *Anemone blanda* in various colourings, snowdrop species, *Meconopsis*, *Pulsatilla*, *Trillium*, *Lilium*, *Cyclamen hederifolium* (*neapolitanum*), the sky blue *Jeffersonia dubia* and many tiny leafed miniature rhododendrons. Among this collection are *R. eclecteum*, 'White Bait', *R. ambiguum*, *R. pemakoense*, *R. trichostomum*, *R. radicans* and *R. forrestii repens*, all fascinating in their miniature flowered forms. Then there are species of *Cassiope*, *Andromeda*, *Phyllo-*

doce; Primula capitata sphaerocephala and *P. heucherifolia*, among many members of the great *Primula* family, and the dainty alpine of the high meadows, *Soldanella*.

Just across the path the weather-worn limestone of the rock garden provides a differing habitat for *Dianthus, Lithospermum, Euryops*, thymes, geraniums, *Helichrysum, Diascia, Campanula* in wide variety, *Sedum* and more tiny saxifrages so that in spring the startlingly white stone provides a perfect foil for the intense colour of these inhabitants of both the High Alps and Yorkshire's own high limestone fells.

By some tastefully arranged rustic stone steps at the rear of the peat garden it is possible to leave this level and climb into the woodland, mainly oak and birch, underplanted with daffodils and lilies which provide shelter and home for Harlow Car's noteworthy collection of rhododendrons, many now grown into mature specimens. Here to be seen, and the sight early in the year is quite eye-searing, are rhododendrons, the Himalayan *R. thomsonii, R. fictolacteum, R. fulvum, R. wightii, R. falconeri, R. hodgsonii*, the Chinese *R. calophytum*, the North American *R. vaseyi*, and a mixed bag from China and Burma of *R. campanulatum, R. basilicum, R. bureavii*, the Korean *R. schlippenbachii*, the late flowering 'Polar Bear', the hybrids of *R. griersonianum* and the cultivars of 'Loderi'. With its many friends in the north Harlow Car is ever adding to its collection and the rhododendrons named above are but a small selection of what there is to see. Azaleas add their colour and in *R. luteum* pervasive perfume.

Wide rides through the woodland lead right through to the extensive arboretum where specimen conifers and deciduous trees provide an object lesson in woodland planting.

Returning by the office (which once, when the grounds formed part of a hydropathic establishment, housed sulphur and other medicinal water baths), a climb past the limestone rockery garden to the left brings one to the yew screen and beds containing an extensive collection of hostas, hellebores, including the unusual yellow flowered 'Bowles Yellow', and bergenias. Just below this bed is a newly planted (in 1977) bed for antipodean plants, *Hebe* and *Eucalyptus*. Above the hellebore bed are the model vegetable plot and fruit garden. The vegetable plot (allotment garden size) was started in 1975 and in that year realized from its crops £380 at middle retail shop prices. Planting times, cropping, crop varieties and other relevant details are given on a noticeboard at the top of the plot, near the collection of culinary herbs. Adjacent is a new fruit plot, at the time of writing still to give of its mixed produce of stone and soft fruit.

To the right of the utility plots there is a most attractive border of

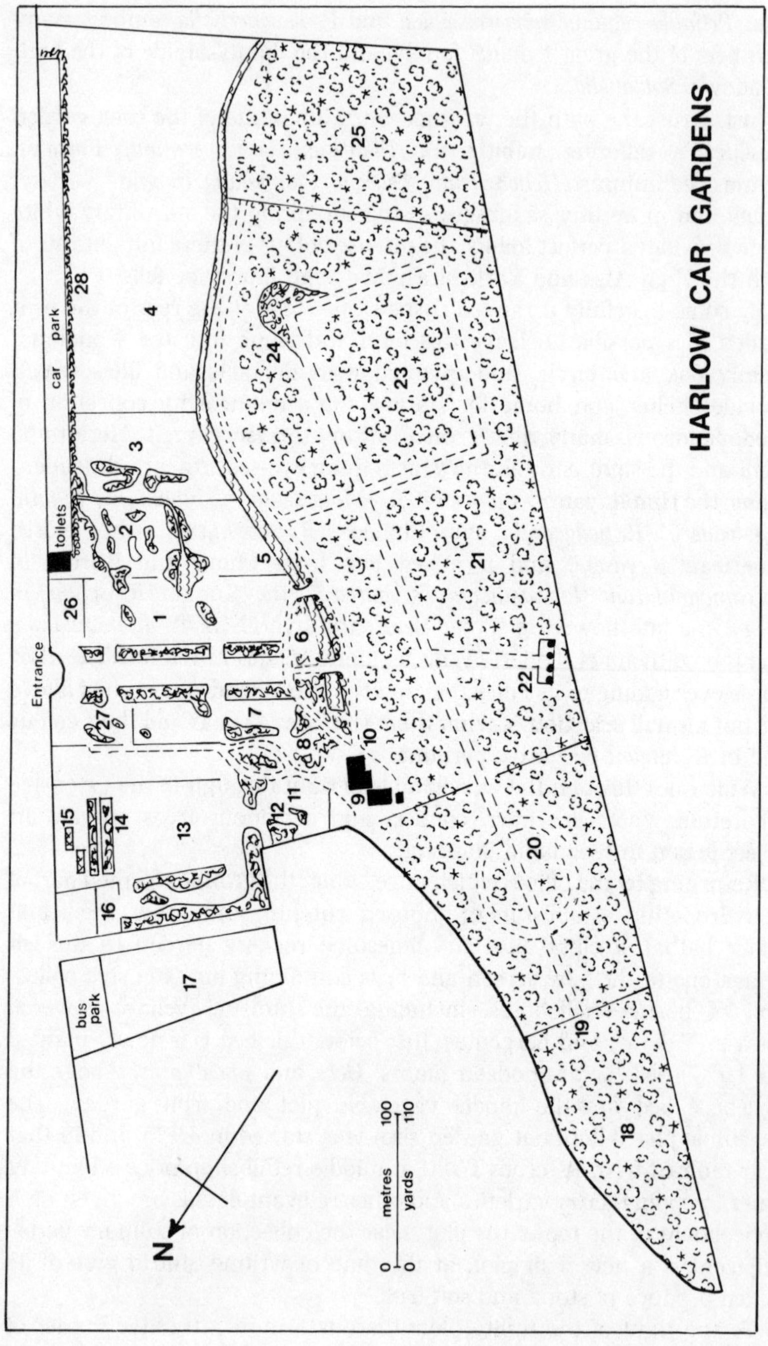
HARLOW CAR GARDENS
car park
toilets
Entrance
bus park
metres
yards
0
100
0
110
N
1
2
3
4
5
6
7
8
9
10
11
12
13
14
15
16
17
18
19
20
21
22
23
24
25
26
27
28

dwarf conifers planted to help the visitor with identification and to show what a splendid display of colour and form can come from discriminate planting of these miniatures of the forest. Nearby are the trial beds for annuals and for perennials, dwarf irises, delphiniums, pansies, sweet peas, pelargoniums, hardy fuchsias and roses, those which are part of the RNRS provincial trials and those from the breeders.

To have gone left up the 'hotel border' between wide beds of old fashioned roses and flowering shrubs would have brought the visitor to a recessed garden of foliage plants. This garden, planted to show what can be done without the benefit of flowers, displays the varied foliage effects of *Rhus*, *Phlomis*, ornamental grasses, rue, *Arum*, dogwoods, variegated weigelas, *Euphorbia*, the Golden Elder, Purple-leaved Plum and variegated lower-growing herbaceous plants including the coloured leaf herbs such as mint, sage and marjoram.

Straight from this garden runs the old fashioned rose border where a collection of more than 200 different species and varieties is grown, largely those which were popular in the last century and before.

Above this border is the alpine house, a treasury of miniature delight, many of the plants having come from post-war expeditions. Note the raised beds nearby for those rather particular alpines which must have perfect drainage and above these, again in raised beds, a fine collection of silver and grey plants, all named to help the visitor with notebook handy.

It is of course impossible to describe in detail all that Harlow Car has to offer, but from the Society's records it is learned that there are growing here 23 separate genera of *Ericaceae* among which are *Ledum*, *Daboecia*, *Kalmia*, *Enkianthus*, *Pieris*, *Epigaea*, *Arbutus*, *Gaultheria*, *Pernettya* and *Vaccinium*. There are 37 species of *Acer*, while *Fothergilla monticola* and *Parrotia persica* add so much to the blaze of autumn colour at Harlow: 8 of *Amelanchier*, 28 of *Cytisus* and *Genista*, 17 of

---

1. Sandstone Rock Garden
2. Heather Garden
3. New Rose Garden
4. Queens Meadow – Specimen Oaks
5. Stream
6. Stream Garden
7. Kalmia Lawn
8. Limestone Rock Garden
9. Offices
10. Peat Terraces
11. Yew Lawn
12. Yew Beds
13. Trials Area
14. Old Fashioned Rose Borders
15. Alpine House
16. Foliage Garden
17. West Wood
18. Sir William's Dell
19. Sorbus Slope
20. Arboretum
21. Oakwood
22. Portico
23. Birchwood
24. Crescent Bed
25. Future Development
26. Winter Garden
27. Old Rose Garden
28. Conifer Screen

Hydrangea, 29 of *Malus*, 13 different oaks, 34 *Sorbus*, 44 different lilacs, 34 *Berberis*, 50 *Cotoneaster*, 14 *Daphne*, 23 *Viburnum* and 20 *Magnolia*. Conifers are represented by more than 160 different kinds. Not everything flourishes at Harlow Car, but then this is its *raison d'être*, for the site was chosen for its less than average soil, its harsh climatic conditions and its elevated position.

Harlsey Hall

J.B. Barnard Esq

Some 11 km (7 miles) NE of Northallerton turn off A19 at signpost to East Harlsey. Open occasionally for charity. A lawns, woodland and lakes garden of 4 ha (10 acres), situated 156 m (500 ft) above sea level on slightly acid soil. Average annual rainfall 710 mm (28 in.). Staff of one and occasional help.

The view from the stone-paved house terrace is down a steeply sloping lawn to the south, outcropped with rockeries and planted with specimen trees, Copper Beeches, conifers, including larches, and maples, over a wide stream to a delightful eighteenth-century temple with a filigree ironwork dome.

The path down the lawn to the bridge over the stream leads to 1 km (¾ mile) of woodland walk by the side of seven man-made lakes where the sycamore and birch cover is carpeted with woodland floor flowers.

Edging the large lawn on the house level on the side of the house next to the walled garden wall, now no longer open, there is a long border of Hybrid Tea roses. From the hall, to the left, a small gate leads to the Saxon foundation church, passing a fifteenth-century brick dovecote.

Harlsey Manor

Mrs Constantine

Next door, as it were, to Harlsey Hall and approached similarly from Northallerton. Open occasionally during the year for charity. A well laid out garden of 1.6 ha (4 acres), situated 140 m (450 ft) above sea level on heavy loam. Average annual rainfall 710 mm (28 in.). Staff of three.

This is an interest-full garden, well cared for, with views from the house terrace over pleasant pastoral countryside to the broad sweep of the Hambleton Hills.

The slightly sloping kitchen garden, on the village side of the house, is neatly privet hedged with well cut yew hedges and topiary work adding interest at the low end. The greenhouses are used for the growing of carnations and begonias, gloxinias, *Streptocarpus* and a collection of ferns.

Walking down the yew topiary walk the formality is carried on by the *Lonicera nitida* hedged lawn approached from either end by large yew arches and having surrounding raised beds from which, early in the year, *Aubrieta* and *Alyssum* make sumptuous curtains of colour. Four flanking beds at the two entrances carry herbaceous plants and a small piece of statuary completes the prim picture. The formal pattern is broken by a tree studded lawn (mainly Silver Birch) in which, framed in cherries and spruce, is a lily pond planted round with the striking foliage and flower stems of an ornamental rhubarb, a form of *Rheum palmatum*. Marsh Marigolds and a large bed of polyanthus at one side offset the cooler tones of the pool.

Through the yew arch nearer the house is seen the long crazy-paved and planted terrace, all manner of ground-hugging plants breaking up the surface. A few steps down from the terrace are two trim lawns, each quite different in character. One is unplanted and divided from the other by a screen of trees, shrubs and a herbaceous border while the second lawn is broken by a variety of trees in a pleasing pattern of cherries, conifers *Prunus cerasifera* 'Pissardii' and a kidney-shaped pool for lilies, fringed with hybrid rhododendrons back to the field edge. Both lawns are sheltered from the countryside around by a screen of mature trees, mainly birch and beech.

Through the tree boundary is a rockery walk with views over the green pastureland to the Hambletons and on the walk are a mixed planting of delphiniums, phloxes, annual rudbeckias, ferns, monkshoods, spring bulbs, the sinuous line of the walk being emphasized by the planting, on either side, of hybrid rhododendrons, maples, cherries, Silver Birch and flowering currants.

A chain of hybrid rhododendrons and borders of shrub roses fill the lower end of the far lawn, hiding the drive to the house.

A belt of foliage colour at the rear of the house comes from an artistic planting of *Picea pungens glauca, Prunus cerasifera* 'Pissardii', cherries, laurels and various ivies in clumps.

The Hutts

Major-General Sir Charles and Lady Dalton

Take the Ripon-Grewelthorpe road, turn left in the main street of Grewelthorpe and follow signposts to 'The Hutts' for 1.6 km (1 mile). Open occasionally for charity when light refreshments are served and picnics allowed in the woodland. A high moorland garden, situated 240 m (800 ft) above sea level. Average annual rainfall 1,150 mm (45 in.).

Called by its owner 'a wild shrub garden', this eyrie of a site commands magnificent long ranging views over a horseshoe lawn and herbaceous and shrub borders down into a deep valley and through woodland and conifer clad hillsides. The woodland drive from the road through groves of rhododendrons is daffodil strewn in spring. And, in due seasons the view from the front lawn is of massed rhododendrons cascading down the hillside in a riot of bloom, clumps of bamboo giving touches of lighter green and of softness to an otherwise solid mass of mixed high colouring.

The borders to the house lawn gain their interest from the silver Willow-leaved Pear, the purple *Cotinus coggygria,* the grey-silver of *Senecio,* with Copper Beech, heaths and *Hibiscus.*

Way below in the valley are two quiet lakes ensconced in thick woodland where the visitor may stroll or picnic in absolute peace.

Kepwick Hall

Mrs A.M. Guthie

Some 7 km (4½ miles) N of Thirsk. Turn E off A19 5 km (3 miles) E of Leake. Open occasionally for charities, when light refreshment is served. Ornamental garden of 1.2 ha (3 acres), part of a large estate, situated 150 m (500 ft) above sea level on slightly acid soil on heavy clay over limestone. Average annual rainfall 660 mm (26 in.).

Nestling under the Hambleton Hills, this magnificently landscaped and planted garden is protected from the east and north by a great sweep of these outlying bastions of the North Yorkshire Moors. The house and garden are in a natural bowl which shuts them off from the world around like a Shangri-la, yet from the house terrace to the south-west are sweeping and beautiful views over the neatly planted parkland to a small lake surrounded by rhododendrons, yews and alders, and to the left, on the flanks of the steep hillside, the rich brown of the bracken in spring is colourful with great masses of *Rhododendron ponticum* which in turn give way to the conifer woodlands and the Hambletons stretching away into the blue distance.

A chance overheard conversation in a train led the owner to bring Mr Robert Wallace from the home counties to landscape these grounds in 1936 and he made a superb job of it. To the left of the house the terrace leads to the yew hedged and sloping kitchen garden which gives way imperceptibly to the ornamental gardens and pleasure grounds. Near the house is a long yew hedged, sloping walk, edged by a herbaceous border terminating in a striking group of spiring conifers behind which mixed woodland climbs the hillside.

The greenhouses at Kepwick are in tip-top order, surrounded by beds of spring flowers including a red anemone *Pulsatilla vulgaris* which has been propagated from a chance seedling. Under the glass there is a melon house for the old 'Blenheim Orange' variety, a carnation house, a nectarine and peach house with space for camellias, Arum Lilies, the sweetly scented *Rhododendron* 'Lady Alice Fitzwilliam', a fine show of *Streptocarpus, Gerbera jamesonii, Agapanthus* and a large old sweet smelling *Jasminum polyanthum*. Many potted plants are grown for house use and for cutting, *Alstroemeria* 'Ligtu Hybrids' being favoured for the latter use. A large bush of the Wintersweet *Chimonanthus praecox* provides scented delight.

In the vegetable garden outdoors expertly trained espalier apples and plums flank the walls, old favourites among the apples here being 'Lord Derby', 'Bramley's Red' and 'Bramley's Seedling'. If you walk back towards the house along this fruit flanked pathway you will come to a circular rose garden, yew hedged and centred on a sundial. Nearby a dense thicket of tall yews is cut through to form a dark, green grotto.

Now the view down the slope is over a three-terraced garden, the raised walls of which are alight in spring with *Aubrieta, Alyssum* and the Shrubby Candytuft. Off the top terrace sweeping curved borders climbing the hillside are full of primulas, the candelabra 'Linda Pope', *Meconopsis,* the purple leaved primrose 'Garryarde Guinevere' and drifts of deep blue *Gentiana acaulis*. A planting of the highly scented *Sarcococca* is near a bed of old Hybrid Tea roses which include 'Prinsesse Margrethe', 'Nordlicht', 'Mister Lincoln', 'Ronsard', 'Violinista Costa', 'Henry Morse' and the more modern 'Super Star'. Also nearby are mixed plantings of *Magnolia, Pieris,* azaleas, rhododendrons, including the fiery 'Ascot Brilliant', *Pittosporum, Mahonia, Viburnum carlesii* and *V. davidii.* A large, dark green Holm Oak, *Quercus ilex*, a towering Wellingtonia, *Sequoiadendron giganteum*, cherries and Japanese maples clothe the gentle slope.

Then, embowered under the woodland trees of the hillside, there is a quiet circular pool, stone-paved around, with water issuing from an ornamental fish mouth. Four flights of steps in a long sloping walk, bordered by massed plantings of rhododendrons and Irish Yews, lead from the pool back to the house. But the path on the upper level through the ordered and beautiful landscape ultimately comes to the edge of the bounding woodland and a walk down the slope by its side reaches the terminus of a long 180m (600ft) terrace which leads back to the house by a series of steps, edged on the field side for a long way by a lavender hedge, then by borders of mixed planting.

A stone seat half-way along is backed by a large bush of the fragrant *Osmanthus* × *burkwoodii* (× *Osmarea* 'Burkwoodii'), and on a leisurely progress to the house you will note *Berberis* and many different rhododendrons, herbaceous plants, conifers including yews, the early flowering *Stachyurus praecox*, the unusual shining silver leaved *Celmisia*, great drifts of heather, the coloured foliage of *Stranvaesia davidiana* and hundreds of *Gentiana acaulis*, which evidently find this soil to their liking, among other spring flowers in great variety. On the slope above in spring are masses of daffodils in the grass under scattered plantings of shrub roses, Copper Beech, whitebeams, the Damson Plum, and the dainty *Nothofagus obliqua*. In the paved courtyard at the rear of the house two flanking beds are planted in spring with massed polyanthus, to be followed by dahlias later in the year.

Kiplin Hall

Trustees of the Kiplin Trust

At Scorton, 11 km (7 miles) NW of Northallerton on B6271. House at present (1978) being extensively restored, house and garden will be open to the public in 1979.

Kiplin Hall is of great historic interest, having been built about 1625 by Lord Baltimore, the founder of Maryland. The grounds are appropriately Jacobean in layout and worth a visit for the garden historian. From the entrance front the view is, over the courtyard, through a tall, imposing ironwork gate up a wide grass drive avenued by limes.

To the right, from the house door, a thick yew hedge flaunts topiary peacocks with high outspread tails and encloses a lawn in which strongly geometrical flower beds give interest and a period flavour.

From this enclosure the view opens south to Copper Beeches, Sweet Chestnuts and a very old huge-boled common beech. To the front of the house the view, over a sloping grass lawn, is to a small lake and over cattle and tree studded country where mature willows predominate.

Middleton Lodge

Mr and Mrs J.R. Ropner

At Middleton Tyas, NE of Richmond, 2.5 km (1½ miles) E of Scotch Corner on the old A1. Open occasionally for charity when teas are available and dogs on lead allowed. Well ordered formal garden and kitchen gardens of some 2 ha (5 acres), situated 110 m (350 ft) above sea level on alkaline soils over shale. Average annual rainfall 610 mm (24 in.). Staff of three and occasional help.

Fine open views to the Cleveland Hills are a feature of this garden, which was laid out, by its owners, as late as 1946. They brought to the task unfaltering taste and obviously an artist's eye for colour contrast – Mrs Ropner is herself a botanical artist of no mean achievement.

By the house entrance, lining the drive, a finely blended shelter belt of trees is most attractive with fine beeches, Wellingtonias, graceful larches and a tall black Incense Cedar, *Calocedrus* (*Libocedrus*) *decurrens*, a rarity hereabouts. Hybrid rhododendrons are planted in and among to give early colour.

On the raised balustraded terrace to the south-east valerian springs high from the paving stones; there are hydrangeas in troughs and a small lawn of mixed and flowering thymes, while *Buddleia alternifolia* and the Climbing Hydrangea, *H. petiolaris*, clamber up the wall. Below the terrace a mixed herbaceous bed sports its spiring lupins, the dark blue of anchusa, the scarlet of lychnis and the magenta of *Geranium psilostemon*.

From the neat, thickly yew hedged lawn the view stretches over a peaceful pastoral scene to the far distant hills. To the right of the lawn is a grand old Turkey Oak furnished to the ground and through the bare tracery of branches in the spring can be seen a carpet of all shades of mauve crocus.

Turning left from this enclosure is a pathway to a circular fish pool. Around the pool the planting has been designed to give a Japanese effect, with its matching six patterns of low-growing green junipers and the taller glaucous *Juniperus squamata* 'Meyeri', the junipers at their different heights looking like footstools for the *Chamaecyparis lawsoniana* 'Lutea' in central columns of gold.

Left again from this open walk we turn to lightly planted woodland where shrub roses 'Constance Spry', 'Cerise Bouquet' and 'Boule de Neige' give colour and where oaks, lime yellow in the spring, clematis climbing the trees and the large creamy white flowers of *Cornus kousa* give added pleasure to this attractive walk. Silver Birch and large clumps of laurel serve at this point to shut out the open views. This brings us to the silver and gold garden by the house wall, where the silver of cotton lavender mixes with the dull purple of *Rosa rubrifolia*, and the deep purple of *Cotinus coggygria* 'Foliis Purpureis' intermingles most dramatically with the sparkle of a tall, spreading Golden Privet. The blue of 'Jackman's Blue' Rue and large leafed hostas show alongside the bright silver of *Cineraria maritima*, while two *Eucalyptus* add their ghostly silvers to the picture. Coloured leaf pelargoniums, *Lonicera nitida* 'Baggesen's Gold', pampas grass and hypericums display their golden foliage and flowers. Widely spaced pyramidal yews add dignity to the rather austere eastern frontage of the house here.

Returning to the main yew hedged lawn a break in the surrounding greenery leads into another garden of taste and sensitivity. A piece of yew topiary in the form of a bird is central, island herbaceous beds with hostas for edging are cut into the lawn and an eye-catching feature by the far hedge is the golden foliaged *Ribes alpinum* 'Aureum'.

This enclosed garden leads on again to a woodland glade walk back to the house where among forest trees are path-bordering plantings of *Viburnum plicatum* 'Mariesii', for its frothy white blossom, more roses, conspicuous being 'Nevada' and 'Constance Spry', autumn colouring maples and *Eucryphia.* In spring the glade is spangled with daffodils.

The extensive kitchen garden, open when the garden is open, is well kept, stocked with vegetables and fruit for the table and herbaceous beds for cutting and colour.

Nawton Tower

Mr and Mrs D. Ward

At Nawton, NE of Helmsley, on A170 between Helmsley and Nawton village. At Beadlam turn and drive N 4 km (2½ miles) on this road. Open on special occasions during the year. Meals at Helmsley; dogs allowed on lead. A wild and formal garden of 4 ha (10 acres), situated 180 m (600 ft) above sea level on moorland, acid soil. South sloping and sheltered by belts of woodland to W and N. Average annual rainfall 710 mm (28 in.). Staff of two and occasional help.

A most unusual and fascinating garden, created, nay torn out of high moorland and woodland 40 years ago. Massed plantings of heathers, rhododendrons, flowering trees, shrubs, old shrub roses and brooms give way to the dignity of formal yew hedged and geometrically shaped eighteenth-century compartmented gardens, each with its own statuary or plantings.

Although there is what at first sight appears to be indiscriminate planting in the wild garden, entered from the wide lawn in front of the house, it is soon apparent that here is a most tastefully and carefully planned arrangement of plant associations for colour, form and dramatic garden effect.

Huge drifts of miniature undulating 'mountains' of *Erica carnea* and *E.* × *darleyensis*, punctuated with the taller and vividly coloured brooms *Cytisus* × *praecox*, *C. scoparius* and *C.* × *kewensis* are the overture to a symphony of tiered rhododendrons. To the left of the first serpentine grass walk the ground base is composed of masses of blues and purples, including the rhododendrons 'Blue Diamond', *R. fastigiatum, R. impeditum, R. keleticum, R. saluenense,* while the high notes come from the sharply contrasting colours and heights of the brilliant scarlet of 'May Day', the yellow-apricot of 'Souvenir of W.C. Slocock', the apple blossom shades of *R. charitopes,* the rose pink of 'Hebe', the tall and spreading form of pink *R. racemosum*, the scarlet of 'Ivanhoe' and the creamy yellow of 'Ivansii'. In and among to give variety are high, spreading plantings of bright orange gleaming *Berberis darwinii*, the flaring beauty of tall *Pieris formosa forrestii* 'Wakehurst' and the more sober greens and glaucous blues of spring conifers in variety.

For a good half of its way the central walk, lined up on the front door of the house down to the far distant wild boar statue, spreads its floral delights. On either side are a conglomeration of hybrid and species rhododendrons, 'Temple Belle', 'Sussex Bonfire', *R. saluenense,* 'Blue Tit', 'Blue Diamond', *R. concinnum, R. pseudoyanthinum,* 'Humming Bird' (this last a beautifully striking deep ruby red), their primary colours contrasting well with the skilfully associated planting of magnolias – *M. stellata, M.* × *soulangiana* 'Lennei Alba', and *M.s.* 'Rustica Rubra', a host of flowering cherries, crab apples, dark columnar yews and the narrow spires of conifers dotted here and there. On the winding side-paths leading off the main walk, colourful vistas and features reward the visitor, the giant parasol of a Weeping Cherry underplanted with forget-me-nots and old shrub roses, among which are seen wide ranging bushes of forms of *R. rugosa, R. pimpinellifolia* (*spinosissima*) and *R. moyesii,* the white froth of *Amelanchier* and *Osmanthus* × *burkwoodii* (× *Osmarea* 'Burkwoodii'), the beautiful blue of *Picea pungens* 'Koster' and the green neatness of *Picea glauca albertiana* 'Conica'. A side-path to the right leads to the top of the azalea avenue ablaze in the late spring with the glorious colourings of hundreds of Ghent and Mollis azaleas.

Having taken our fill of colour and variety, the strict formality, on

---

1. House
2. Courtyard
3. Lawn
4. Peat Rockeries
5. Temple
6. Grass Circle
7. Yew Hedged Garden
8. Sundial
9. Boar Statue
10. Temple
11. Rose Garden
12. Walled Garden

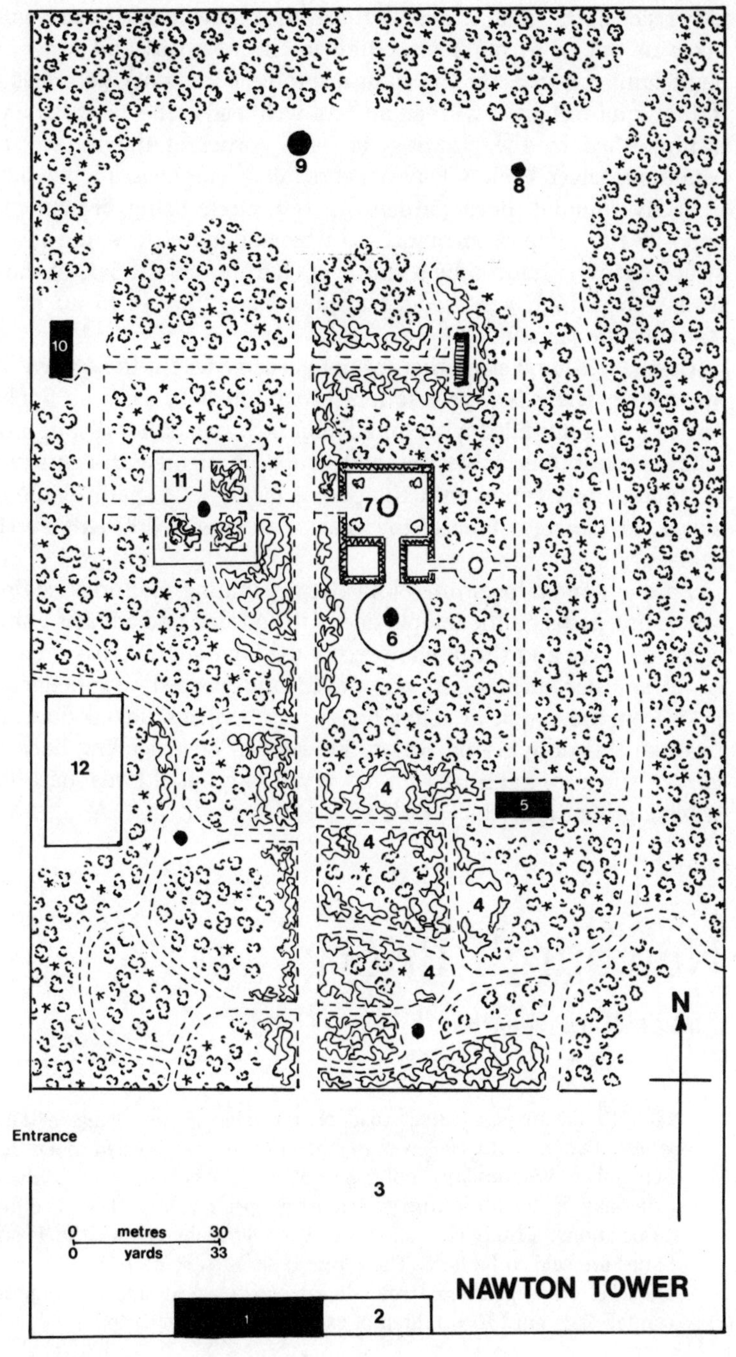
9
8
10
11
7
6
12
4
5
4
4
4
N
Entrance
3
0 metres 30
0 yards 33
NAWTON TOWER
1
2

either side of the main walk, of square, dark, yew hedged secret gardens takes us out of a romantic setting to the neatness and order of the eighteenth century. On the right a wrought ironwork gate leads to a formal square of grass with an ancient wellhead in the centre, the whole distinguished by the planting, at each corner of the square, of the pendulous silver Willow-leaved Pear, *Pyrus salicifolia*. To the side is a perfectly round hedged garden, its yew circle being broken directly opposite the stepped entrance, by a blossoming cherry and its green-sward centre enhanced by a statue of cherubs. On the side of the main walk, too, a high yew hedged avenue leads the eye to an arboured statue at the far end.

On the left-hand side other formal gardens delight the eye with their symmetry. There is a yew square broken at both sides by finely patterned iron gates filled with spirally cut box and, either through the far gate or continuing down the main walk, an eighteenth-century semi-circular temple comes into the period picture, the path leading to it ablaze, at the right time of the year, with over 1,000 Exbury Hybrid azaleas.

As one almost loses oneself in the fascinating plantings edging the serpentine paths on the temple side of the garden and admiring the long views and tree and shrub plantings of the boar statue cross-drive, there is yet another surprise. A long paved and stepped yew hedged walk leads from the temple area to a heavy pedimented solid oak door. We go through this only to find we are in an open lawn leading back to the garden entrance gates past an old Wych Elm full of birds'-nest-looking witch's groom growths.

Newburgh Priory

Captain V.M. Wombwell

Off A19 Easingwold-Thirsk road on the edge of the village of Coxwold, where Laurence Sterne was rector. House and garden open May to September Wednesdays only 2–5.30pm. Teas available. This house, originally a twelfth-century Augustine priory, has close Cromwellian associations; Cromwell's daughter Mary lived here, and the Protector's bones are said to be here. The estate is situated some 67m (220ft) above sea level on well drained soil, slightly on the acid side. Average annual rainfall 760mm (30in.). Staff of two and occasional help.

A fascinating garden with two principal features, the massive and unusual yew topiary work in various parts of the grounds and the 2 ha (5 acre) winding pathed wild water garden and 'rockery'.

Entered through a finely patterned iron gate the 0.8 ha (2 acre) kitchen garden has a rose pergola gravel walk to a central lily pool edged about by a neat circle of *Lonicera nitida.* The old favourites 'American Pillar', 'New Dawn' and 'Dorothy Perkins' roses climb the pergola. On the tall brick walls between trained pears, mostly luscious 'Comice', and a tall, most flourishing pineapple-scented broom, *Cytisus battandieri,* are *Ribes speciosum,* a grand old Sweet Bay, and variegated *Euonymus.*

If we make our way past the nicely proportioned stable block to the house the shaped yew and shrub studded lawn has views through mature beeches and limes up the sloping hillside where cattle and horses graze. On the centuries-old masonry of the house are growing *Actinidia,* a wisteria, more *Euonymus* and magnolias. Along the wide gravel walk at the front of the house we come to cherries, planted in the lawn just beyond the terrace gate, which herald the start of a cherry and crab apple walk through closely planted woodland. Turning to the right through an extensive upward-sloping lawn, tree studded, we come to the entrance to the wild water garden. It would be impossible to reach this point, however, without first noticing the plaques on the trees, for here is royal history. There is an oak planted by Queen Mary on her first visit to Newburgh on 22 August 1923; a Wellingtonia planted by the Prince of Wales in September 1877; a beech given its start in life by Prince Albert Victor in November 1887; an elm bearing the Duke of Cambridge's title and the date December 1851; another oak planted by Prince Albert Victor, also in November 1887; and a Scarlet Oak nearby planted by Princess Mary on 22 August 1923.

At the top of this lawn, before entering the water garden, there is a mixed planting of maples and a *Parrotia persica* to add its own version of autumn colour.

Blessed with several sources of running water at all times, the Newburgh wild water garden is almost a tangle of lush greenery embowering and hiding the many intriguing paths winding their various ways uphill to the top of the garden. The way in is bordered by raised alpine beds full of *Gentiana acaulis* for early flowering and *Gentiana septemfida* for later in the year. By the path, among the golden conifers at this low end of the garden, are seemingly scores of troughs and ornamental containers full of miniature alpine treasures, among which can be seen *Achillea argentea* (*Tanacetum argenteum*), *Artemisia lanata, Campanula pusilla, Draba aizoon, Scutellaria alpina, Teucrium,*

Tanacetum, Calocephalus brownii and a host of saxifrages, stonecrops, houseleeks and many other alpine plants relishing the conditions provided for them.

Through the green thickets of bamboo surrounding the several pools edged with the giant leaved *Gunnera manicata*, the American Bog Arum, *Lysichitum americanum*, the architecturally foliaged *Ligularia spp.* and drifts of Asiatic primulas, we mount the paths to find in one corner a collection of the small leaved rhododendrons, while the various forms of Japanese maple foliage edge the paths here and there. Enjoying the shade and shelter is a varied planting of Kurume and Japanese azaleas, and a big bush of *Rosa moyesii* helps in the screening in from the outside world of these quite enchanting gardens.

If we make our way back over the royal tree lawn, down the sloping greensward we have a magnificent view to a lake edged with a collection of mature trees at one corner but quite free of planting in the centre, so that the eye is taken over the countryside to the dramatic view of the White Horse, a great animal sculptured into the limestone of the Hambleton Hills some miles away.

Flanking the entrance courtyard, overlooking the lake, is a roofless and ancient building where Captain Wombwell has paved the floor and planted in the pavement and borders a lovely serene garden of lilies of the valley, irises, soft spreading drifts of *Alchemilla mollis*, ivy climbing the walls, pink hydrangeas with roses to match and, in an angle of the walls, a pear and a flourishing fig. On the back wall is a touching reminder of the love we can have for animals for here on a conventional tombstone above the grave of a horse are these words:

> In memory of The Turk. He went to the East in the Spring of 1854 and carried Sir George O. Wombwell, Bt., at the battles of Alma and Inkerman. Died at Newburgh aged 26 years.

Newburgh has much to offer to the garden lover.

Newby Hall

R.E.J. Compton Esq

At Skelton-on-Ure, 6 km (4 miles) SE of Ripon on B6263 Boroughbridge road, 5 km (3 miles) W of A1. House and garden open Easter Saturday to second Sunday in October Wednesdays, Thursdays, Saturdays, all Bank Holidays 2–6 pm, garden only Monday, Tuesday, Friday 11 am–6 pm. Car park; teas available in orangery. Fine Adam-decorated house attributed to Sir Christopher Wren, containing superb tapestries, furniture and rare collection of classical sculpture collected in the eighteenth century. Garden of 10 ha (25 acres), situated 23 m (75 ft) above sea level on differing soils, mostly neutral. Susceptibility to spring frosts modified by wall and hedged shelter. Average annual rainfall 690 mm (27 in.). Staff of three or four.

A variety of soils from light sandy to heavy clay and alluvial deposits, mainly lime-free, enabled the owner's father, the late Major Compton, in 1925 to create, from a stylized Victorian layout and an Ellen Wilmott period-piece rock garden, one of the finest all-round interest gardens in Yorkshire, as full of varied and rare plantings as one could wish to see.

As you enter the garden from the formality of the south terrace (with its Queen Anne mirror shaped lily pool and its four magnificent Adam urns in clipped yew frames), and walk over the yew hedged lower lawn, the main axis of the garden is revealed. This is the famed long border, 320 m (1,050 ft) of it, leading in a gentle, south-facing slope to the River Ure, which borders the garden. The other compartmented gardens can be reached from this long floral walk.

But first let us stay on the long walk, edged on both sides by walls of yew, with its very wide herbaceous and shrub-planted borders designed for their effect, in bands of differing colour, by Major Compton. As well as the usual and favourite herbaceous flowering plants there are other unusual and interesting plants, such as the rare purple *Delphinium cashmerianum atropurpureum*; the yellow dwarf Kniphofia 'Gold Else'; *Romneya coulteri*, the Californian Tree Poppy; Newby's own selection of *Alstroemeria* 'Ligtu Hybrids' in great drifts; the not often seen False Hellebore, *Veratrum nigrum*; paeonies *P. mlokosewitschii*, *P. peregrina* (*lobata*), *P. delavayi* and *P. veitchii* 'Woodwardii'; a fine *Campanula latiloba* 'Highcliffe', and edging them all the feathery silver of *Artemisia ludoviciana* 'Silver Queen', while the tall feathery blooming large

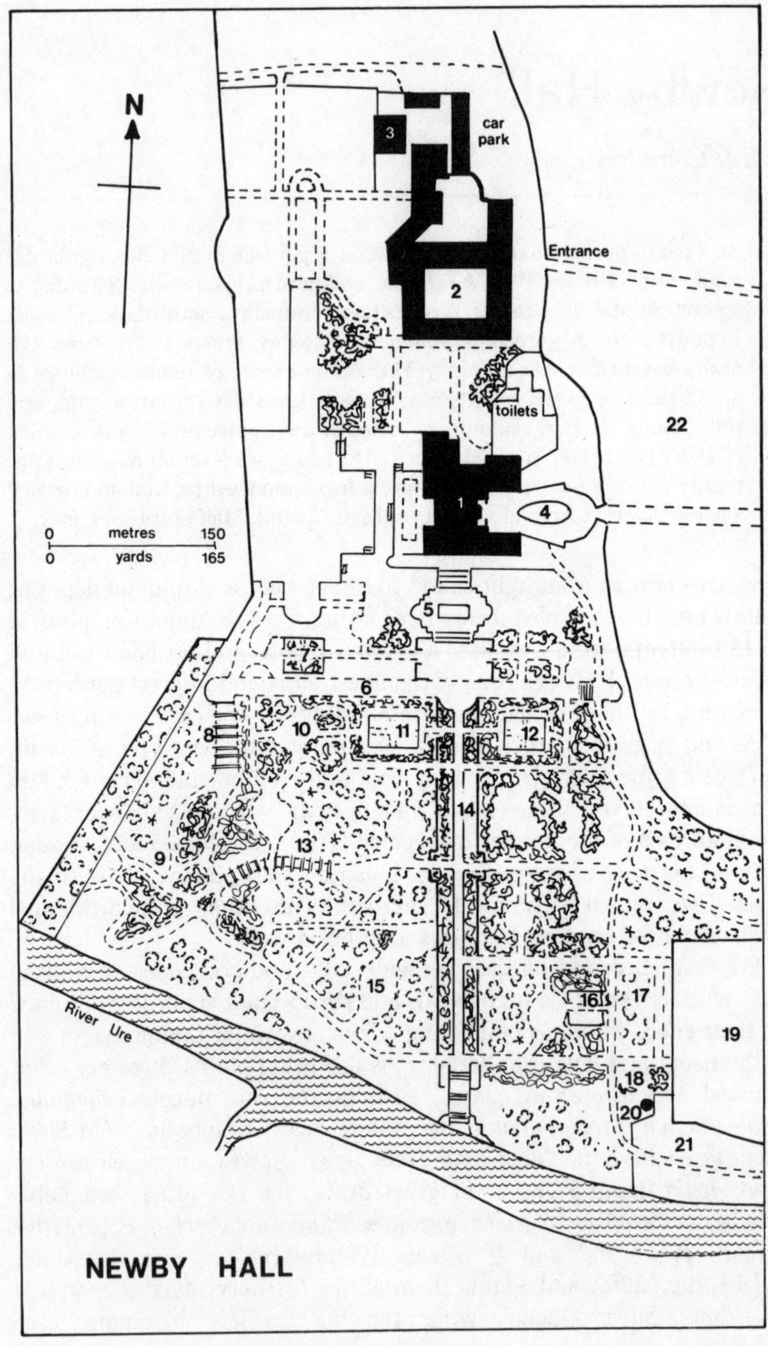
N
car
park
3
2
Entrance
toilets
22
1
4
0 metres 150
0 yards 165
5
7
6
8
10
11
12
14
13
9
15
16
17
19
18
20
21
River Ure
NEWBY HALL

leafed *Crambe orientalis* fills in the background. To give colour, contrast and height are plantings of the rose 'Iceberg', the red leafed *R. rubrifolia*, the variegated blooms of *R. versicolor*, a weigela with purple leaves, *Genista virgata*, *Philadelphus*, *Potentilla* and *Hypericum* in variety.

Running east-west at right angles to the long border is the statue walk, a wide gravelled path lined with seventeenth-century Venetian stone statues on pedestals, their whiteness staining the red leafed *Prunus cerasifera* 'Pissardii' and the dark Irish Yews planted behind. The pedestals rise from tangles of *Cotoneaster horizontalis*.

Hydrangeas do well here, particularly the Lacecaps, Major Compton's favourite being *H. macrophylla* 'Veitchii'. Here also grow *Eucryphia lucida* (*billardieri*), *E. glutinosa* and *E.* × *nymansensis* 'Nymansay' and the large pendant white cups and claret coloured flowers of *Magnolia sinensis*. This semi-open woodland has also proved congenial to some of the camellias, in particular 'Tricolor de Siebold', *C. saluenensis*, *C. japonica* 'Magnoliiflora' and 'Cornish Snow', though the Major plumped for *C.* × *williamsii* 'Donation' and 'Elizabeth Rothschild'as the two best for Yorkshire gardens. There are various hybrid rhododendrons and, a plant effect its late owner was very fond of, a 3 m (10 ft) high *Erica arborea alpina* at the foot of two or three tall Scots Pines with, as neighbours, *Camellia japonica* 'Latifolia', *Stewartia koreana* and the hostas *H. undulata univittata* and 'Thomas Hogg'.

Below the statue walk are delightful compartmented gardens, the western one being a sunken rose garden, neatly paved with York stone and full of low-growing, smothering and mounded plants. This is surrounded by a Copper Beech hedge planted by Major Compton 'as a foil to the delicate charm of the rose leaf'. The central circular bed is occupied by *Rosa chinensis* 'Old Blush' underplanted with *Viola cornuta* and in the four main beds grow many of Major Compton's favourite old fashioned roses – 'William Lobb', 'Tour de Malakoff', the Scotch Rose 'William III', 'Fantin-Latour', 'Nuits de Young', *R. farreri persetosa*, the Threepenny Bit Rose, a collection of Hybrid Musks including 'Penelope'

---

1. Newby Hall
2. Stable Block
3. Orangery Tea House
4. East Front
5. Lily Pond
6. Statue Walk
7. Sylvia's Garden
8. Iris Pergola
9. Rock Garden
10. July Garden
11. Species Rose Garden
12. Autumn Garden
13. Curving Pergola
14. Herbaceous Borders
15. Rhododendron & Wild Garden
16. East Rock Garden
17. Orchard Garden
18. Tropical Garden
19. Kitchen Garden
20. Wheel House
21. Children's Playground
22. Parkland

and 'Nur Mahal' and the *rugosa* hybrids. Next to the rose garden is the July garden, filled with midsummer blooming plants.

On the eastern side is the autumn garden, a collection of plants to give of their best in August and September – *Buddleia, Fuchsia, Phlox,* heathers, yuccas, *Crocosmia, Poncirus trifoliata* (*Aegle sepiaria*), late roses, *Hoheria, Ceanothus* and dahlias bedded out annually.

Another small sunken garden on the north side of the statue walk is called Sylvia's garden, named for Major Compton's late wife, a sunken, paved, period garden, surrounded by yew hedges and containing many of Sylvia's favourites – pinks, aubrieta, thyme and other cushioning plants, lavender, catmint and the silver leafed plants *Senecio* and Cotton Lavender, and, in and among, the lustrous white trumpets of *Lilium regale*.

Near the river to the west of the long border is the garden filled with species rhododendrons.

More unexpected treasures of Newby are in the walled enclosures and on the walls to the east of the main border where the alluvial soils of the river and the shelter of the appropriately south-facing walls, including the long stretch of the kitchen garden wall (the kitchen garden is not open) give protection and encouragement to a host of tender plants normally found in the south and west country – *Viburnum × bodnantense*, a cloud of pink in January; *Xanthoceras sorbifolium*, whose white, carmine-eyed flowers bloom in May; *Wisteria sinensis* 'Alba', that rarity *Magnolia dawsoniana*, 7.5 m (25 ft) high, which flowered in 1971 after years of anxious waiting, along with other magnolias, *M. sinensis*, *M. × soulangiana* 'Lennei', *M.s.* 'Alba Superba', *M.s.* 'Brozzonii', the aristocrat of the *soulangiana* types, and *M. Lypoleuca*. *Ozothamnus rosmarinifolius*, rarely seen, grows well here. Other plantings worth looking up are *Clethra delavayi, Osteomeles schweriniae*, of the rose family, and *Stranvaesia davidiana*, which berries well each winter. *Azara lanceolata* and *A. microphylla* bloom happily along with the Californian shrub *Carpenteria californica*.

From the long herbaceous border towards the river there is a heritage from the Victorian garden, a curving, stone-paved, stone-pillared pergola, covered in old roses, honeysuckles, laburnum, wisteria and quince. By the walk side are alpine beds to link up with the rock garden, beyond which, through light woodland and shrubs, we look over the river. This rockery, with old steps leading down to and around pools and streams, is the romantic setting for all manner of tiny rock plants, as well as the taller more lush moisture-loving subjects. In the woodland, underplanted with all the spring flowers and designed to give shelter to a host of the more tender shrubs and trees, is a multiple planting of *Acer griseum* with its colourful peeling bark, *Prunus serrula*, whose polished mahogany red bark attracts the hands to stroke, a collection of flowering cherries and lilacs and the tender *Viburnum japonicum* (*macrophyllum*), which has seen near on 40 Yorkshire winters and still flowers profusely. In the east rock garden there is *Embothrium coccineum lanceolatum*, alight each June with vivid red blossoms, and a collection of *Pieris* represented by *Pieris floribunda*, *P. japonica*, *P. taiwanensis* and the most delectable of all, which early in the year bears the scarlet shoots that fully earn it its name of 'Forest Flame'. An iris walk, where paeonies and old French roses intermingle with the iris, leads from the rock garden back to the statue walk.

In the orchard garden, sheltered on three sides by high brick walls, the apples, alternate standard and half standard, were planted years ago not so much for their fruit as for their blossom. Major Compton had them underplanted with alternate rows of hellebores and paeonies for their foliage and flower effect. An old horse-powered 'wheel house' nearby once drew water for the gardens.

The gardens at Newby Hall are a plantsman's delight and an inspiration to the northern gardener, who can see just what successful inroads the gardener can make into the harshness of the northern climate by providing shelter and microclimates.

Norton Conyers

Sir Richard and Lady Graham

---

6 km (4 miles) SE of Ripon off A61. Open 1 June to 30 September every Wednesday and occasionally on differing dates for charity. For hours see current issue of *Historic Houses, Castles and Gardens*. Teas available; dogs allowed on lead. The seventeenth-century house, with family portraits, fine oak staircase and associations with Charlotte Brontë, is also open. Walled kitchen and ornamental gardens of approximately 0.6 ha (1½ acres), situated 30 m (100 ft) above sea level on dry, sandy, gravelly soil. Average annual rainfall 640 mm (25 in.). Staff of one and occasional help.

The attraction here is the walled kitchen and ornamental garden sloping to the south-west. A wide path leading to a gate with views over flat parkland is edged on either side with fine walls of yew sheltering wide herbaceous borders in old world cottage style, the planting being predominantly silver, grey and gold. Lady Graham has used for her colouring lavender, rosemary, irises, *Eremurus, Thermopsis, Camassia, Trollius*, the cranesbill geraniums, *Fritillaria*, hellebores, double Day Lilies, poppies and those finely decorative paeonies *Paeonia lutea* and *P.l. ludlowii*. The early flowering *Clematis macropetala* and Morello Cherries cover the end wall.

To the right of the yew hedged border is a long path bordered by *Aquilegia* in variety, an unusual border subject, but one which contrasts well with the yew. A lovely old orangery is the background to a small but effective grey and silver garden and a small bed nearby is home for a collection of alpine auriculas.

The old vinery glass on the same level as the orangery has been stripped and the area turned into a fascinatingly planted sitting-out room-cum-arbour. Climbers obviously relish the site for rampant on the walls are the old rose 'Gloire de Dijon', the Potato Vine, *Solanum crispum, S. jasminoides* and the scarlet-trumpeted honeysuckle *Lonicera × brownii*. Up the wooden pillars supporting the open roof clambers a vigorous *Clematis macropetala*, the fragrant, red-purple flowered *Akebia quinata* and *Passiflora coerulea*. In ornamental pots are the evergreen white flowering *Nerium oleander* and *Agapanthus*. In the paved garden area around is the rich blue flowering *Ceratostigma willmottianum*, with stocks, tobacco plants and a lovely white daphne for scenting the air.

By the side of the vinery, where *Gentiana acaulis* thrives, are planted three old shrub roses, *R. hugonis*, the fern leaved *R. × cantabrigiensis* and the Threepenny Bit Rose, *R. farreri persetosa*. Near the rear wall is a bed of the new dwarf irises and close by a fine plant of the white flowered Bleeding Heart, *Dicentra formosa* 'Alba'. The old world character of this part of the garden is echoed by large clumps of lily of the valley, hostas, fritillaries and variegated mint in a bed by the greenhouse.

The terrace to the front of the house with its long ha-ha has wide ranging views over flat, pastoral countryside.

Otterington Hall

Miss M. Furness

On A167 near South Otterington village, 6 km (4 miles) S of Northallerton. Open occasionally for charity. A series of ornamental gardens, walled kitchen and fruit garden covering 1.2 ha (3 acres), situated 35 m (120 ft) above sea level on slightly acid, clayey loam. Average annual rainfall 640 mm (25 in.). Staff of two.

One of the finest topiary gardens in the county and kept in perfect trim, these pleasure grounds provide a series of differing and intriguing garden pictures.

Starting out in the old walled garden, with a southerly aspect, the greenhouses there still provide for the house excellent peaches, nectarines, grapes and, for decoration, Arum Lilies, orchids, mimosa and roses 'White Ensign' and 'Madam Butterfly'.

The wall panels are picture frames for meticulously fan trained Morello Cherries, gooseberries, red and white currants, while espalier trained apples and pears form neat, useful edges to the paths. In the sheltered square at the rear of the house is an old world brick-paved garden planted with old fashioned tulips, *Iris unguicularis* (*stylosa*) and herbs, the house walls providing shelter for figs, apricots and a 100 year old Greengage Plum.

At the upper end of the kitchen garden is a rose hedge made up of the thornless 'Zéphirine Drouhin', 'Hugh Dickson' and climbing 'Gruss an Teplitz'. An openwork iron gate by the hedge leads through the wall into the pleasure grounds.

By the south wing of the house to our right is a rose garden of ordered squares planted with six differently coloured roses. A hedge of briar roses is planted for protection and on the house and the back of the kitchen garden wall are flourishing magnolias and clematis.

If we come now to the front of the house, the lawn here is terminated by a high wall of yew, the ironwork gate in its centre being flanked by yew pillars with round balls of yew atop them and in two sunken circular beds at either side are hoop shaped yews like the Michelin tyre man! Looking through the gate and between buttressed and topiary worked yew hedges, the eye is led to a small statue at the far end of the walk.

If you go round this yew wall you will see that the central pathway dividing the lawn is for part of its length a stone-pillared chain-linked rose pergola carrying 'American Pillar', 'Climbing Dorothy' the old (1924) 'Clematis' and the newer 'Dortmund'. The lawn is backed by a planting of lilacs, cherries, crab and shrub fuchsias. Five spiring Lawson Cypresses give foliage and form a contrast against the tall blackness of the yew wall.

Then we come to a completely round rose bed divided into four by stone paths and planted for effect with lighter and darker coloured roses. At the far side of the tight circle is an arched yew arbour with a seat in its curved recess.

Down some steps to the left is a half-moon pool with a small boy and fish fountain. Pink cherries give colour at this end of the lawn. To the left again one of the glories of Otterington is the long 45 ml (150 ft) grass carpeted yew garden with two great arches in yew at one end and another single, wide spanning arch at the other. Hard against the tall, meticulously trimmed yew hedges on either side are squared yew pedestals on which have been 'carved' 11 figures on one side and 8 on the other – birds, animals, spirals and tiers, a most accomplished piece of the topiarist's art.

Through the yews and down towards the extreme edge of the pleasure grounds another surprise awaits us, for behind a tree screen there is a walk overlooking open countryside, planted with hybrid rhododendrons, azaleas, heathers, daffodils, clematis, herbaceous plants and, in their season, yellow crocuses. Leaving this pleasant glade for the house we walk on the lower terrace lawn tastefully planted with cherries, *Magnolia* × *soulangiana* and *M.s.* 'Lennei', a mulberry, maples and the Handkerchief Tree, *Davidia involucrata*. It should be noticed that in the two curving beds at each side of the ironwork gate the plantings are exactly matching – lilacs, crab apple and cherry.

On the stable block wall as we leave this garden there is a fine old heavily trunked 'Beurré Bedford' Pear and at the rear another early pear which has been there so long the gardener cannot name it.

Parcevall Hall

Walsingham College Trust

Just 1.6 km (1 mile) NE of Appletreewick in Wharfedale off B6265 Pateley Bridge-Skipton road. Gardens open regularly during year. Teas available. A most unusual 3.2 ha (8 acre) garden of terraces and wild woodland, situated 180 m (600 ft) above sea level on light loam over limestone. Average annual rainfall 1,020 mm (40 in.). Staff of two.

At this seventeenth-century manor house hidden away in a deep rift of Wharfedale the late Sir William Milner (who bought the property in 1927) created two gardens; a massively buttressed and terraced garden in front and at the back a wild woodland garden following the natural contours of the hillside and planted with rhododendrons, many of them from China.

From the front, facing south, the giant, craggy bulk of Simon's Seat, 476 m (1,544 ft) topped by the jagged teeth of the Hen Stones, is silhouetted against the sky making a dramatic *mise-en-scène* to the garden. Between the house and the mountain runs the fertile wooded valley of the Skyreholme Beck, taking the eye sweeping down Wharfedale to historic Barden Tower in the far distance.

On this steep hillside Sir William threw up his imposing terraces, each with its own character both architecturally and in its planting.

We approach the hall and its garden up a steeply sloping walk to the courtyard, with on one side lilacs and *Escallonia* backed by Scots Pines and larches. By cottages on the other side the tender pink flowers of *Nerine bowdenii* bloom in the wall borders and in the hedge there is an unusually deep yellow flowered jasmine which blooms in July, most probably *Jasminum revolutum*.

Through a wicket gate on the left we find the chapel garden, a charming, restful oasis, a paved and sheltered enclosure where beds in the stone are filled with fuchsias and marguerites. A tiny stream coming from the dense woodland behind runs through a carpet of primulas to foam into a small but deep pool.

Well worn stone steps at the far end of the chapel garden lead to a path to the orchard where, by a tall hedge of dark conifers, there is a stone porch, the entrance to the rose garden. Once again the great hulk of Simon's Seat looms over the tall conifers that surround and shelter this Persian carpet square of colour, which slopes quite steeply to the south. In the beds separated by paved paths are roses 'Kerryman', 'Iceberg', 'Frensham' and 'Tom Tom', and over the porch sprawls an old Pompom rose. The wide borders all around are filled with old fashioned roses and *Phlox*.

From the orchard the path winds uphill through the rhododendrons in the thickly planted woodland which in spring is carpeted with *Narcissus cyclamineus*, bluebells and *Orchis maculata*, pale purple spotted and brownish flowered. In among the mixed plantings of ash, sycamore, larch and oak are *Acer griseum* with its peeling bark, *Magnolia × soulangiana, M. sieboldii, M. campbelli* and *M.c. mollicomata*. Rhododendrons which Sir William planted here profusely have so crossed naturally that experts find their nomenclature puzzling, but there can be seen one of the noblest of the Chinese species *R. calophytum*, as well as *R. × caucasicum* 'Cunningham's Sulphur', now rare, *R. auriculatum*, which flowers in August along with the hybrid 'Polar Bear'; *R. williamsianum* of the small round foliage; June flowering *R. lepidostylum* and hybrids 'Rex'; 'Cilpinense', a Bodnant raised plant, and one of the choicest of the hybrids, 'Penjerrick' with its fragrant, creamy yellow flowers.

Thc path, climbing all the time, next comes to a natural limestone outcrop serving as a ready-made cascade for spring water falling into a lily pond surrounded with *Primula florindae*, grown from seed sent by Kingdon Ward, as well as ferns and astilbes. A second cascade pool is higher up the hillside. Planted for their foliage effect to surround the pools in an exotic enclave are White Spruce, *Picea glauca, Thuja occidentalis* 'Rheingold', *Juniperus × media* (Pfitzerana', *Chamaecyparis lawsoniana* 'Fletcheri' and *C.l.* 'Stewartii'. Large, mounded bushes of *Potentilla, Cotoneaster, Ilex × altaclarensis* 'Camelliifolia' and *Salix lanata* help with foliage contrast at this picturesque spot.

There are Three Paeonies, *Mahonia* and *Erica carnea* growing around, but the ever uphill path beckons on, passing through mainly ash woods, until it terminates at a wooden gate. Through this there is another dramatic Wharfedale view, this time of Trollers' Gyll, seen 30m (100ft) below, where a swiftly running stream has cut a steep sided valley, leaving it scarred, studded and patterned with imposing limestone outcropping.

The way back to the house is by a higher path which descends to the courtyard level where a Wilson introduction, *R. sutchuenense*, is underplanted with Asiatic primulas, a natural combination.

Through a wooden door in a high wall here and, hey presto! Sir William's bird's eye view of this secluded corner of Wharfedale is revealed; the door opens on to the top one of four terraces which descend to a paved garden. The house terrace to the left is also paved and on the house walls a giant spreading 'Albertine' rose, a trained laburnum, *Viburnum farreri (fragrans)*, and a wisteria. Small beds cut into the paving of the terrace are planted up with annuals appropriate to the season and in the border under the walls the tender South African *Phygelius capensis* is quite happy.

A flight of imposing steps leads to the second terrace where a round lily pool, dignified, cool and light-reflecting, with white flowers only, is the principal feature. The central portion is separated from the two ends of the terrace by neat yew hedges. At the left end of the terrace is a wood and stone pergola over which old fashioned roses grow in abandon, along with the clematis 'E.W. Gladstone'. A variety of camellias grows underneath the shelter. Beds in the terrace paving hold, in a lovely colour combination, the deep orange *Crocosmia masonorum*, a deep red variety of montbretia, yellow Day Lilies, white marguerites, dark red astilbes, bright yellow *Lysimachia punctata*, lavender and roses. On the terrace wall are a wide spreading *Solanum crispum* with its blue potato-like flowers, vines, *Jasminum nudiflorum*, *Actinidia kolomikta* of the pink splashed leaves. *Hamamelis mollis*, the Chinese Witch Hazel, which throws up its spidery blooms in January/February, and two large *Eucryphia* × *nymansensis* 'Nymansay', which embower a seat at the other end of the terrace.

The descent to the third terrace is by a pair of stone steps built around a recessed arch in the terrace wall from the centre of which water flows gently into a deep semicircular pool. Four old dome-topped cherries form a central feature on this terrace. To the right through screening yew hedges is an oblong stone-rimmed lily pool in which white and cream lilies echo the serenity of the top pool and demonstrate the superb taste of Sir William's plantings. On the walls here, surprisingly for this elevation in the north, are found the Chilean beauty *Crinodendron hookeranum*, of the scarlet Japanese lantern flowers, *Magnolia* × *soulangiana*, *Buddleia globosa* with its tiny orange pompon balls of flower, the grey tassels of *Garrya elliptica*, the pineapple-scented broom *Cytisus battandieri*, the sun-loving *Abelia*, climbing roses and *Escallonia*.

Grassed and bounded by beech hedges, the final terrace has a contrasting simplicity. A deep recessed arch encloses a seat which is so warmly sheltered it can be used at Christmas time. To the left the terrace level is raised, steps leading to raised beds of *Meconopsis* and polyanthus. The terrace wall is again clothed with interest – *Chaenomeles japonica*, *Ceanothus thyrsiflorus*, a variety of *Buddleia* including the deep rose *Buddleia colvilei* and white flowered *B. davidii alba*. Wide steps down to a long lawn set between conifers lead the eye, or the feet if one is energetic, to the thick band of woodland hiding the beck and the start of the long climb to Simon's Seat.

There is still another feature of Parcevall we should see before we leave, the camellia walk, under the great flying buttresses of Sir William's massive terrace walls where fuchsias, rhododendrons, including the original *R. forrestii repens*, azaleas and, of course, camellias are growing. Even edging the car park there are one or two more surprises: the Chilean evergreen with holly-like leaves and scarlet tubular flowers *Desfontainea spinosa*, the shining gold leafed *Gleditsia triacanthos* 'Sunburst' and the bottle brush flowered and autumn colouring *Fothergilla monticola*.

Ripley Castle and Gardens

Sir Thomas Ingilby, Bt

At Ripley, 1.6 km (1 mile) from Harrogate off A61 Harrogate-Ripon road. Gardens and castle open Easter Sunday and Monday then all Sundays and Banks Holidays from May to September, gardens only open Saturdays 2–6 pm. Parties by arrangement. Teas available; dogs allowed on lead. Walled and pleasure gardens, parkland and lake of 72 ha (180 acres), situated 75 m (240 ft) above sea level on well drained medium loam over millstone grit. Average annual rainfall 690 mm (27 in.) Staff of two.

A notable mid-eighteenth century Brown landscape in which the fourteenth-century castle is set. Before entering the spacious cobbled square leading to the 1450 gatehouse, with its village stocks and market cross, notice the model village with its Hôtel de Ville (1854) and its cottages of Gothic and Tudor style reconstructed between 1780 and 1861. On entering the castle grounds spare a glance to the right for the battlemented stable block with its clock and clock-faced wind direction indicator.

From a battlemented terrace there is a fine view of the parkland split by a serpentine lake, the upper lake 2.8 ha (7 acres) in extent and the lower one 11 ha (26½ acres). Looking south-west the vista is over the narrow neck of the lake, in spring over hosts of daffodils, to a pretty

Victorian ironwork bridge where the waters of the lake fall down a steep cascade and out into the surrounding countryside.

Looking north from the other terrace the lake opens out into a fine sheet of placid water in which two wooded islands lead the eye to a three-arched stone bridge through which, over a sparkling cascade, the waters of the upper lake descend. In the middle distance, looking up Nidderdale to the blue, hazy hills of Yorkshire moorland, can be seen the picturesque roofs of the village of Bishop Thornton. On the sloping greensward of the lakeside are fine old beech and oak trees, planted in Brown's time. Together with the browsing deer and a herd of Black Angus cattle they give today the exact effect which Brown must have envisaged. On the lake Canadian Geese, swans, coots and waterhens make a pleasing pattern.

From the north-facing terrace a path leads past an old summerhouse into the walled pleasure garden. Here, facing south-west on the far wall, are two terminal balustraded stone summerhouses and, in the centre, a handsome 1820 orangery with semicircular iron and glass roof. Some very old and very thick stemmed wisteria clothe half of the wall under which is a wide herbaceous border. In front the two spacious lawns have been cut into ornamentally shaped beds for roses, mainly Hybrid Teas, with one bed of 'Hugh Dickson' planted 70 years ago. Peaches and nectarines can be seen in the lean-to greenhouses which fill the other half of the rear wall. If the path is followed round a disused fountain basin comes into view amidst tall yews, the fountain head an upright boar, the Ingilby crest.

If you go through the glass door of the orangery, and the one opposite, you will discover a delightful view of a four-pillared classical temple at the end of a wooded walk some 320m (1,050ft) long. In spring the margins of this sanded walk are bespangled with primroses and daffodils and behind, confining the view to the terminal temple, are some of the original Brown plantings of beech, oak and Portugal Laurel, with later additions of Wellingtonias and large clumps of hybrid rhododendrons. A path to the left of the temple gives on to the ridge above the lake and a path leading back to the house terrace. But if the return walk is made through the orangery there is the opportunity to climb the cleverly built steps in its back wall to get a 'captain on the bridge' view of the pleasure gardens and the village from a platform. The central path in the large walled garden passes under a short avenue of fastigiate yews and through an artistically worked iron gate into the reserve garden, part of the extensive kitchen garden. The gate leads straight into an old circular brick-pillared rose pergola with York stone paving and on either side, box edged parterres planted with lupins, delphiniums and paeonies. Dividing this small garden from the kitchen garden proper is a well trained hornbeam hedge which makes a recessed ending to the pergola path.

On the extensive walls of the kitchen garden are to be seen meticulously fan trained fruit trees including the pears 'Doyenne du Comice', 'Conference', 'Pitmaston Duchess', 'Williams' Bon Chrétien' and 'Victoria' plum. By the side of the far walk are old but expertly pruned apple trees, the varieties including 'Arthur Turner', 'Bramley's Seedling' and 'Lord Suffield'. Against the wall nearest the castle are double stemmed cordons of red currants and gooseberries. Through a wooden door in this wall a path leads into another long, narrow, sheltered wall garden where globe artichokes, peas, onions and the overwintering sprouts and cabbages and broccoli relish the extra warmth. But the *raison d'être* of this narrow walled enclosure is the long row of neatly trained fruit trees on the wall, again mainly the pears of the kitchen garden next door, but probably advanced by a week or so.

Rudding Park

Mackaness Organization

Some 5 km (3 miles) out of Harrogate, off A661 Harrogate-Wetherby road. Open 29 May to 12 September daily 12–6 pm. Refreshments available Saturdays and Sundays only. Park, landscaped by Repton, and woodland rhododendron garden, situated 110 m (360 ft) above sea level on light soils, boulder clay over sandstone. Average annual rainfall 760 mm (30 in.).

Rudding Park is one of those parklands and gardens fortunate in garden history in being the subject of one of Humphry Repton's Red Books, made up for the layout around 1790. The parkland, apart from the very oldest trees (some oaks are part of the original Forest of Knaresborough) must be much as Repton planned it. The views to the east and the north are enlivened and framed by dense plantings of trees. From the front of the house to the east there is a panoramic view looking far away over the Plain of York to the Wolds, framed by belts of fine beech and dotted with red tiled farmhouses. Captain Sir Everard Radcliffe, Bt, M.C., developed the garden from 1945 until he sold the estate a few years ago.

Although formality plays little part in this garden, there is a rectangular parterred herb garden following the line of the house walls at the side. Here the wide paths, paved with York stone, lead to a garden room on a raised terrace and on either side of the path are lawns punctuated here and there with *Agapanthus* in tubs. From the lawn edges to the yew hedges bounding the parkland and to the house walls are geometrically shaped beds of low clipped box and yew filled with lavender, rue, thyme and sage, their blues and purples contrasting with the silver and grey foliaged cotton lavender and *Senecio*. A large *Garrya elliptica* screens the masonry of the house walls at the back of the garden and the side walls provide anchorage for wisteria, *Jasminum polyanthum* and a fine large *Magnolia* × *soulangiana* with *Nerine bowdenii* flowering at their feet. The brilliant colours of strutting peacocks add animation to the scene.

From the garden room terrace azaleas and rhododendrons, with a variety of *Meconopsis* growing among them, lead in a bold line up a sloping lawn into the woodland glades and gardens. Unfortunately the great gale of 11 and 15 February 1962, which did so much damage at Bramham Park, only some 16 km (10 miles) away, took with it the famed cedar avenue at Rudding, but this only spurred Captain Radcliffe on to repair the damage with more planting in island beds of a great variety of shrubs and young trees. The grassy glades lined by high beeches lead to a central pleasance where a tall marble vase in a ring of greenery, outlined by lime and beech, makes a meeting place of all the woodland paths and vistas.

Beyond at the end of a long narrow walk is a delicately patterned ironwork gate leading to the walled garden. At the far end of a broad path leading from the gate is a small brick-built orangery on a plinth flanked by statues of two female figures. Through the gate the path leads between wide herbaceous borders in which the silver pear *Pyrus salicifolia* grows with the lavender blue and silver foliaged *Buddleia* 'Lochinch', the dark purple leaved *Prunus cerasifera* 'Pissardii' and *Cotinus coggygria* 'Foliis Purpureis', the big, single flowered white rose 'Nevada', the flaming yellow 'Rêveil Dijonnais', the crimson 'Will Scarlet', the purply coloured foliage of *Rosa rubrifolia* and the scented Musk 'Penelope'. The *rugosa* roses 'Belle Poitevine' and 'Conrad F. Meyer' add to this ceiling of colour. The contrasting underplanting, chosen for its form and foliage effect, includes the silvers of *Perovskia atriplicifolia*, *Artemisia* 'Silver Queen', *Stachys lanata*, the reds of *Potentilla* 'Gibson's Scarlet', the greens of *Euphorbia sikkimensis*, the vivid blues of *Anchusa caespitosa*, the pinks and creams of the late flowering stonecrops, Japanese Anemones, *Lavatera*, and the unusual floral architecture of the graceful Wand Flower, *Dierama pulcherrima*, the thistle-topped *Echinops* and steel blue *Eryngium*.

Retracing our steps to the woodland glades we first come to the rose garden among whose worthwhile plantings are a variety of Hybrid Musks, particularly the soft pink 'Felicia', the fragrant citron yellow 'Erfurt' and the ever popular long flowering 'Buff Beauty'. The newer Floribunda 'Fashion' grows tall and spreading here, while *R. moyesii* covers a lot of ground side by side with 'Ferdinand Pichard', striped and marbled crimson and white.

To the left of the central path is a glade mass planted with hydrangeas, among them being the Lacecap forms of *H. serrata* 'Bluebird' and 'Veitchii', *H. sargentiana* with moss covered stems, *H. serrata* 'Grayswood', first white, then rose and later deep crimson, the later flowering lilac blue *H. aspera* (*villosa*) and the autumn colouring oak leaved *H. quercifolia*.

Interconnecting green paths lead to further beauty, particularly rhododendrons in a grassy opening between tall Douglas Firs and Wellingtonias, and a fine collection of specimen trees – the American Snowdrop Tree *Halesia monticola*, the Tulip Tree, *Liriodendron tulipifera*, the white and pink barked *Betula ermanii*, snake barked maples, the mahogany barked *Prunus serrula*, large and vigorous *Eucryphia*, both *E. glutinosa* and *E.* × *nymansensis* 'Nymansay', *Eucalyptus gunnii*, *Sorbus* in variety, an old Strawberry Tree *Arbutus unedo*, the Blue Spruce, chestnuts, oaks, clumps of bamboo, all of interest. Under a clump of sober yews there are shelter and shade for hostas, *Meconopsis*, astilbes and the lacy green *Alchemilla mollis*, used as a path edging.

Rhododendrons are here planted both *en masse* and individually in the shelter beds of other trees. The large leaved species do well in such conditions, as is seen by the healthy state of the many *R. sinogrande*, *R. basilicum*, *R. macabeanum*, *R. fictolacteum*, the blue foliaged *R. thomsonii*, the red *R. cinnabarinum*, and its glaucous foliaged variety *R.c. roylei*. Interesting also among such a grand collection of the genus

---

1. Rudding House
2. Chapel
3. Tea Room
4. Herb Garden
5. Rhododendrons
6. Rose Gardens
7. Herbaceous Borders
8. Orangery
9. Duck Pond
10. Parkland Picnic Area
11. Woodland Walks
12. Azaleas & Lilies
13. Hydrangeas

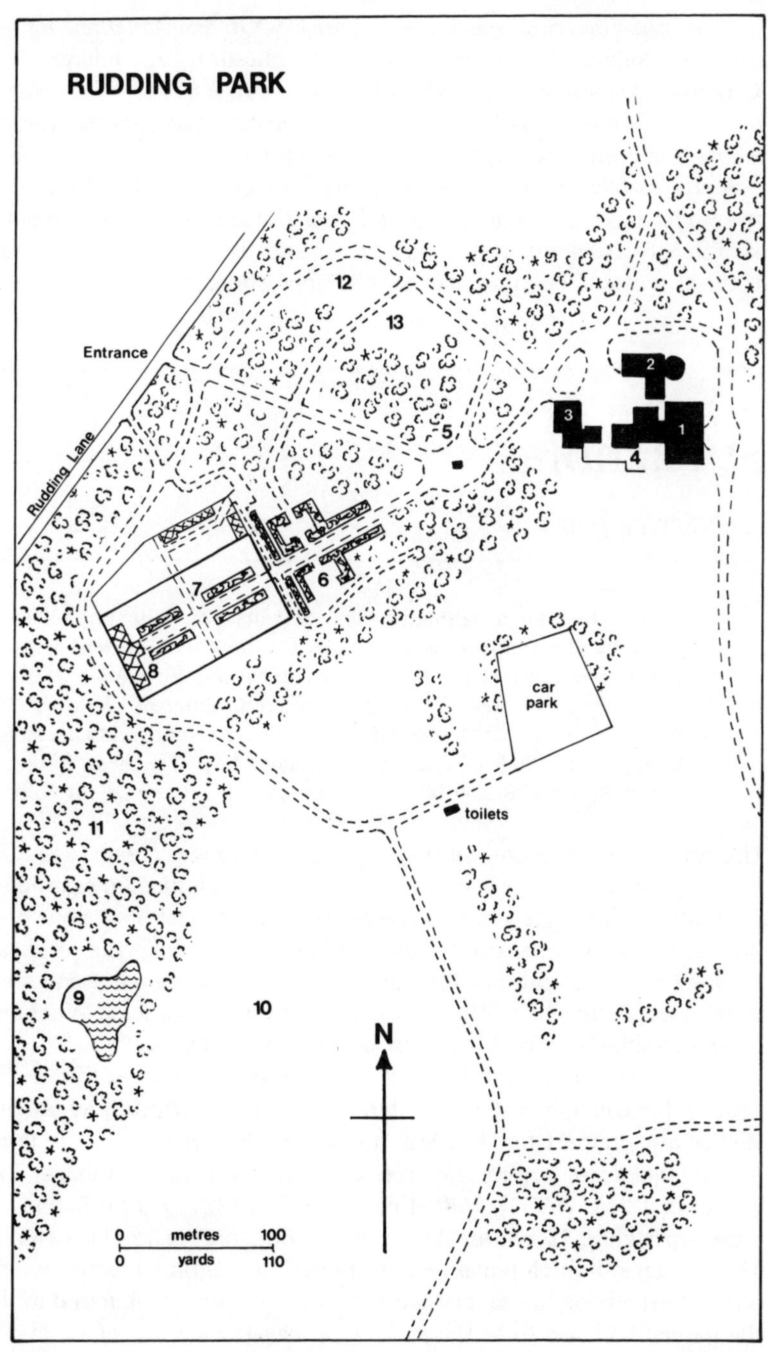
RUDDING PARK
Entrance
Rudding Lane
12
13
5
2
3
1
4
7
6
8
car park
toilets
11
9
10
N
0 metres 100
0 yards 110

are the free-flowering species *R. oreotrephes, R. desquamatum,* for its aromatic foliage, *R. yunnanense,* with chestnut-like foliage and *R. xanthocodon* of the cigar-shaped yellow flowers. There are many good hybrids too – 'Aladdin', 'May Day', 'Idealist', the curious orange-yellow 'Dido' and the large white flowering 'Loderi'.

A stream falls down shallow steps at right angles to the main walk and under it, and here in damp and cool shade grow hosts of Asiatic primulas. Rudding will repay visits at various times of the year so that its multi-seasonal beauties can be fully appreciated.

St Nicholas

Lady Serena James

On A6108 Richmond-Darlington road on outskirts of Richmond town. Open during the summer months daily. For hours see current issue of *Historic Houses, Castles and Gardens.* A compartmented garden of some 2.8 ha (7 acres) of great horticultural interest, situated 150 m (500 ft) above sea level on light soil over limestone. Average annual rainfall 760 mm (30 in.). Staff of one and occasional help. The head gardener trained at St Nicholas as a boy, when five gardeners were on the staff.

This series of gardens on a site sloping to the south was created some 70 years ago by the late the Hon. Robert James. It is a plantsman's paradise, fascinating in its variety and for the unusual and tender plants one does not expect to see so far north. There is an extensive collection of shrub roses and rhododendrons too, the rhododendrons raised from seed, some of it from the expeditions of George Forrest and Kingdon Ward and other expeditions to which Robert James contributed.

The garden surrounds a fine old Tudor house on the site of thirteenth-century Benedictine hospital, the buttressed walls of which now provide shelter and support for *Actinidia arguta, Buddleia alternifolia,* the large leaved *Hydrangea aspera,* the roses, mostly of ancient lineage, like 'Gloire de Dijon' (1853), 'Alfred de Dalmas' (1888), 'Fantin-Latour', a large, sprawling 'Zéphirine Drouhin' (1868), one called by Graham Thomas after Robert James 'Bobby James', a fragrant creamy white, one named for the house 'St Nicholas', a semi-double pink found in the the garden and said to be the progeny *R. damascena* × *R. gallica,* and, a comparatively new one, 'Godfrey Winn'. Then there are the Mexican Orange, *Choisya ternata*; the Mount Etna Broom, the late flowering *Genista aetnensis*; the Himalayan *Buddleia colvilei*, and profusely flowering *Cistus*. Sheltering nearby under the lee of the forecourt wall are several subjects rare for this climate – the Cape Figwort, *Phygelius capensis*, the cinnamon colour barked *Myrtus apiculata* and the late flowering Asiatic shrub *Abelia* in three species – *A. floribunda*, *A. schumannii* and *A. uniflora*. Over by the entrance drive is +*Laburnocytisus adamii* with its tricoloured flowers.

Separated from the house by high and ornamental topiary yew hedges is a paved and grassed enclosure which leads through tall yew pillars to a formal garden gay with flower beds in complete contrast to the sombre dignity of the yew lawn. A massive arch of yew at the other end of the yew enclosure leads to a long herbaceous border hemmed in by green walls of privet.

Through a wooden door at the end of the herbaceous walk we enter a very long, hornbeam hedged shrub rose border where the occupants grow large and spreading in bewildering variety. To name but a few there are to be seen 'Aloha', 'Conrad F. Meyer', 'Nevada', *Rosa virginiana*, forms of *R. rugosa* in variety, 'Pink Pearl', *R. gallica* 'Versicolor', *R. californica*, 'Nymphenburg', 'Canary Bird', *R.* × *cantabrigiensis*, 'Dusky Maiden', 'Sarah Van Fleet', 'Chapeau de Napoléon', Moss and Musk roses, 'Duplex' ('Wolley-Dod's Rose'), 'Schneezwerg' ('Snowdwarf'), *R. ecae* (1880) and forms of *R. canina*.

To the left, at the top of the rose walk, is Her Ladyship's Garden where stone paths cut the mixed flower and rose beds into oblongs and where again a wealth of roses is on display, among them being the Threepeny Bit Rose, *R. farreri persetosa* and the York and Lancaster Rose, in white and red. There are beds of lilies and many of the ornamental onions, the *Allium spp.* with their globular and pendant blooms, as well as the unusual Hen and Chickens Daisy where a rim of miniature daisies, the chickens, surround the larger central flower, the hen. Other unusual plants to be found at St Nicholas are the white daisy flowered shrub from Chile *Chiliotrichum diffusum* (*rosmarinifolium*), the yellow buttercup flowered *Meconopsis chelidoniifolia*, St Bernard's Lily, *Anthericum liliago*, with its sprays of small white lily-like flowers, the rosy pink hyacinth-scented *Lonicera syringantha* and, flowering for the first time in 1976, the rare evergreen species of *Decumaria sinensis*, related to the hydrangeas, with honey-scented green and white flowers.

At the end of Her Ladyship's Garden are planted specimen trees, *Acer griseum*, *Arbutus unedo* and *Hydrangea sargentiana*, with mossy covered stems and shoots and large leaves.

There is a gate in a wall here leading into the old Orchard Garden where one finds that one-time favourite of our early fruit growers, the Medlar, *Mespilus germanica*; pink flowered and large leaved *Rodgersia*; the tiny yellow flowered and black fruited *Jasminum fruticans* and the beginning of the rhododendron feast that awaits in the rockery below. As an appetiser here is the late flowering large white *R. auriculatum*, the Himalayan species *R. thomsonii*, noticeable for its plum coloured bark; the sweet smelling and tender *R. lindleyi* and 'Lady Alice Fitzwilliam'; *R. yakushimanum*, dome-shaped with silvery young growths, and only found in the wild on the peaks of the Japanese island of Yakushima; the white and pink funnel flowered *R. decorum*; *R. fictolacteum*, one of the most striking of the large leaved species, and the similarly coloured *R. monosematum*.

Weathered old steps lead down into the dell of the densely planted and winding pathed rockery, almost natural in its sprawl, where many rhododendrons find shelter, plants almost all grown from seed by the late Mr James and now so crossbred as to make identification difficult. But there are *R. oreodoxa*, one of Fortune's discoveries; the floriferous *R. racemosum*, the heart-shaped, bronzy foliaged *R. williamsianum*, *R. sutchuenense* with its long sword-shaped leaves and, from Forrest's seed, *R. neriiflorum*. Filling in with their small but profuse blooms are the one or two rhododendron hybrids allowed in this garden, 'Blue Tit' and 'Blue Diamond'. Providing shelter for many of these comparatively tender rhododendron species are sprawling shrub roses – the violet stemmed *R. rubrifolia*, *R. omeiensis*, whose pear-shaped fruits are edible, and *R. moyesii*, whose fruits are flask-shaped and sealing-wax red. Also benefiting from the shelter are the sweet scented shrubs *Sarcococca*, which blossoms in January, and *Osmanthus delavayi*.

The lilac walk at the lower slope of the rockery, and our way back to the house, looks over open country and down the steeply sloping hillside to Easby Abbey in its picturesque setting by the swiftly running Swale.

1 Sledmere House, Humberside: the broad sweep of Brown's landscape seen from the South East Terrace; note the characteristic 'belting' and 'clumping' of the trees

2 Beningbrough Hall, North Yorkshire: the clean lines of the house and garden front are clearly apparent here. The walls are filled with 'climbing' plants and there are paved gardens behind the trim yew hedges

3 Castle Howard, North Yorkshire: Vanbrugh's magnificent first essay into architecture reflected in the South Lake

4 Castle Howard, North Yorkshire: the Temple of the Four Winds, Vanbrugh's last work here and one entirely his own design without Hawksmoor's help. The approach by Terrace Walk was once the lane of Henderskelf, a village demolished to make way for the landscaping

5 Harlow Car, North Yorkshire: rhododendrons and ferns in the woodland, remains of the ancient forest of Knaresborough

6 Harlow Car, North Yorkshire: an unusual, leafless parasitic plant, *Lathraea clandestina*, growing over tree roots in the Streamside Garden

7 Kepwick Hall, North Yorkshire: looking from the kitchen garden area over the terraced lawns with their imposing planting of fine trees and rhododendrons

8 Kepwick Hall, North Yorkshire: rhododendrons by a grass walk giving long views to the bracken covered slopes of the Hambledon Hills

9 Middleton House, North Yorkshire: one of the yew enclosed lawns here, enhanced by colour associated herbaceous plantings and its central piece of topiary

10 Nawton Tower, North Yorkshire: a lovely corner of this so skilfully merged modern and 18th century landscaped garden created by the late Lord Feversham from wild moorland

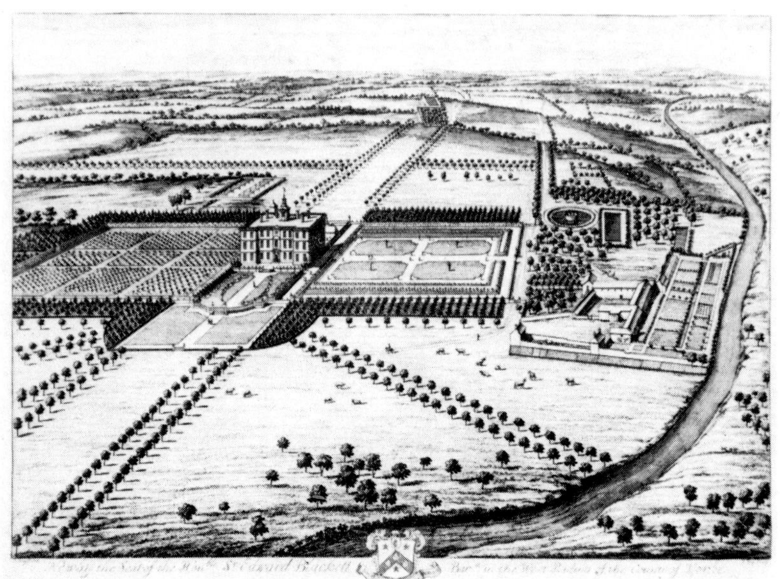

11 Newby Hall, North Yorkshire: the early 18th century lay-out, the epitome of formality, swept away in mid-century to give the informality of the present gardens

12 Newby Hall, North Yorkshire: a corner of the sunken rose garden, one of the several enclosed gardens created by the late Major Edward Compton

13 Studley Royal, North Yorkshire: 'the encircling theatre of the vale' surrounds the Moon Ponds and embowers the Doric Temple of Piety

14 Studley Royal, North Yorkshire: the principal vista of this green and watery landscape, the 'Surprise View' of Fountains Abbey from Tent Hill

15 Thorp Perrow, North Yorkshire: birches make a cathedral aisle, only one of the many imposing uses of trees in this Yorkshire arboretum

16 Sheffield Botanical Gardens, South Yorkshire: the Paxton domed roof pavilions (greenhouses) near the main entrance to this well stocked and planted display garden

17 Bramham Park, West Yorkshire: looking across the lawns and sunken garden to James Paine's Ionic porticoed orangery, now a chapel, at once the terminal point of the Broad Walk to the Obelisk Ponds and the start of the long beech avenue lay-out

18 Bramham Park, West Yorkshire: the 'Four Faces' so called because of the carvings which depict the seasons on the four sides of the vase. It is placed at the meeting of five beech avenues at one of the key points of the view

19 Canal Gardens, Roundhay Park, West Yorkshire: the formal rose garden and Coronation Greenhouse, always with its all-year-round display of flowering plants and shrubs

20 Harewood House, West Yorkshire: the Brownian landscape displayed, a view from the Barry Terrace across the lake

21 *Below* Harewood House, West Yorkshire: by the lakeside, a haven, under fine trees, for rhododendrons, many Harewood's own hybrids

22 *Right* Lotherton Hall, West Yorkshire: a dignified, formal approach across the lawns to the 'temple' summerhouse

23 Nostell Priory, West Yorkshire: an aerial view showing the tree-lined lake and the Adam stable block to the right

24 Parceval Hall, West Yorkshire: order brought into an otherwise wild natural landscape by the hillside terraces created by the late Sir William Milner

25 Parceval Hall, West Yorkshire: the paved lily pool terrace over-looking the craggy bulk of Simon's Seat in Wharfedale

Sharow Hall

Mr and Mrs T.S. Lucas

Between Ripon and Boroughbridge. From Ripon via A61 Thirsk road. N of Ripon first turn right over river, signposted. From A1 6 km (4 miles) N of Boroughbridge turn left for Sharow. Open occasionally for charity when tea is served in the house. Parkland of 60 ha (150 acres) and 0.8 ha (2 acres) of lawns, trees and ornamental and kitchen garden, situated 50 m (160 ft) above sea level on medium loam with neutral pH. Average annual rainfall 690 mm (27 in.). Staff of one and occasional help.

The house terrace at Sharow was obviously designed for its extensive views, to the right to the towers of Ripon Cathedral, and to the front to the blue haze of the Yorkshire Pennines over planted parkland and a thickly wooded copse screening a small lake.

Walking left from the terrace along the wide grass sward to the kitchen garden we have to our right the long distance view while to the left is a thick screen of old oaks and breeches underplanted with large massed hybrid rhododendrons. In the walled kitchen garden is a period greenhouse sheltering figs and grapes while in the extensive enclosure, part grassed down, are beds of roses and herbaceous plants.

By the house entrance the walls are covered with clematis and quince, while in a curving herbaceous border following the sinuous drive to the estate entrance is a mixed planting. *Euphorbia characias* (*wulfenii*) is prominent. Across the drive, opposite the house, is a fine stand of mature oak, Copper Beech and a fine specimen of the Monkey Puzzle Tree, *Araucaria araucana*.

Sleightholmedale Lodge

Mrs Gordon Foster

At Sleightholmedale on North Yorkshire Moors, 1.6 km (1 mile) from Fadmoor, 5 km (3 miles) from Kirbymoorside off A17 Helmsley-Pickering road. Open occasionally for charity, when dogs allowed on lead. A hillside garden of some 1.2 ha (3 acres), situated 90 m (300 ft) above sea level on acid soil, over limestone base in some parts. Sheltered from N but subject to severe winters, hard frosts and heavy snowfalls. Average rainfall 760 mm (30 in.). Staff of one and occasional help.

Finding this garden hidden away in the steep folds of green and wooded Sleightholmedale, an outrider of Bransdale higher up the valley, is an adventure in itself.

The gardens were first laid out in 1910 by the present owner's father, who at that time built the high walls of the rose garden and planted the avenue of cherries and limes. It was Mrs Foster, however, who from 1935 onwards set about much of the present planting, including the spring garden at the rear of the house where in season the avenue of Geans, *Prunus avium*, throws a white veil over the daffodil carpet and where various crab apples and pink cherries, *Prunus sargentii* mainly, give further colour.

On the same level, but safely behind high brick walls, the one-time rose garden climbs steeply up the moorside, a central path leading to the summerhouse at the top. Cottage garden planting on either side of the path is bright with colour most of the summer – the sweet disorder of *Rudbeckia, Helenium, Monarda*, delphiniums, catmint, perennial cornflowers, montbretias, *Liatris*, monkshoods, golden rod. *Phlox, Lythrum* and the pale yellow *Achillea*. Behind each wide border an oak timbered fence runs uphill, heavily laden with many climbing roses and especially with honeysuckles, *Lonicera × americana* of spectacular midsummer display, as well as Late and Early Dutch and the coppery yellow *L. × tellmanniana*.

The terrace in front of the house, facing south-west, commands a fine view of the valley, where sheep graze in the lee of a mass of forest trees stretching away to the north and south on the far side of the Hodge Beck.

Despite the garden's elevation and its quite northerly situation, a large Mexican Orange, *Choisya ternata*, grows by the front door and against the walls are clematis, *Cotoneaster horizontalis*, honeysuckles, and the grey leaved, lavender blue flowered labiate, *Perovskia atriplicifolia*.

Away from the house terrace to the right a wrought iron gate leads by a few steps to a tennis court, not seen from the house, into almost a secret garden surrounded by old shrub roses. Making an almost impenetrable barrier are high, spreading bushes of *Rosa moyesii*, 'Frühlingsgold', the Himalayan *R. webbiana*, the Threepenny Bit Rose, *R. farreri persetosa*, two *R. pimpinellifolia* (*spinosissima*), *R.p. altaica* and *R.p. hispida*, and the fern leaved *R.* × *cantabrigiensis*. Interplanted are *Buddleia alternifolia*, azaleas, both Exbury and Ghent, lilacs in variety, *Acer griseum* and *A.* × *coriaceum* and large bushes of the Witch Hazel, January flowering *Hamamelis mollis*.

On the terrace west of the house are drifts of heather, relishing, as one might expect, this moorland garden soil, where Dorset and Irish Heaths rub shoulders with *Erica tetralix*, the Cross-leafed Heath, *E. vagans*, the Cornish Heath, the winter flowering varieties of *E. carnea* and the tree heaths *E. arborea* and *E. arborea alpina*, which raise the floral level. Planted here and there for most effect are the variegated dogwoods, adding their stem colour in winter and foliage charm in summer, *Pernettya mucronata* and *Cotoneaster bullatus*, while a large, spreading *Berberis thunbergii* positively sets itself afire in the autumn.

A sloping piece of lawn leads by stone steps from the heather down to the second grass terrace where, under the drystone walls, so much in keeping in this rural setting, are Moss Roses, red and white forms of *R. rugosa*, a selection of Hybrid Musks in pink, white and red and *Cistus* × *purpureus* and *C.* × *cyprius*.

In the centre of the terrace roughly hewn stone steps lead down either side of an old stone cistern into which water falls from a lion's head. Two young *Chamaecyparis pisifera* 'Boulevard' act as 'gateposts' to further steps which lead through an iron gate into the meadows below.

Another gentle sloping grass path to the right points the way to the delight of lily pools, two of them, rock rimmed and under a rock wall behind, from which water flows and up which a winding 'goat' path leads the way among more shrubs, alpines and roses back to the house terrace. A massive piece of native stone forms a bridge between the two ponds around whose lily-padded surface grow masses of primulas, the Water Hyacinth, a large foliaged *Ligularia*, bushes of white flowering *Potentilla*, irises and low-growing willow.

Within two minutes of leaving this ideally situated and secluded garden it is lost from sight, but the most pleasant of memories remain.

Smeaton Manor

Brigadier the Hon. and Mrs R.G. Hamilton-Russell

Near Northallerton, 1 km (½ mile) W of Great Smeaton village. Open occasionally for charity during the year, when teas are served. A medium sized, well laid out garden, situated 90m (300ft) above sea level on a heavy loam over a clay subsoil. Average annual rainfall 610mm (24in.). Staff of three.

The warm brick house (built 1875–8) is by Philip Webb and the garden layout near the house, with its pantile wall copings and elegant use of paving, is reminiscent of the work of Lutyens and Jekyll.

The garden to the south was reconstructed by its owners some 17 or 18 years ago and the creation does them every credit. From the semi-circular lawn around the formal house terrace the view is over two natural ponds to the far Cleveland Hills. To the right the view is even more extensive to Lower Swaledale.

The house terrace is cut into geometrically shaped beds full of Hybrid Tea and Floribunda roses and was constructed as a raised site with the soil excavated from the swimming pool on the side terrace. Stone steps lead down from this terrace to the lower lawns and to a border, at the foot of the retaining wall, full of massed roses and lavender.

To the left are irregular beds of azaleas backed by taller bushes of *Rhododendron luteum*, hybrid rhododendrons and massed plantings of *R. ponticum*. Grass paths have been cut into these thickets so that in the spring the garden stroller finds himself walking between high walls of colour and greenery. A satisfyingly irregular line of this planting leads to a copse of Red May, the golden tasselled, dark foliaged oak *Quercus ilex* and the silver foliaged pear *Pyrus salicifolia*. The natural pond here is edged with yellow flag irises, reeds, bullrushes and a spotted orchid. From the second pond a wooded walk, neatly edged with birches, is between oaks, Copper Beech, Scots Pine, crab apples, a walnut tree and cherries.

Turning off to the left towards the long extension of the lawn below the house terrace is a shrubbery planted for a very varied colour effect from both bloom and foliage, with weeping cherries, more Willow-leafed Pear, *Pieris formosa forrestii*, *Berberis × stenophylla*, *Weigela*, *Viburnum* in variety, *Kalmia*, a coppery coloured form of *Cotinus coggygria* and magnolias. The curving line of this shrubbery leads naturally to the far end of the garden where a beech hedge screens the kitchen garden wall and where an unusual double flowered lavender coloured rhododendron, *R. catawbiense* × *ponticum* 'Fastuosum Flore Pleno', is of interest.

The kitchen garden wall turns at right angles, after a short walk, to make a sheltered corner for climbing roses on the brick of the wall and a well planted herbaceous border. From here the formal paved path edged with roses leads to the large stone-paved patio terrace and swimming pool. Rather unusual are three beds of tall lupins through the centre of which grow bush lilacs.

Among the roses are 'Ice White', 'Romany Rose', 'Elizabeth of Glamis' 'Pink Perfection' and 'Tabarin', all chosen to make a shaded colour picture. An old yew hedge, over 100 years old, adds dignity to the scene.

The long swimming pool patio backed by a cosy red high brick wall topped by a 'roof' of pantiles is a sun trap for a furnishing of climbers, the roses 'Albertine' and 'Nevada', *Clematis lanuginosa* 'Henryi', the early flowering *Magnolia denudata*, the Lily Tree, *Ceanothus* and, in a narrow border under the wall, a sun-loving collection of silvery foliaged plants, white *Buddleia*, lavender, *Cistus*, stonecrops, Cotton Lavender, *Ballota pseudodictamnus*, thyme and *Stachys lanata*.

In the centre of the long wall is a semicircular niche enclosing a dolphin spouting water for the pool.

The kitchen garden, approached through a handsome clock-turreted stable block, is a satisfyingly neat enclosure with trained cherries, pears and currants on the walls, strawberry beds, and an extensive planting of sweet peas, as well as the usual household vegetables.

Studley Royal – Fountains Abbey

North Yorkshire County Council and Department of the Environment

3 km (2 miles) SW of Ripon, 14 km (9 miles) N of Harrogate. Approach to Studley via Studley Roger. Take B6265 Ripon-Pateley Bridge road, turn at sign for Studley Roger. Open all year daily: March, April 9.30–5.30 pm, May and September closes 7 pm, June to August closes 9.30 pm, November to February closes 4 pm, Sundays all year 2–4 pm. Car park; meals available; dogs allowed on lead. A unique land- and waterscape of some 40 ha (100 acres), situated 60 m (200 ft) above sea level. Average annual rainfall 640 mm (25 in.).

Studley Royal's landscape and water features are a unique and original design of the early eighteenth century carried out by John Aislabie (1640–1747), the Chancellor of the Exchequer discredited when the South Sea Bubble burst. Aislabie retired to his Yorkshire estates where at Studley he found a wild, wooded ravine through which the turbulent Skell ran from Fountains Abbey towards its confluence with the Ure beyond Ripon.

From 1718 until his death in 1747 Aislabie worked to transform this unkempt wilderness into a thing of quiet and beauty. In this green and shimmering landscape he captured all the elements of formalism, the picturesque and the romantic before the latter two aspects of landscape had become acknowledged forms of the art. For John Aislabie first dammed the Skell to form a large artificial lake, next, by means of an underground channel, caused it to issue through a grotto spring into his formal canals, cleverly contrived so as never to be seen in their full length, and then used it to feed his Moon Pools, one circular, with the classical Temple of Piety on its rim, the other two crescent-shaped and marked by the appropriate lead statuary.

A canal leaves the Moon Pools to fall down the ornately stepped cascade between two Venetian fishing lodges and stone-balustraded margin into the great lake with its central island, once the site of a tall obelisk fountain discharging jets of water.

Velvet lawns line the canal with unusual grass buttressed sides, like early earthworks. On one side rise steep woodlands while on the other more gently sloping woodlands and tall yew hedges enclose the landscape.

The house was burned down in 1964, but the contemporary Colen Campbell banqueting house or orangery (*c*.1726–30) on its high lawn, to the right after entering the gate, must have been the eyrie from where guests could get their bird's eye view of the landscape. And how exciting that must have been, for from his recent researches Mr W. Walker, in charge of Studley for the North Riding, has shown how unique was John Aislabie's triangulation of its many features.

Even now from the banqueting house lawn through the trees can be seen the formal canal, the Moon Pools, the Grotto Springs and rustic bridge above them and the Temple of Piety. In the days of both John and his son William, it was possible to see, on the same side of the water as the banqueting house, an obelisk, a steeply rushing cascade which tumbled down the hillside into the great lake and, before the trees had grown so tall, a 'Gothic' building and a 'Chinese' temple.

If we go over the stepping stones between the fishing pavilions we have a choice of route, either following the edge of the Moon Pool and the large lake to Fountains Abbey or up the steeply wooded hillside by a path almost immediately in front of us, by which we come to a grotto tunnel, long, dark and winding, climbing uphill to a ridge walk. Here, by the top entrance to this typical eighteenth-century conceit, we come across a 'Gothic' octagonal tower, built by John's son William, probably used as a picnic resort from which visitors could look down on the waters and across to the banqueting house, for only a short time ago Mr Walker uncovered by its side what he considers to be one of the earliest barbecues, with hearth and oven.

The walk with its differing views of the water features, rather reminiscent of Rievaulx and Duncombe Terraces, passes a classical open-domed rotunda erected by William Aislabie (*c*.1730) notable for the fact that its 'solid stonework' is really cleverly camouflaged wood. The woodland path leads on to where, just before the steep descent, we take a narrow path into the depth of the greenery on Tent Hill where we discover the *raison d'être* of the exercise, for here, after passing through the rear door of a small wooden summerhouse, we come to the superb surprise view. Far below is the most magnificent Gothic ruin in Christendom, the romantic pile of Fountains Abbey (*c*.1135), revealed for the first time on our garden perambulation. While John Aislabie made possible this most picturesque of vistas it was not until 1768 that his son William was able to buy the abbey buildings and estate and preserve the vista for posterity.

Coming down from the surprise view we can go forward by the Skell side to Fountains Abbey and Hall, a beautifully proportioned Jacobean manor built from the very stones of the abbey, and make our way back to Studley Royal going on the other side of the Skell through woodland walks past high yew hedges and on a path giving different view of the canal, Moon Ponds and the Temple of Piety embowered in woodland. A shorter walk is to turn right at the bottom of the Tent Hill descent and follow the lakeside and the Moon Pools walk past the Temple of Piety and back to the stepping stones.

As you enter Studley Park with its herd of roe deer and before going downhill to the entrance gate, do look up towards the church (designed by William Burgess), to the obelisk, and then look backwards, for here is another of those breathtaking vistas designed by John Aislabie. The eye is carried through an avenue of ancient trees down the main drive and out beyond to the countryside and to the twin towers of Ripon Cathedral in exact alignment many miles away. A magnificent prospect indeed.

Sutton Park

Major and Mrs E.C.R. Sheffield

In the village street of Sutton-on-the-Forest, 13 km (8 miles) N of York on B1363. Open April to 10 October, usually Tuesdays, Wednesdays, Thursdays, Sundays and Bank Holidays 2–6 pm. House of 1730 with fine furniture, porcelain and pictures open also. Teas available; dogs allowed on lead. A terraced and woodland walks garden of character, situated 34 m (110 ft) above sea level on heavy loam over clay. Average annual rainfall 640 mm (25 in.).

This gracious garden, with wide ranging views over parkland reputedly landscaped by 'Capability' Brown (but not listed in Dorothy Stroud's definitive work) and the Plain of York, seems as old world as the village street which runs by the imposing entrance gates. Yet it was only taken in hand by Mrs Sheffield in 1962 when the family moved into this lovely Georgian house (the wings are by Thomas Atkinson). Two fine cedars flank the entrance drive where also, for Mrs Sheffield planted the garden for scent, stand Balsam Poplars. On the west side the white rose

'Iceberg' is planted thickly in beds in startling juxtaposition to dark old yews and a large oak with deeply serrated foliage.

On the way to the south front with its three linked terraces the path goes through a charming conceit, a small paved garden on the west side of the house, partly enclosed by a high brick wall and gaining much of its charm from the contrast of paving and cobblestones in which space has been claimed for small beds of lavender and lilies and two 'Amanogawa' cherries. Against the wall two large white orange-tree tubs, which come from Blenheim and were given to Mrs Sheffield by the Duke of Marlborough, contain large bush hydrangeas.

But the terraced garden and its view over the plain is Sutton Park's particular pleasure. The top house terrace is paved with old York stone from demolished houses at Otley, patterned by larger rectangular areas of grass. Flowers and shrubs abound in the borders. At the far side of the terrace the colouring is kept mainly to mauves, greys and pinks by the plantings of old fashioned and shrub roses, 'Maiden's Blush', 'William Lobb', 'Reine des Violettes', 'Lavender Lassie', 'Felicia' and 'Chaplin's Pink'. Creamy 'Félicité et Perpétué' shares the house walls with *Jasminum polyanthum*, wisteria and clematis. In the borders are the softer greys, silvers and mauves of *Artemisia arborescens*, *Ceanothus*, *Anaphalis*, *Acanthus*, rosemary, the sweet smelling *Clematis* × *jouiniana*, Cotton Lavender and Sweet Lavender. Six standard wisteria stand boldly in the far border above a froth of white hydrangeas, tobacco plants, *Salvia horminum*, mints, spurge and more lavender.

Wide stone steps lead to the rose garden on the second terrace. Percy Cane, the celebrated landscape architect, advised Mrs Sheffield in the laying out of this part of the garden and here, set in trim turf, is a series of geometrically shaped beds, now of mixed plantings, though roses are still much in evidence with 'Blessings', 'Prima Ballerina' and 'Canary Bird'. Richly purple leaved *Vitis vinifera* 'Purpurea', with bunches of small, intensely blue grapes forms a fringe by the side of the steps where spreading bushes of the yellow Tea rose 'Mermaid' luxuriate. The series of matching beds is centred on a large stone basket filled with scented pelargoniums which when touched in passing release delicious odours. Some of the beds are edged with pinks; others with *Alchemilla mollis*, *Nicotiana*, and low-growing dahlias. The grey Willow-leaved Pear, *Pyrus salicifolia*, is planted in some of the beds to give vertical interest. The beds under the retaining wall are filled with shrubs and perennials: white *Buddleia*, *Rosa rugosa*, *Echinops*, lilac, *Philadelphus*, delphiniums and more silver foliaged plants, *Phlomis fruticosa*, *Senecio* 'Sunshine' (*greyii*), catmint, Cotton Lavender, *Artemisia* and roses. Two female bronze statues are almost completely surrounded by the not often seen autumn flowering Virgin's Bower Clematis, *C. flammula*, whose small panicles of white flowers are almond-scented. Shrubby *Potentilla fruticosa* cultivars are nearby, and two delicate ironwork 'gazebos' at each end of the terrace are almost completely covered in climbers.

The third terrace is a wide expanse of open lawn separated from the well copsed parkland beyond by a high beech hedge, its formal line being broken centrally by a large semicircular niche with a classical white marble seat from which, looking back up the terraces, the garden layout can be seen and admired as an entity.

Immediately at the foot of the steps to this terrace is a rectangular lily tank, its angularity broken by a semicircular arc on the far side, matching the curve of the hedge beyond. Here the pleasing combination of grass and water is punctuated by the verticals of well spaced, dark columnar conifers against the retaining wall, flanking the shallow descent of the steps and the stone seat.

The terrace border with its many *Echium* is backed by old shrub roses such as *R. moyesii*, a varied planting of *Buddleia*, and a Judas Tree, *Cercis siliquastrum*. One of the largest Monkey Puzzle Trees hereabouts is a feature of this lawn and through trees along the terrace wall the roses 'Kiftsgate' and 'Wedding Day' run riot.

But this is not all Sutton Park can show, for the bottom terrace merges on both sides with wooded glades broken by island beds and trees jutting out of the embracing woodland. The beds on the east side hold unusually apricot coloured foxgloves; there are tall mulleins, *Crambe cordifolia*, planted for their greyish-green heart-shaped foliage, *Bergenia* and Cardoons. From here starts the 400m ($\frac{1}{4}$ mile) Temple Wood walk, aglow in spring with daffodils and white cherries among the native trees.

Swinton Castle

Earl and Countess of Swinton

On A6108 Ripon-Masham road 1.6 km (1 mile) SW of Masham village in Wensleydale. Spring garden only open occasionally for charity. Teas in Masham; no dogs. Situated 140 m (450 ft) above sea level on heavy loam over millstone grit. Sheltered by extensive woodlands. Average annual rainfall 810 mm (32 in.).

The spring garden is approached through a lime avenue from the rear courtyard of Swinton Castle. Totally enclosed by tall forest trees and yew hedges this pleasance of some 0.8 ha (2 acres) has been planted especially for the early blossom of trees, shrubs and bulbs. Its central feature, a stone sundial, gives some idea of the date, for it was erected by Samuel Cunliffe Lister, later Baron Swinton, a notable Yorkshire textile magnate, to commemorate the coronation of George V in June 1911.

Two wide gravel paths between gently sloping lawns provide the platforms for viewing the long double avenue of cherries and the sinuous line of massed rhododendrons and azaleas at the top of the enclosure, carpeted right to their feet by masses of daffodils, which are also thickly planted under the lilacs, laburnums and Mock Oranges skirting the bottom boundary in a broad band.

An ornamental ironwork gate at the far end of the lower walk leads into a cathedral aisle of tall limes, where high yews fill in the spaces between the trunks with impressive effect.

From a winding path which runs by the foot of the lime avenue, at the other side of the green aisle, distant vistas of the lake and castle are seen over parkland trees, venerable oaks, beech and elms planted in copses, dotting the landscape. Rhododendrons *en masse*, an impenetrable green wall, fill the other side of the walk between the aisle and the garden which is entered again to return to the castle. By the sundial, and guarding the top entrance gate, are two imposing bronze statues of athletes, their formality softened by the planting of two mop-headed cherries by their side.

As this garden is only open in springtime its full beauty is always seen.

Thimbleby Hall

Sir Richard and Lady Barwick

E of A19 between Thimbleby and Osmotherley, 11 km (7 miles) E of Northallerton. Open occasionally for charity when light refreshments are served. Natural woodland and ornamental gardens of 12 ha (30 acres), situated 180 m (600 ft) above sea level on acid woodland soil. Average yearly rainfall 690 mm (27 in.). Staff of one and occasional help.

Thimbleby Hall is for lovers of woodland walks and fine trees. It is entered by way of an old lime tree avenue. A kitchen garden and rose garden away from the house, at the rear, is entered from the stableyard.

This garden has a quaint concentric circled box parterre planted up with annuals and a modest-sized rose garden mostly of Hybrid Teas sheltered on the east by a large beech and conifer woodland. The shaven lawns in front of the house are reached down a steeply sloping walk edged by massed rhododendrons on the one side and daffodils on climbing greensward on the other.

From the front the view has been skilfully landscaped to lead the eye down the steeply sloping lawn to a picture of foliage colour with fine beeches predominant, contrast coming from Copper Beeches, conifers, bamboo, cherries and large clumps of hybrid rhododendrons. The picturesque roofs of Osmotherley village are just glimpsed through the trees on the opposite slope.

The stream dividing the house lawn from the woodland has the odd appearance of running uphill at the far left, for the Jenny Brewster stream which has been steeply cascaded by the centre of the lawn flows to the left, while the Cod Beck coming in from a beech glade runs in the opposite direction.

On the main entrance drive can be seen a grand old oak of massive proportions, underplanted with daffodils, which is matched by a gnarled and twisted ash on the opposite side of the drive.

From the house terrace a steep path leads through beech and sycamore with here and there Scots Pines and Douglas Firs, the woodland floor being carpeted with daffodils, wood anemones, primroses and bluebells. Far below we catch glimpses of the stream and with us all the way is the incessant murmur of running water. About 1.6 km (1 mile) through the woodland is a large lake (now used as a reservoir) from which a waterfall feeds the stream below. Notice the gamekeeper's 'warning line' hung with the remains of rooks, stoats and grey squirrels.

If instead of taking the steep woodland walk you cross a bridge at the east end of the house, you will find a walk along the streamside where the great bare roots of beech trees grip the steep sides. Midway along this walk the steep cascade can be seen amidst great clumps of rhododendrons. A little further on is the junction of the two streams and another walk, almost level, through woodland beeches.

Thorp Perrow

Sir John Ropner, Bt

At Firby, 3 km (2 miles) S of Bedale. Leaving Bedale on B6268 Masham road almost immediately take left turn signposted 'Thorp Perrow'. Open occasionally during year for charity, when light refreshments are available. Arboretum, ornamental and kitchen gardens and lakes of some 28 ha (70 acres), situated 76 m (250 ft) above sea level on a slightly acid soil. Average annual rainfall 760 mm (30 in.). Staff of five.

A long drive through grazing sheep and Highland cattle in well wooded parkland leads to this sylvan retreat where, some 40 years ago, the late Sir Leonard Ropner was given some rough fields by his father. He turned them into a woodland of delight and one of the finest arboreta in the north of England, notable for its collection of rare trees.

The ornamental gardens are to the front of the house, a yew hedge screening the kitchen gardens at the rear. A broad gravelled walk with herbaceous borders on either side is punctuated by urns holding, unusually, large clumps of the greeny-gold *Euphorbia polychroma*, followed in summer by pelargoniums. To the left is a tree girt lawn planted with shrubs and trees among which is a beautifully shaped *Cedrus deodara*. To the front is the trout stocked lake with more flower filled urns on the bank on the house side and, on the opposite bank, a fringe of gold, light green and purple from the willows, alder and Copper Beech, through which the eye is led by a long avenue leading into the far distance among the closely planted trees of the arboretum. On the front lawn to the left and forming a frieze above the water is an interesting collection of tonsured yews cut into a variety of shapes and behind, forming a boundary and embowering the large summer pavilion, is a vari-toned stand of conifers including *Chamaecyparis nootkatensis* and *C. lawsoniana*, a giant Wellingtonia, Golden Yew, *Juniperus chinensis*, *J. squamata* and *Cupressus glabra* (*arizonica*).

Once in the arboretum over the lake bridge it is possible to see the skill and taste with which it has been planted, with avenues and glades of different kinds of trees leading off the main drives. Through an avenue of beeches and by a smaller lake can be seen the light gold of maples, crab apples and cherries underplanted with myriads of daffodils. A screen of green beech opens into an avenue of deep red *Prunus cerasifera* 'Pissardi', the Purple-leaved Plum, and one notes with pleasure the more recent interplanting of specimen conifers.

On the western boundary and ride of the arboretum, reached from a Red Chestnut avenue and planted for shelter, is a long 230 m (750 ft) cypress avenue. Against a background of Douglas Fir and Western Red Cedar is first a golden wall of *Chamaecyparis lawsoniana* 'Lutea', *C.l.* 'Hillieri' and *C.l.* 'Stewartii'; then the avenue becomes more sober with its dense plantings on both sides of the common green Lawson Cypress, *C. lawsoniana*. To give variety of colour and a foretaste of the arboretum proper, the right-hand side of the ride is planted with *Pyrus salicifolia*, the white and green variegated maple *Acer negundo* 'Variegatum', Red May, laburnums, lilacs, the Black Spruce, *Picea mariana* (*nigra*), *Prunus cerasifera* 'Pissardi', *Cotinus coggygria*, both the green and the purple foliaged, *Crataegus oxycantha* 'Paul's Scarlet', *Berberis thunbergii*, *Sorbus* 'Mitchellii', green above and white below, the Box Elder, *Prunus × blireana*, with its coppery purple foliage, the golden stemmed willow *Salix alba* 'Vitellina' and *Acer platanoides* 'Schwedleri', of the rich crimson-purple foliage.

From the long cypress avenue there opens out an extensive green glade both sides of which have been skilfully planted for foliage colour contrast, one side being lightly planted with golden cream and white

---

1. House
2. Walled Garden
3. Red Oak Avenue
4. Back Park
5. Lake
6. Cascades
7. Spring Wood
8. Elm & Laburnum Avenue
9. Foliage
10. Chestnut Avenue
11. Lodge
12. Cricket Field

THORP
PERROW
0 metres 100
0 yards 110
1
2
3
4
5
6
7
8
9
10
11
12
N
Entrance

while the other, in complete contrast, is more heavily planted with deeper colourings. In the 'Golden' border are large clumps of *Weigela florida* 'Variegata', *Cornus alba* 'Elegantissima', a grand specimen of the Golden Hazel, *Corylus avellana* 'Aurea', and the tiny double rosebud flowered *Crataegus oxycantha* 'Masekii'.

Opposite the scale as well as the colour alters, with the Weeping Larch, *Larix* × *pendula, Chamaecyparis obtusa* 'Lycopodioides', with its dark bluish-green mossy foliage, the golden yellow of *C. obtusa* 'Crippsii', the conical gold of *C. pisifera* 'Plumosa Aurea', the sulphur yellows of *C.p.* 'Squarrosa Sulphurea', the string-like green sprays of *C.p.* 'Filifera' and the grey-green of *Cupressus glabra*.

A cherry walk, claimed by arboriculturists to be one of the finest in the north, is notable for its variety and its glory of pink and white clouds of blossom in the spring. Among the species and varieties here are *Prunus incisa*, the Fuji Cherry, autumn colouring *P.* × *yedoensis* with the arching branches, the Flag Cherry, *P.* 'Hatazakura', so called because of the tattered edged petals, Cheals Weeping Cherry, the Spring Cherry in its pendulous form *P. subhirtella* 'Pendula', the Ernest Wilson Cherry *P. lannesiana, P. scopulorum*, rare and of upright habit and *P. padus* 'Watereri', the Bird Cherry, with long racemes of flowers.

The surprising and intriguing feature about Thorp Perrow is the way one ride leads to another as full of interest as the last. Here, for instance is a laburnum avenue. Laburnums are, of course, common to many gardens, but this avenue is a collection of *L.* × *watereri 'Voissii'*, the not often seen tricoloured +*Laburnocytisus adamii*, the twice flowering *L. anagyroides* 'Autumnale', the Scotch Laburnum, *L. alpinum, L. alpinum* 'Pendulum', one named *L. anagyroides alschingeri* but not in the catalogues, as well as the common form, *L. anagyroides*. A well grown *Magnolia grandiflora* is by this ride and at the end of it there is *Abies magnifica*, the Red Fir, planted for contrast against a tall Weeping Birch *Betula pendula* 'Youngii'.

What one could well call the Blue Spruce grove, for the superbly coloured specimens of *Picea pungens* 'Koster' which fill one end, is another foliage bay, made even more exciting by a central island of different young cedars, the rare Cyprian Cedar, *Cedrus brevifolia, C. atlantica* 'Fastigiata', *C.a.* 'Glauca Pendula', *C. deodara, C.d.* 'Albospica', with creamy white leaf shoots, *C.a.* 'Aurea', *C. libani*, of course, and a unique one known here as *C. fletcheri*. At the end of this bed is a thicket of the small *Buddleia globosa*, with its small orange-shaped flowers.

The side plantings of this glade are for spring and autumn effect, the tiny leafed upright *Acer palmatum* 'Ribesifolium'; *A. davidii*; *A. japoni-*

cum 'Aureum'; *A. palmatum* 'Heptalobum Osakazuki'; *A. griseum*, with the flaking bark; *A. palmatum* 'Senkaki', the Coral Barked Maple; *A. palmatum* 'Septemlobum' and *A. japonicum* 'Aconitifolium'. Large trees as a backloth include Scots Pines, *Cupressus glabra*, *Chamaecyparis lawsoniana* 'Lutea', Red Oaks, the columnar decorative *Chamaecyparis lawsoniana* 'Pottenii' and the *C. lawsoniana* 'Kilmacurragh', which is so like the Italian Cypress.

Next is an avenue called the 'Peep' because down an avenue of limes and Wheatley Elms a glimpse of the house over the lake can be seen. Notice the original giant sized oaks and ashes which were mature trees when Sir Leonard started the arboretum. Going left again are tall slim pillars of Silver Birch backed by massive beeches. At the rear of this avenue is another surprise, for in a green opening there is a planting of the tall, the short, the pyramidal, the weeping and the globular of the genus *Chamaecyparis*: *C. lawsoniana* 'Pendula', *C.l.* 'Intertexta', *C. obtusa* 'Albospica', *C. nootkatensis*, *C. lawsoniana* 'Wisselii', the most ornamental *C.l.* 'Fletcheri' and *C.l.* 'Ellwoodii', *C.l.* 'Triomf Van Boskoop', a lovely glaucous blue, *C.l.* 'Westermanii', brilliant yellow in spring, *C. nootkatensis* 'Variegata', noticeable for its almost white tipped foliage, as is *C.l.* 'Silver Queen'.

Nearby is an unusual avenue of Yukon Cherries and crab apples in variety. There is also a long grassed avenue of lilacs, the purple in its season extending into the distance.

Three wide grassed bays opening out of the woodland are specially planted for foliage colour and separated by stands of deciduous and coniferous trees. In the extensive borders to the bays are specimen maples: *Acer rufinerve* with striated bark; *A. monspessulanum*, the Montpelier Maple; *A. cappadocicum*; the snake barked *A. hersii*; *A. hyrcanum*; *A. truncatum*; and the striped barked *A. pensylvanicum*. Then there are *Cotinus coggygria*, the Smoke Bush, impressive stands of Golden Privet, *Parrotia persica*, Golden Elder, Red Oaks, *Cornus controversa*, *Berberis* in variety, *Enkianthus*, and the rare native Wild Service Tree, *Sorbus torminalis*. Illustrating the interest found in these woodland glades is the White Avenue made up of white flowering Chestnuts, *Aesculus turbinata*, the Japanese Horse Chestnut, and *A. parviflora*, the upright, multi-stemmed *Betula medwediewii*, *Crataegus prunifolia* with its polished oval leaves, an unusually tall *Malus tschonoskii* and species of *Cornus* and *Viburnum*.

There is a collection of walnut trees, not so often seen in gardens, comprising the Common Walnut, *Juglans regia*, *J. mandshurica*, *J. ailantifolia* and *J.a. cordiformis*.

Another green way, flanked by weather-worn pieces of statuary which came from the Palace of Westminster, leads to a large grassed circular clearing from which radiate six long avenues each with its individual interests and attractions. On the edge of the lawn is a specimen of the fastigiate Dawyck Beech. One avenue is of Red Oaks, another of the fastigiate cherry 'Amanogawa'. Whichever avenue one takes there are unusual and different trees to see, London Planes beside Camperdown Elms or a collection of oaks including *Quercus frainetto*, the Hungarian Oak, *Q. phellos*, the Willow Oak, and the rare *Q. canariensis*. The Wing Nut Tree, *Pterocarya fraxinifolia*, stands among tall Balsam Poplars and willows. *Acer saccharum*, the Sugar Maple, famous for its highly coloured autumn foliage, has its place near the birch *Betula maximowicziana*, with large heart-shaped leaves, a huge specimen of the Cut-leaved Beech, *Fagus sylvatica heterophylla*, and the Cock's Comb Beech, its leaves deeply lobed and curled, *F.s.* 'Cristata'. There are the Chinese *Sorbus vilmorinii* with its fern-like foliage; the Red Elm, *Ulmus rubra*, with velvety leaves; the Hoary Willow, *Salix elaeagnos*, with rosemary-like foliage; the Snowdrop Tree *Halesia carolina*; New Zealand native related to the mallow, *Hoheria lyallii*; the shaggy barked birch *Betula nigra*; and two *Ulmus pumila*, whose catkins are produced in autumn.

Specimen conifers among so many worth noting are *Cupressus duclouxiana*; the Bhutan Pine, *Pinus wallichiana*; *P. ponderosa* with the cinnamon bark; *Picea omorika*, so distinctly branched; the long 'skirted' *P. brewerana*; the Tiger-tail Spruce, *Picea polita*; *P. smithiana*, a beautifully foliaged tree; the Spanish Fir, *Abies pinsapo*, and a representative of the species which is the oldest living tree in the world, *Pinus aristata*. Douglas Firs rear their heads above the other greenery.

For those who can tear themselves away from the trees the kitchen garden is worth a visit. It is well kept behind its high brick walls which are covered with trained pears, plums and apples, while the glass houses vines, early pears and plums. Part of the ground is laid out as a nursery standing ground for shrubs and trees for sale and the remainder, not used for vegetables, carries a collection of paeonies and herbaceous plants.

Upsall Castle

Lord and Lady Tranmire

Turn E off A19 about 5 km (3 miles) from Thirsk at signpost marked Knayton and follow signs to Upsall. Open occasionally for charity. Teas in Thirsk. Ornamental garden and planted woodland, situated 73 m (240 ft) above sea level on medium to heavy loam. Average yearly rainfall 640 mm (25 in.). Staff of one.

This garden with extensive views south and west over the Plain of York is built round the ruins of the fourteenth-century castle, the home of the historic Scope family. In the old walled garden there are Greengage plum and Morello and sweet cherries on the walls.

On the house terrace is a sunken, circular thyme garden reached by steps, once the entrance to the old castle itself, and on the crumbling stone walls grow white and pink valerian and a veteran yellow Scotch Rose. This terrace gives way to the main lawn, from where it can be seen that the upper terrace is retained by the ancient walls of the old castle, which give shelter to a large bush of the Mexican Orange, *Choisya ternata*, a huge Sweet Bay, and the climbing roses 'Albertine', 'Golden Showers', 'Fashion' and 'Ena Harkness'.

Rhododendrons and fine mature trees line the entrance drive.

Valley Gardens

Harrogate Borough Council

In the centre of Harrogate, main entrance near Pump Room Museum. Open at all times. Car parks; meals available; dogs allowed. Ornamental garden, streamside, open parkland and pinewood walks of some 28 ha (70 acres), situated 135 m (446 ft) above sea level on slightly acid soil over millstone grit. Average annual rainfall 790 mm (31 in.). Staff of six.

The Valley Gardens, for many years a resort of lovers of garden and woodland walks is part of the 120 ha (300 acres) of gardens and Stray (open greensward) which earn Harrogate the name of 'Floral Spa'. The gardens comprise ornamental streamside, bog and water, heath and peat, rose, New Zealand and rockery gardens, open grassland and pinewood.

At all times of the year the long walk by the stream has some floral colour to show and in high summer it is ablaze. At dahlia time a long curving border with a host of decorative and cactus varieties is the mecca for all lovers of the flower and of floral spectacle. The limestone rock garden houses a very fine collection of alpines including the dwarf types of *Fuchsia, Hypericum, Aquilegia, Penstemon, Potentilla,* many different kinds of gentians and *Aethionema.* In the peat garden there is to be seen a comprehensive collection of rhododendrons, primulas, heathers, hellebores and lilies. The sheltered New Zealand garden has its antipodean inhabitants – *Senecio,* myrtles, *Cordyline, Callistemon, Pittosporum, Phormium, Hebe, Eucalyptus* and *Celmisia.*

South Yorkshire

Greenery Amid the Bricks and Mortar

Cannon Hall

Barnsley Metropolitan Borough Council

8 km (5 miles) W of Barnsley on A635 and 1.6 km (1 mile) NW of Cawthorne. Open daily all the year round 10.30–5 pm in summer, to dusk in winter. Car park. The parkland of 34 ha (85 acres) and the hall were bought by Barnsley Corporation from the Spencer-Stanhope family in 1951, the first time they had changed hands in 300 years. The hall, now a museum, houses good furniture, paintings, plasterwork, glass and the Regimental Museum of the 13/18th Royal Hussars. Situated 115 m (370 ft) above sea level on slightly acid soil over clay. Average annual rainfall 760 mm (30 in.). Staff of five.

Cannon Hall, the ancient home of the Spencer, later Spencer-Stanhope family, stands (on the site of a house mentioned in the Domesday Book) on sloping ground looking to the south. The hall, a characteristic lesser country house of the Georgian era, is principally by John Carr of York. The present day landscape is the creation of John Spencer the third, who in 1761 spent £30,000 on improvements effected by Richard Woods, a landscape gardener of the Brownian school, and Thomas Peach, the head gardener.

There are fine views from the house terrace over long sloping lawns to three long lakes in the valley bottom, connected by picturesque cascades. Over the lakes the landscape rises again to the well wooded hillside of Bentcliffe Hill, Hoyland Swain and a charming view of Cawthorne village and church.

The house approach is from the west by a tall lime avenue skirted by old plantings of clumped rhododendrons backed by fine mature and very tall beeches.

To the east of the house, with views to the last cascade and Cawthorne, is a sunken rose garden 'fenced in' by a massive yew border. The path runs by the side of the red brick of the kitchen garden wall into which is let a round-windowed brick conservatory, an alternative entrance to the kitchen garden, which is filled with decorative plants in summer. Also piercing the wall, which is covered with climbing roses and forsythia with free-standing magnolias in front, are three 'Italian gates' with delicate ironwork. Between two of the gates stands the now glassless eighteenth-century orangery which in autumn is aflame with its covering of Virginia Creeper, wisteria and forsythia clothe the back wall.

Before proceeding further it might be as well to enter through the last Italian gate into the kitchen garden, for here is one of Cannon Hall's main attractions – the long stretch of garden wall, filled with hardly an inch to spare, with the espalier trained pears – many said to be nearly 200 years old. Against the tall red brick wall of an outbuilding are espaliered trees more than 6 m (20 ft) high – 'Doyenné du Comice', 'Jargonelle' and 'Fondant de Cuerne'. Then right round the three walls are a range of noble sounding pears including 'Buerré Hardy', 'Jargonelle', 'Williams' Bon Chrétien', 'Durondeau', 'Louise Bonne of Jersey', 'Beurré Diel', 'Laxton's Early Market' and 'Laxton's Superb', a magnificent sight in blossom. There are roses in beds, more pears trained as hedges and several greenhouses, one of which houses the famous grape vine the Cannon Hall Muscat, some 150 years old, now a much prized commercial grape in Australia and a favourite with connoisseurs of the grape everywhere.

But to return to the main walk, this now leads between tall, almost impenetrable borders of hybrid rhododendrons, hedged in by mature forest trees – beech, oak, Sweet Chestnut, Holm Oak and conifers. In a clearing is a colourful bank of tall heathers. The path ahead terminates in a romantic stone gateway through which the visitor is attracted to find he is on a wooden bridge over the ha-ha which extends completely round the garden to the south. Here he has a surprise view over open country to the hillside of Cawthorne. From the bridge the path continues downhill to an oval lily pool hemmed around on the south with mouldering, ivy covered church window masonry taken from Silkstone and Cawthorne churches when they were renovated by the family. Uphill now the path carries on through groups of azaleas and rhododendrons, with yews as high as forest trees which separate the garden from the landscape outside, to where, under an arch of cedar, the region of the rose garden is reached once more.

To the rear of the house, by a giant screen of yew and some very tall mature beech, there are more winding paths through old established thickets of rhododendrons and high forest trees. In a clearing is a circular stone pool backed by a designed frieze of varying tree forms. The main path to the west of the house leads to a break in the estate wall and over the metalled main drive to the walls of another kitchen garden not now part of the estate, but which housed, contemporaneously with the pear garden, more pears on the walls and free-standing apples.

Oakes Park

Major and Mrs T. Bagshawe

At Norton, 6 km (4 miles) S of Sheffield on B6054, 3 km (2 miles) from A61 at Meadowhead Junction. Open Easter, then 22 May to 18 September Saturdays and Sundays and Bank Holiday Mondays and Tuesdays. The Georgian house with old furniture, tapestries and paintings is also open. For hours see current issue of *Historic Houses, Castles and Gardens*. Teas available. Garden of 1.2 ha (3 acres) in 40 ha (100 acres) of parkland, situated 240 m (800 ft) above sea level on acid soil. Average annual rainfall 760 mm (30 in.). Staff of one and occasional help.

The garden at Oakes is said to have been designed by John Nash, of Regent's Park and Buckingham Palace fame, and the house terraced by the nineteenth-century sculptor Sir Francis Chantrey. While the passage of time and violent storms have left their mark on the trees and layout, enough remains to appreciate, for the view from the Chantrey terrace (with Chantrey urns) takes in gently sloping south-facing lawns cut into by beds of rhododendrons, azaleas and heathers and a long sinuous lake with a willow and rhododendron planted island, and then away across miles of countryside towards Chesterfield.

Of two sentinel cedars at each side of the lawn one is dead, but because house records show it to have been bought for £2 3*s*.6*d*. and planted in 1770 (it survived until 1967, nearly 200 years) its gaunt frame has been preserved and clothed with clematis. Other links with the past are the 150 year old *Magnolia acuminata*, which reaches to the eaves of the house, the rectangular canal pond behind the stable block (this is mentioned in a 1753 survey) and the nearby eighteenth-century dovecote in the turreted Derbyshire style.

A path from the terrace leads by the end of the lake through an iron gate, fashioned from ore mined on the estate, to the privy, pear-shaped garden which houses the bothy where the gardeners lived. One side of this garden is enclosed by a high holly hedge; old brick walls enclose the rest. Low box edged beds hold roses and on the walls are old thick stemmed climbing roses 'Albertine' and 'Golden Showers', *Eucryphia* × *nymansensis* 'Nymansay' and old trained pears.

There is a huge holly tree in the lawn, some new planting of specimen trees on the ha-ha edge with its view to the faraway home of the

Sitwells at Renishaw and, by the side of the house, the wall of which is almost covered by an old Sweet Bay, is the stump of a *Robinia pseudoacacia* so huge that a miniature garden has been made within its circumference. Close by, a seedling from the original tree preserves its continuity. The house walls are covered with a variety of *Clematis*, 'Jackmanii' and 'Ernest Markham' being prominent.

Sandbeck Park

Lord Scarbrough

Off A634 Maltby-Blyth road. Open occasionally for charity when the eighteenth-century mansion is also open: note fine marble fireplaces, sporting pictures, Rose ceilings, a chapel with one window of mediaeval glass unearthed at Roche Abbey. Dogs allowed on lead. A Lancelot Brown landscape, situated 140m (450ft) above sea level. Average annual rainfall 640mm (25in.). Staff of one and occasional help.

At Sandbeck Park a James Paine mansion of *c.*1763, said to be one of his most dramatic designs, is set in a landscape designed by Brown from a plan, dated 1774, still in existence in the house. At this time Brown also altered the grounds of nearby Roche Abbey, a Cistercian monastery of *c.*1147, now owned by the Department of the Environment but once a part of the grounds. His contract laid down that he had 'To finish the valley of Roach Abbey in all its parts according to the idea fixed on with Lord Scarbrough with poet's feelings and with painter's eye'. The abbey in its eighteenth-century setting may still be visited.

The imposing house front looks over greenery to the lake designed by Brown and many of his original tree plantings. Seen from the front and from the piano nobile of the house in spring the lawns to the lake are a sea of bulbs including fritillaries and the Lenten Lily, *Narcissus pseudonarcissus*. There is a small bridge across the lake and the high walls and iron paling round the park once contained a herd of fallow deer.

Near the house are a rose garden and a secret garden laid out in 1908 which has run wild, but Lord Scarbrough has plans to bring this delightful period piece into a semblance of order.

Sheffield Botanical Garden

City of Sheffield

On Clarkehouse Road, off A625 Ecclesshall-Sheffield-Chapel-en-le-Frith road. Open throughout the year Monday to Saturday 7.30 am–dusk. Sunday 10 am–dusk, except for November to January when the opening hours are 8.30 am–dusk. Dogs allowed on lead. Gardens of 8 ha (19 acres), sloping to SW, situated 140 m (450 ft) above sea level on clay soil of a fairly acid character. Average annual rainfall 810 mm (32 in.).

The Sheffield Botanical Garden was established in 1833 by public subscription, Robert Marnock, of Regent's Park, London, considered by Repton and Loudon the best exponent of the gardenesque school of landscaping, being its first designer and curator. As you enter by the imposing stone gateway of 1836 the first feature of interest is the long range of Paxton Pavilions, three beautifully proportioned, curved, glass roofed conservatories of 1837, linked laterally by a colonnade wreathed in climbers – *Solanum crispum* 'Glasnevin', *Ceanothus* × *veitchianus*, *Garrya elliptica*, Firethorns, wisteria – and in the beds at their feet the winter flowering iris *Iris unguicularis*, *Cistus* and *Daphne* species. The far pavilion is given over to plants which will grow in this area without heat – *Fremontodendron californicum*, *Camellia japonica* and *C.* × *williamsii* in variety, the Lobster Claw, *Clianthus puniceus*, *Convolvulus cneorum* and *Passiflora caerulea*. On the wall border behind the Paxton Pavilions grows the Sheffield collection of lilacs, some 40 species and hybrids.

Not far from the entrance gate are two species of *Arbutus*, the Strawberry Tree *A. unedo*, and the not so often seen *A. andrachnoides* with cinnamon red branches and flowering October-November.

The garden is of an irregular shape divided principally by a long herbaceous border reaching from the Paxton Pavilions to a large piece of Victorian statuary commemorating the Crimean War. Many winding paths and walks lead to the various sections of the garden devoted to roses, woodlands, Victorian bedding plants, trials, peat-loving plants, rock gardening, heathers and demonstration gardens, and large grassed areas studded with specimen trees and shrubs of which there is an excellent and comprehensive collection.

On the left of the entrance is the historic Victorian garden where a

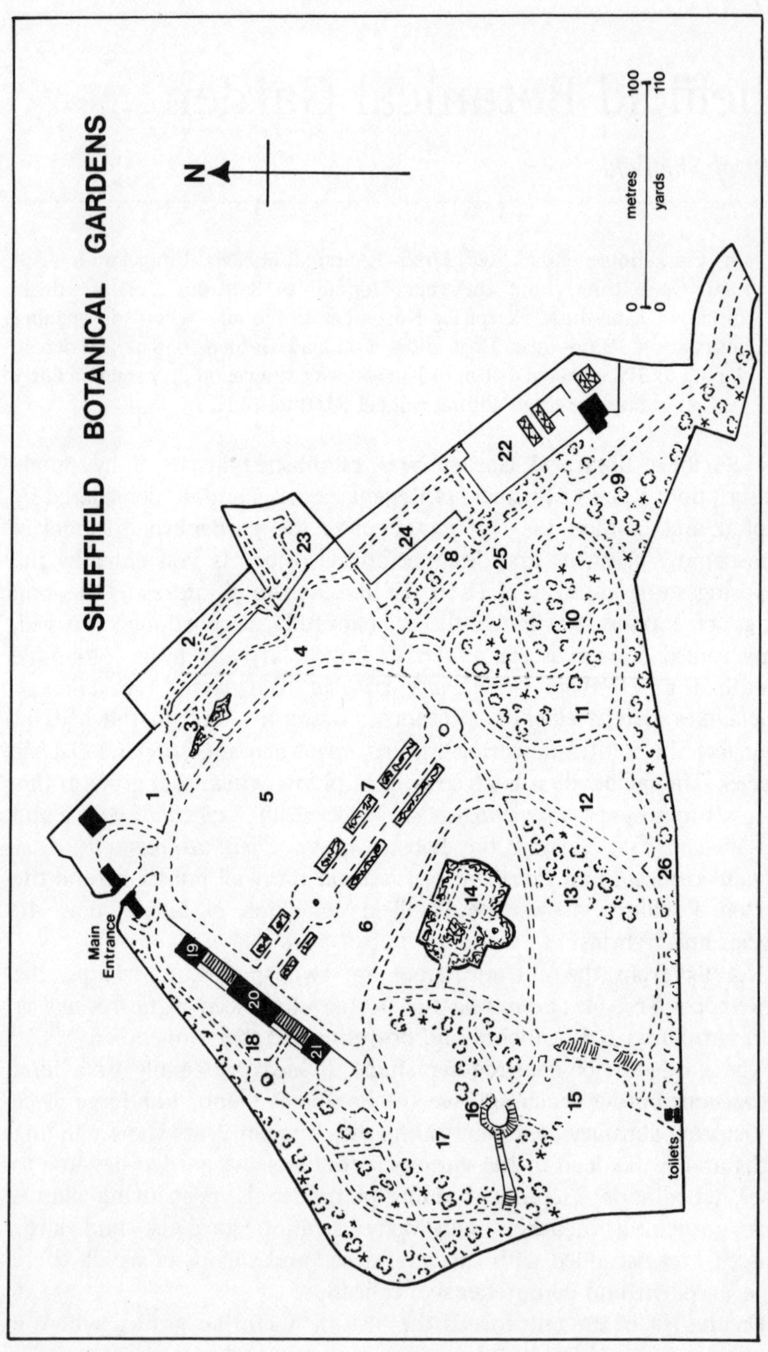
SHEFFIELD BOTANICAL GARDENS
N
0 metres 100
0 yards 110
Main Entrance
toilets
1
2
3
4
5
6
7
8
9
10
11
12
13
14
15
16
17
18
19
20
21
22
23
24
25
26

series of intricately shaped beds cut into the lawns are filled with low-growing subjects – *Echeveria*, stonecrops and low-growing annuals peculiar to Victorian bedding-out displays. The back screen is composed of a collection of *Escallonia* species and many of the newer Donard cultivars. The path following on from this garden is full of interest, passing as it does Osborn's Field where trials of new annuals are carried out each year. This section is separated from the main path by a border principally of plants of the family *Leguminosae*, among which grow *Cytisus battandieri* the pineapple-scented broom, *Salix matsudana* 'Tortuosa' the twisted stem form of the Pekin Willow and some fine specimens of the somewhat tender *Erica terminalis*, the Corsican Heath.

Opposite is the rock garden with a series of ponds and paved areas backed by rock faces in which grow *Saxifraga*, *Androsace*, a fine collection of *Dianthus*, *Geranium*, *Helianthemum*, *Aubrieta*, *Bruckenthalia*, *Daboecia*, *Draba* and a host of primulas, gentians and other alpine subjects. In the grass around the rock garden are a wide range of the shorter-growing maples, *Salix irrorata* with white-grey bloomed stems, *Cornus*, *Cistus*, a comprehensive collection of *Genista* and many dwarf conifers.

The heath garden which follows on contains a wide selection of species of *Erica* and named cultivars, *Corylopsis spicata*, whose primrose-fragrant flowers come early before the foliage, *Fothergilla monticola*, an autumn colouring subject, the Buffalo Berry, *Shepherdia argentea*, the uncommon Tasmanian conifer *Podocarpus alpinus*, a pendulous *Chamaecyparis nootkatensis* 'Pendula', an agreeable variety of coloured bark birches including *Betula lutea*, *B. utilis* and *B. papyrifera*, the Paper Birch. There are also *Cryptomeria japonica*, *Juniperus conferta*, *Leiophyllum buxifolium*, with box-like leaves, and the London Plane, *Platanus acerifolia*.

The largest areas of grass are the east and west lawns flanking the

---

1. Victoria Garden
2. Osborne's Field Trials
3. Rock Garden
4. Heath Garden
5. Main East Lawn
6. West Lawn
7. Herbaceous Borders
8. Award of Garden Merit Collection
9. Sorbus Lawn
10. Woodland Garden
11. Peat Garden
12. Cedar Lawn
13. Copse, Shrubberies & Malus Lawn
14. Rose Garden
15. Bear Pit Garden
16. Bear Pit
17. Birch Hill
18. Clarke House Walk
19. East Pavilion/Aquarium
20. Main Pavilion/Aviary
21. West Pavilion/Plant House
22. Nursery
23. Demonstration Garden
24. Botanical Supplies
25. Bottom Lawn
26. Long Wall Borders

long herbaceous border, the setting for large collections of trees and shrubs. On the east lawn can be seen the Tulip Tree, *Liriodendron tulipifera,* the Tree of Heaven, *Ailanthus altissima, Acer pseudoplatanus* 'Corstorphinense', the formidably thorned white flowering *Colletia armata* and *C. cruciata,* many varieties of *Potentilla* and *Deutzia, Viburnum* × *juddii,* the Dutch Elm *Ulmus* × *hollandica* 'Major', *Ulmus procera* 'Louis van Houtte', with golden yellow foliage, *Senecio, Salix alba* 'Chermesina', a scarlet stemmed willow, *Sorbus aria, S.a.* 'Handsworth Variety', *S. decora,* and, a few of the many pines in the garden, *P. contorta,* with twisted needles, *P. nigra* and *P. sylvestris,* the Scots Pine. There is also a particularly good selection here of *Chamaecyparis.*

The herbaceous border is representative of an old style perennial-full border.

The west lawn, on which there is a wide range of *Forsythia,* is divided into six beds with an educational theme. The first houses plants whose shape or form is distinctive, such as the Corkscrew Hazel, *Corylus avellana* 'Contorta', and the weeping cherry *Prunus subhirtella* 'Pendula'. The second bed displays silver and gold foliaged plants; the third contains dwarf conifers and the fourth is filled with flowers which do well in the Sheffield area. The fifth bed is for those subjects best suited to floral art and the sixth is a foliage bed in which *Ajuga, Mentha,* small maples and other plants show their leaf colouring to advantage.

On the perimeter of this lawn and in the woodland garden is the Sheffield collection of *Magnolia* – *M. liliiflora* 'Nigra', *M. sieboldii, M. wilsonii, M.* × *soulangiana, M.s.* 'Lennei', *M. stellata, M.* × *highdownensis, M. kobus, M.* × *loebneri* 'Leonard Messel', *M. acuminata,* 'Charles Coates', *M. obovata, M. salicifolia, M. sargentiana robusta, M. sinensis, M.* × *soulangiana* 'Alexandrina', *M.* × *thompsoniana* and *M. virginiana.*

To the south of the east lawn is the ornamental rose garden, yew hedged on three sides. This has an all-embracing collection of species, shrub roses and old fashioned varieties as well as the more modern Hybrid Teas and Floribundas. Here are represented most of the progenitors of our modern roses – Teas, Hybrid Musks, Hybrid Perpetuals, forms of *gallica,* Bourbons, and cultivars of *R.* × *alba* and *R. pimpinellifolia* (*spinosissima*).

To the east of the rose garden is the bear pit which was on the site when the garden was established. The approach to this is near Birch Hill where the *Viburnum* collection includes the winter flowering *V. farreri* and *V.* × *bodnantense.* Birch Hill itself commands fine views over the lawns, the sloping sides of the hill being filled with naturalized bulbs. At the bottom a bed is filled with many of the newer coloured foliage varieties of *Calluna vulgaris*.

To the east again of the rose garden and bear pit and running along the eastern boundary of the garden is an extensive collection of rhododendrons – some 60 species and 50 hybrids – as well as a representative collection of Mollis and Ghent azaleas. In the extreme eastern corner is what is termed the 'South of France', planted with Mock Orange, lavender, mignonette, stocks and hyacinths. Immediately in front of this fragrant border is a selection of lesser known trees commemorating the 1972 conference of the Horticultural Education Association held in Sheffield – *Liriodendron tulipifera* 'Fastigiatum', the silver foliaged *Pyrus nivalis*, the Choke Cherry, *Prunus virginiana*, and a tall maple with ascending branches, *Acer × lobelii*.

Between the main rhododendron garden and the woodland are the peat garden, the cedar lawn and the copse shrubberies. Created from a dark shrubbery of Victorian laurel the peat garden houses a host of *Primula, Ledum, Cassiope, Meconopsis* and dwarf rhododendrons. Next door the cedar lawn is marked by a well shaped *Cedrus atlantica, Pseudolarix amabilis*, the Golden Larch, *Calocedrus* (*Libocedrus*) *decurrens*, the Incense Cedar, rarely seen hereabouts, and two specimens of the Dawn Redwood, *Metasequoia glyptostroboides*. A small bed is the site of a collection of hellebores, *Helleborus niger*, the Christmas rose, *H. atrorubens, H. viridis, H. foetidus* and *H. corsicus*. Some camellias also find a congenial home here – *Camellia japonica* 'Elegans', *C.j.* 'Furoan', and *C. × williamsii* 'St Ewe'.

The copse shrubberies, underplanted with heathers, lilies and cyclamen, are the home of some of the garden's most unusual and rare shrubs, planted in irregular beds interwoven with broad grass walks. More camellias are found here – *C. japonica* 'Donckelarii', *C.j.* 'Latifolia', *C.j.* 'Mathotiana Rubra', *C. × williamsii* 'Donation', *C.w.* 'Citation', *C.w.* 'J.C. Williams', and *C.w.* 'Mary Christian'. The *Hamamelis* are happy here in their winter blooming and the later flowering rhododendrons and azaleas keep the colour going as well as early flowering daphnes. Among shrubs of particular interest are *Pachysandra terminalis*, a dark evergreen ground cover flowering in February-March, the evergreen *Osmanthus* of fragrant bloom, *O. armatus* and *O. delavayi*, the holly-like *O. heterophyllus* and the tender *O. suavis*. There are the ericaceous *Leucothoe fontanesiana*, with racemes of pitcher-shaped flowers and bronze-purple shoots, *L. keiskei* of the cylindrical white nodding flowers, and the Black Huckleberry, *Gaylussacia baccata*. Finding their required shelter here are the Chilean natives *Desfontainea spinosa*, with scarlet and yellow tubular flowers, *Crinodendron hookeranum*, the Japanese Lantern Tree, and *Embothrium coccineum* and

E. coccineum lanceolatum, aflame with orange-scarlet flowers all along the branches in May and June. Autumn tints come from *Clethra barbinervis* (as well as fragrant white bloom in spring); *Coriaria japonica*, red fruited, and *C. terminalis*, black fruited, both with fronded leaves; the erect branched *Enkianthus campanulatus*, *E. chinensis* and *E. perulatus*, all with wonderful autumn leaf colour as well as lovely drooping urn-shaped flower in spring. Also good for autumn effect is *Clerodendrum trichotomum*, with its maroon calyx, fragrant white flowers and blue berries. The Winter Sweet is represented by yellow flowered *Chimonanthus praecox*.

The blue flowers of *Ceratostigma willmottianum* contrast with the waxy paper flowers of *Eucryphia glutinosa*, *E.* × *intermedia* and *E.i.* 'Rostrevor', the heavy blooming New Zealander *Hoheria glabrata* and the spiraea-aping *Holodiscus discolor*. *Pittosporum tenuifolium* brings a change with its black stems and chocolate-purple honey-scented flowers, as does *Ptelea trifoliata*, yellow flowered and of the best honeysuckle fragrance. Here too are *Staphylea pinnata*, with pinnate leaves and bladder fruits, *S. colchica* 'Coulombieri', *Styrax japonica* and *S. hemsleyana*, named 'Snowbells' for their pure white pendulous flowers, and *Pieris formosana forrestii*. There are also *Gaultheria*, hollies in many variegated varieties, *Skimmia*, *Mahonia* and *Elaeagnus* to fill in with their evergreen foliage.

The tree cover is varied; specimens include the Snowdrop Tree *Halesia carolina*, the Indian Bean Tree, *Catalpa bignonioides*, *Koelreuteria paniculata*, yellow flowered and bladder fruited, the Handkerchief Tree, *Davidia involucrata*, *Castanea sativa*, the edible Sweet Chestnut, a diversity of *Malus* and the thorns *Craetagus laciniata sanguinea*, with large deep red haws, *C.* × *lavallei*, orange-red fruited, *C. monogyna* 'Pendula', the Weeping Thorn, and one named as *C. kansuensis aurantiaca*.

The woodland, formerly the site of an old quarry, with its overhead canopy of beech, gives dappled shade and shelter to hydrangeas, many rhododendrons, spindles, *Abeliophyllum distichum*, whose fragrant white flowers tinged with pink blossom in February before the leaves appear, clumps of the sweet smelling early flowering *Sarcococca hookerana*, *S. humilis* and *S. rusicolia*, the palm *Trachycarpus fortunei* and *Eucalpytus gunnii*.

On the *Sorbus* lawn by the Thompson Road entrance are planted various rowans to show off their different coloured fruits and foliage. The principal species are *S. hupehensis*, *S. serotina*, *S. pluripinnata*, *S. prattii*, *S. vilmorinii* and *S. wilsoniana*. An interesting feature here on the roots of a poplar is *Lathraea clandestina*, a parasitic plant with purple hooded flowers.

There is a demonstration garden of which one half simulates a well planned small house garden with rockery, paved area, pool and stream, a shrubbery and climbers on a woven wood fence. The other half serves as a trial garden for seed and bulbs. At the rear is an area where unusual vegetables are grown and just a little further down the path is the A.G.M. border, showing plants which have been awarded the Royal Horticultural Society's Award of Garden Merit.

'A day in the garden' at the Sheffield Botanical Garden is one way of getting to know better the tremendous wealth of plants this island is blessed with.

Wentworth Castle

Barnsley Metropolitan Borough Council

At Stainborough, near Barnsley. Off M1 at Junction 37 on minor road signposted Stainborough and Gillroyd. Garden open by appointment only. Teas in Barnsley. Extensive early-eighteenth-century landscape initially created by the first Earl of Strafford (second creation) from 1708 to his death in 1739; now grounds of teachers' training college. Situated 110 m (360 ft) above sea level on good loam over coal measures. Average annual rainfall 690 mm (27 in.).

Described in an article in the Garden History Society *Journal* as a 'forgotten landscape', Wentworth Castle, once the home of the Earls of Strafford, has still much of what made it, in Walpole's words in 1789, 'my favourite of all great seats, such a variety of ground, of wood and water; almost all executed and disposed with so much taste'.

Today the visitor can still walk up the wide slope behind the house, hemmed in on both sides by rhododendrons in woodland, to the obelisk put up by the second Earl in 1739 and dedicated to his near neighbour Lady Mary Wortley Montagu, commemorating the fact that in 1720 she introduced into England inoculation against smallpox.

Turning to the right by the obelisk, where there are fine views over rolling countryside, for the walk is high on a ridge, the visitor comes upon the 'Gothic' castle built by the first Earl, certainly before 1730, which makes it a precursor of the romantic ruins of many later eighteenth-century gardens. Although the castle is in a sad state of disrepair, the battlements and towered gateway and the long encircling wall with other towers are there. The visitor might well have passed, on his way into the castle grounds, what at first sight appears to be a small church. This too was an early piece of romantic 'Gothic' building, designed as a gatehouse and still lived in.

At the rear of the house there is still in use a fine example of a spacious and elegant Victorian conservatory and to the right, among the shrubbery and lawns, is a concealed entrance to a secret garden.

To the south-west of the terrace of the house is an open temple, Corinthian in style (*c*.1730) from which fine views over well wooded countryside and parkland take in another obelisk to Queen Anne, erected by the first Earl, her soldier and diplomat, in 1734. There can also be seen the top of a now, alas, ruined Corinthian temple dome, a rotunda with twelve Ionic columns, said to have been designed by the Earl as his mausoleum, and as noble in its day as any in an eighteenth century garden. To the rear of the terrace temple and across the rough parkland is yet another soaring Corinthian column erected in 1743 in memory of the second Earl's father-in-law, the Duke of Argyll.

From the east terrace can be seen, now with difficulty, the course of what was once a fine serpentine 'river', tree margined and disappearing from view under a finely ornamented bridge of Brownian design and date. Local historians have it that Lancelot Brown did indeed work here on the stream and on building the bridge, but there is no documentary evidence to substantiate this. Certainly the formal garden shown in Kip's engraving of 1714 was swept away at about the time when the second Earl, in 1764, was adding new features to the estate. Attributable to this period is a Horace Walpole designed 'Gothic' cross, now a ruin in Menagerie Wood, and, gone these many years now, one of the boldest picturesque landscape designs of its era, a long line of mock fortifications on Worsborough Common (*c*.1765–6) which was to be seen in the distance from the house and its south terrace.

Again this is a historic garden for the student of garden evolution. Set in the midst of the South Yorkshire Coalfield and within sight of the night-time infernal glow of the Sheffield and Rotherham steel furnaces, this landscape, still with views over farmland and woodland, is something we should endeavour to preserve. Even the M1 down in the valley below (the house can be seen on its hill to the right as cars rush Londonwards) has not desecrated this green blessing in an otherwise industrial landscape.

Wentworth Woodhouse

Earl Fitzwilliam

At Wentworth, 6 km (4 miles) from Rotherham, off M1 at Junction 36 to Wentworth. The house is now a teachers' training college and open by appointment only, but the major part of the ornamental gardens surrounding the house (7 ha, 18 acres) is being opened as part of a garden centre complex. Car parks. Situated 110 m (350 ft) above sea level on good loam over coal measures. Average annual rainfall 690 mm (27 in).

On the opposite side of the well wooded valley from Wentworth Castle, this historic house and epic landscape were created and built by the rival branch of the Wentworths to that at the castle, the Wentworth Woodhouse family being that of the ill-fated first Earl of Strafford. The house has still intact its gloriously decorated, nobly proportioned state rooms and the famous east front, at 180 m (600 ft) long the longest façade of any stately home in the country, can still be seen and admired in all its Palladiun pomp and splendour. It was the work of Henry Flitcroft, whose drawings for it are dated 1737.

The house can best be seen from the public footpath which runs from the main gate in Wentworth village to Greaseborough. This path also gives an opportunity to see the John Carr (1768) stable block with its finely proportioned inner square and gigantic fountain basin. The path passes through the vast parkland with the herd of deer browsing under mature parkland trees, mostly indigenous and, pleasing to see, much new planting. The path to Greaseborough goes by footbridge over the stream linking two lakes in the valley below the house. Dominating the skyline are the features for which Wentworth Woodhouse is well known – the mausoleum, circular and Corinthian pillared, designed by John Carr (1788), Hoober Stand, triangular in shape with a lantern, designed by Flitcroft (1746), Keppel's Column, by John Carr (1778) in memory of Admiral Keppel's court martial acquittal and the Needle's Eye of 1780.

The ornamental gardens and garden centre to the west of the house are reached by Hague Lane from the village. Here the extensive walled kitchen garden area has been laid out as a young tree plantation, sales centre and car park. The long terrace walk overlooking part of the ornamental gardens has been given over to the display of container trees, shrubs and plants.

Outside the kitchen garden walls an old, heavy branched and twisted hornbeam hedge bounds what was once the iris garden with a central pool. A path here by the side of the high walls lead through an ivy covered archway into the sunken Japanese garden (created in the late eighteenth and early nineteenth century), where skilful advantage was taken of an old quarry, its craggy face and lichen covered outcropping forming a natural boundary. A steep cascade, fern banked, tumbles into a large pool under the shelter of the looming rockface, giving an atmosphere of brooding and mystery. Crumbling life-size eighteenth-century stone figures, Japanese garden ornaments and troughs and massively heavy stone seats stand among plantings of autumn maples, azaleas and spreading junipers. Two Weeping Crabs flank the cascade, looking down on the winding stepped paths leading from one level to another. A thick-boled cherry at the top of the pool has reached the unusual height for the genus, of almost 15m (50ft).

A path from the Japanese garden leads to a wildly ornamented stone doorway of *c.*1630, its pilasters and open segmented pediment heavily decorated with carved fruits of improbable origin. The doorway is the entrance to a long curving grotto tunnel bringing us to the bottom of the bear pit, part of the original eighteenth-century garden layout. From the circular niched (for the bears?) floor the way out is by a spiral staircase to the higher level of the camellia house garden where willows, more maples and cherries dot the grass. The doorway of the bear pit is completely overrun by the Russian Vine, *Polygonum baldschuanicum.* Just before reaching the camellia house there is the old Menagerie Paddock (which may soon once again hold its animals for the pleasure of the visitor), at the far boundary of which is an Ionic open temple on a mound.

By a large copse of rhododendrons and a semicircular holly hedge the path leads to the glass roofed early-eighteenth-century camellia house, which houses many tree-high camellias. The nine-bayed front is topped by a delicately balustraded frieze. The area round the camellia house is well wooded and at the rear of the house is a crumbling stone summerhouse.

Through the woodland a path leads by a round pool which feeds the Japanese garden cascade, and by steep stone steps to the summerhouse garden, a more formal extension of the Japanese garden proper. The steps lead through a wide paved area to the simple stone summerhouse, almost entirely covered in wisteria. The back wall of this garden, supporting the long terrace, is, in autumn, aglow with the fiery foliage of one of vines, the border in front being planted with many buddleias, bringing a butterfly invasion at blossom time to add to the Japanese atmosphere. To the side of the summerhouse is a small lily tank and by its side garden troughs, Japanese stone ornaments, low-growing cherries and a low-growing Copper Beech (forming a foliage 'kennel' for a statue of a dog', as well as a large *Prunus triloba* and more spreading junipers. Another feature of the garden here is a long narrow stone-edged canal fed from a small round pond filled with irises.

At right angles another long canal, with two zigzag stone bridges crossing it, runs parallel to the garden wall. Steep steps lead up from the canal to a terrace which looks over another sunken Japanese garden with a long water feature, the water entering from a triangular basin, flowing into a wide oblong one, then into a narrow oblong canal before entering a pear-shaped pool and disappearing from sight under greenery at the far end. The garden down to the pools is in three terraces, bare now, but to be planted up in keeping with the character of the garden.

From the top terrace, or by steps, if we are going from the pool level, paths lead to the high garden with its fine view over the first Japanese garden. The lawn here is bounded by a topiary worked hedge and has island beds filled with heather and low-growing shrubs.

On the walk out into the woodland glade by the kitchen garden wall is a row of beeches pointing the way back to the garden centre and Wentworth village.

West Yorkshire

Public and Private Gardens

Arthington Hall

Mr and Mrs C.E.W. Sheepshanks

Off A61 Leeds-Harrogate road on A659 to Harewood Bridge and Otley. Open occasionally for charity when light refreshments are served. A finely planted and well kept garden of some 2.4 ha (6 acres), situated 45 m (146 ft) above sea level on alluvial soil. Sheltered by woodland and walls. Average annual rainfall 690 mm (27 in.). Staff of two and occasional help.

A garden of absorbing interest to the plantsman, where the traditions of the old walled gardens are upheld and new plantings, by the owner particularly of trees, have a care for foliage colour, form, and bark and stem features to provide year-round interest.

The view from the west front of the hall would be any landscape designer's envy, for over massed plantings of heathers enlivened by columnar conifers and between woodland trees the eye is carried to the meandering course of the River Wharfe in the valley beneath, to the splendid architectural frieze of the long curving Arthington railway viaduct and then away into the far distance up the broad shouldered valley of Wharfedale.

One of the plants on the house wall is the unusual sweet smelling *Clerodendrum trichotomum fargesii* and in the conservatory-type entrance hall there are Oleander, Bottle Brush, and tender *Eucalyptus*. To the right of the house entrance is a sloping lawn, daffodil strewn in spring and with a *Rhamnus alaternus* which, surprisingly in this northern climate, can match the holly for berries. At the top of the lawn is one of the most recently planted parts of the garden, as fine an arboretum as one could expect to see in a comparatively small space. Since 1969 Mr Sheepshanks has planted an incredible number of specimen trees, among them being a fine range of maples for autumn colour and bark interest – *Acer rubrum*; the paper barked *A. griseum*; the snake barked *A. pensylvanicum*; the marbled bark *A. hersii* and *A. grosseri*; *A. palmatum* 'Heptalobum Elegans'; *A. japonicum* 'Aconitifolium' with its ruby-crimson foliage; *A. japonicum* 'Vitifolium', of brilliant autumn colour; *A. maximowiczii* with striated stem; *A. cappadocicum* 'Aureum', of butter yellow foliage; the Silver Maple, *A. saccharinum*; the Hornbeam Maple, *A. carpinifolium*; *A. platanoides* 'Drummondii'; *A. davidii*, another species with green and white striated bark, and *A. capillipes*, striated also and with young red growths. Several *Cornus* add to the overall autumn blaze, *C. controversa*, *C. nuttallii* and *C. kousa* with its white spring bracts.

Among this fine stand of maples are interspersed *Ginkgo biloba*, the Maidenhair Tree; a very fine specimen of the Dawn Redwood, *Metasequoia glyptostroboides*; that fine golden foliaged tree *Robinia pseudoacacia* 'Frisia'; the shrubby *Euonymus alatus*; noted for its autumn colour and, almost as fiery, *Fothergilla monticola*. The rhododendron 'Sir Charles Lemon' contributes its bright rust coloured indumentum. There are also *Magnolia* × *veitchii*, *M. sieboldii* and the ever popular *M.* × *soulangiana* with its varieties 'Lennei' and 'Brozzonii'; the ornamental flowering tree *Paulownia fargesii*; the Snowbell Tree *Styrax japonica* and, much prized by its owner for its autumn tints, *Nyssa sylvatica*. *Embothrium coccineum lanceolatum* 'Norquinco Valley', with its strongest of scarlet flowers, also gives him particular pleasure. Then there are a lovely cone-shaped *Eucalyptus niphophila*, the Snow Gum, and the silver leafed *E. perriniana*, as well as some old shrub roses, 'Stanwell Perpetual' and the sweet smelling red blooms of 'F.J. Grootendorst'.

Malus cultivars, including 'Golden Hornet' and 'Red Sentinel', diversify the planting with their autumn fruiting, while a fern leafed beech, *Fagus sylvatica heterophylla*, helps to give foliage contrast. Rhododendrons and azaleas planted *en masse* contribute to the spring colour, the selection including 'Pink Pearl', 'Cynthia', rose-crimson, and 'Ascot Brilliant', rose-red, several hybrids, 'Jalisco', Loderi, 'Lady Chamberlain', with lovely bell-shaped flowers, and some fine Exbury hybrid azaleas. Conifers and yews also add to the diversity of foliage with *Chamaecyparis lawsoniana* 'Lanei', golden and feathery, and *Gleditsia triacanthos*, both the tree form and its golden cultivar 'Sunburst'. There are *Sorbus* too for their berries, the white berried *S. cashmiriana*, the bright red berried *S. americana* and, for its curious leaf form and surprising flowers, the Tulip Tree, *Liriodendron tulipifera*. Another spot of gold is provided by the poplar *Populus alba* 'Richardii'.

A rose pergola leads to the 65 m (210 ft) long herbaceous border with its terminating view of Harewood House woodlands on the far hillside. The arboretum side of this border is still a place for old roses and colourful shrubs, among which are the colourful Smoke Bush, *Cotinus coggygria*, the sparkle of *Cornus alba* 'Elegantissimia' and more maples. *Acer laxiflorum* and *A. forrestii*, both with striated bark, and *A. buergeranum*. On the kitchen garden wall side there is a well filled 'cottage garden' border of flowers interspersed with many Hybrid Musk roses.

From here the first kitchen garden is entered. It is laid out in Scottish fashion with vegetables surrounded by a border of flowers. There are apples and pears trained on the walls and peaches and nectarines in the houses by the far wall, including a very old white peach called 'Noblesse', 9 m (30 ft) high by 9 m wide. A small lean-to camellia house is a joy in the early part of the year, and behind is an old fernery where years ago soil was placed against the back wall behind netting to provide a footing for the collection. The vinery nearby gives good crops of the old finely flavoured green grape 'Muscat of Alexandria' and the black grape 'Black Hamburgh'. In one small house *Bougainvillaea* and a large 'climbing' zonal pelargonium fill the back wall and the long pink trumpets of *Lapageria rosea* hang from the roof. Two rather tender magnolias are given wall protection here, *M. kobus*, still to flower (some 15 years from planting is usual), and *M.* × *soulangiana* 'Alba Superba'.

A door in the far wall takes us into a second kitchen garden where 'Doyenné du Comice' pears are trained on the wall and the sweet smelling herbaceous *Clematis* × *eriostemon* 'Hendersonii' is in the border. The melons in the melon house bear their precious fruit in net bags, and flowering outside in a large pot (but taken indoors for winter) is the Brazilian Coral Tree, *Erythrina crista-galli*.

On the way back to the house from the kitchen gardens there are several shrubs including the unusual *Photinia glabra*, red stemmed and red fruited; *Cotinus coggygria* 'Notcutt's Variety', one of the best purple leaved shrubs; *Hypericum elatum* (*H.* × *inodorum*), with long, narrow red fruits; the variegated *Weigela florida* 'Variegata'; *Caryopteris clandonensis* 'Ferndown', with aromatic leaves; *Eucryphia* × *nymansensis* 'Nymansay', evergreen with white, paper-like flowers; two more magnolias, *M.* × *watsonii* with saucer-shaped flowers and *M. denudata*, the Yulan or Lily Tree. To complete the picture *Parrotia persica* gives autumn colour to this collection.

Bramham Park

Mr and Mrs George Lane Fox

8 km (5 miles) S of Wetherby to left of northbound carriageway of A1. House and garden normally open four days a week from Easter to end of September, but for details see current issue of *Historic Houses, Castles and Gardens* or apply to the Administrator, Bramham Park. Free Car park; meals available. Queen Anne mansion containing period furniture, pictures and porcelain. Formal garden of some 28 ha (70 acres), situated 65 m (220 ft) above sea level on alkaline soil. Somewhat sheltered by wooded estate land around. Average annual rainfall 690 mm (27 in). Staff of three.

The landscape of Bramham Park remains almost as it was originally laid out over 250 years ago, and it is acknowledged to be one of the finest examples in the British Isles of the French-style garden design of the late seventeenth and early eighteenth centuries. The ornamental avenues and water features were inspired by Le Nôtre's work at Versailles and Vaux le Vicomte and created by Robert Benson (1676–1731), later Lord Bingley. Benson himself was an amateur architect of no mean ability and is said to have known Le Nôtre. His work at Bramham was contemporary with the creation of the Castle Howard and Studley Royal landscapes.

While, unfortunately, a great storm of 1962 destroyed many of the beech avenues which had stood for two and a half centuries, well maintained beech hedges and replanting lead the eye as interestingly as ever to the vista stops of urn, temple or obelisk.

To the north of the house the James Paine Temple (*c.*1750–62), now

1. Chapel
2. Bramham House
3. Rose Garden
4. Obelisk Pond
5. Temple
6. Obelisk
7. Gothic Temple
8. Dog Monuments
9. T Canal
10. Open Temple
11. The Four Faces
12. Black Fen Woodland
13. Parkland

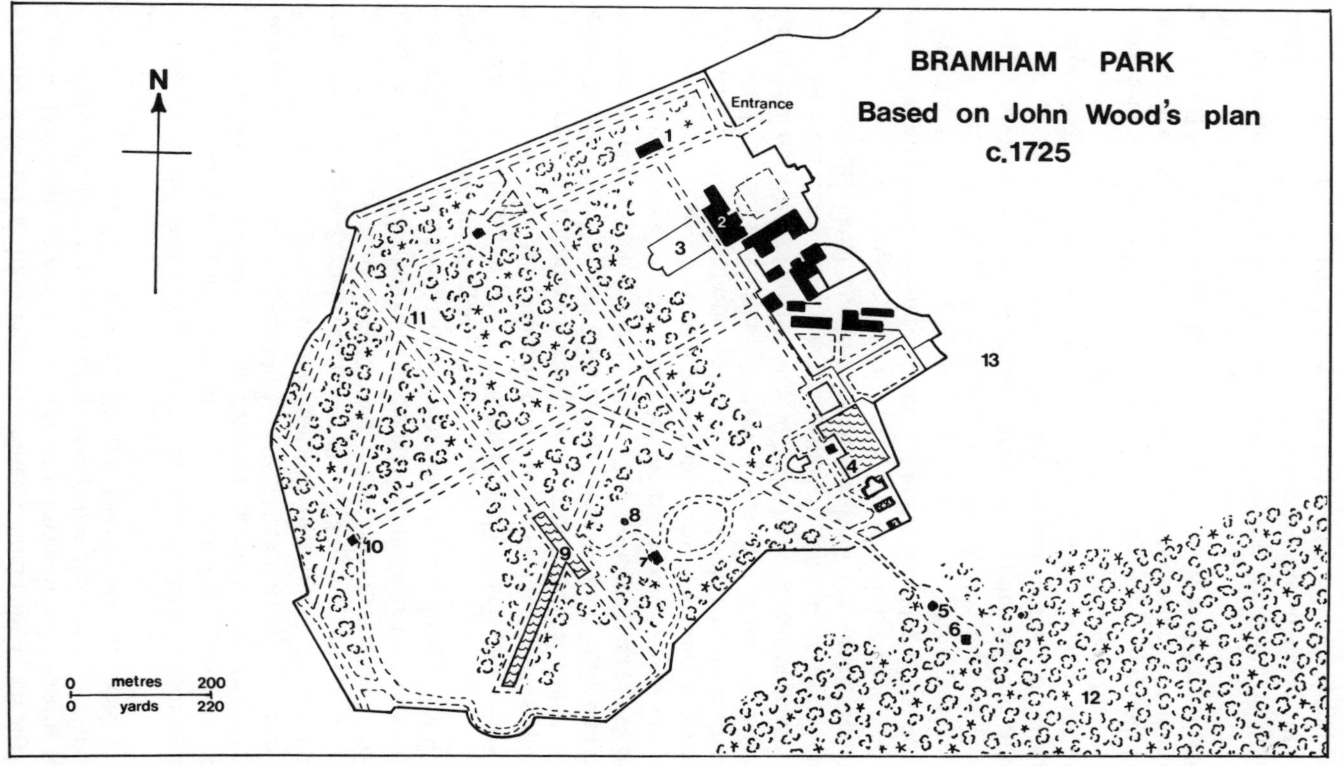
BRAMHAM PARK
Based on John Wood's plan
c.1725
N
0 metres 200
0 yards 220
Entrance
1
2
3
4
5
6
7
8
9
10
11
12
13

a chapel and said to have been an orangery originally, is the architectural start of the southward looking broad walk which, passing the west front of the house, leads to the obelisk ponds and terminates about 1.6 km (1 mile) further on at the Round Temple and the obelisk in Black Fen.

Adjacent to the west front of the house and by the entrance to the gardens, a flagstone garden is full of low-growing, spreading and mounded plants. Opposite is a sunken rose garden, once the formal parterre. The central path, lined by pyramidal yews, leads to a recess in the back wall with basins and a dragon's mouth, which is where, originally, a formal French cascade of 30 shallow steps fell down the gently sloping lawn between an avenue of trees into the sunken garden basin, to be seen and admired from the main windows of the house. The sloping lawn is called the Queen's Hollow and is now being planted with species roses and spring bulbs.

If we start our garden perambulation from the chapel and, facing it, to the left is a 450 m (1,500 ft) long beech hedge avenue. Walking along this we came to a diamond-shaped *salon* with a central statue of a female figure. Then the path leads to the Urn of the Four Faces and the intersection of five avenues. One leads to the T-shaped canal (*c*.1728), the gathering ground for the water for the ponds and cascades. From the side of the T canal there is a picturesque view of the house down a grass walk bordered in spring with daffodils and wild flowers. It should be noted, however, that although there is this view of the house from the T canal the avenues are not aligned to the house in any way, as was usual in eighteenth-century landscaping, but have their own *raison d'être*. From the canal another avenue leads to the Gothic Temple (*c*.1750) beside the bowling green. Across the lawn is the dogs' graves area, with magnolias and ilex in contrast to the formality of the beech avenues.

There are several approaches to the water feature, a series of six ponds, ornamentally different in shape and connected by finely sculptured cascades, from which there is a romantic vista to the Gothic Temple. Across the parkland from the steps leading down to the last pool, looking southwards, an avenue of beech connects the garden with Black Fen, leading to the Round Temple and the obelisk beyond. For those who wish to venture further, Black Fen is a complex of radiating avenues of beech, Spanish Chestnut and lime, many of the trees being over 200 years old.

While the straight lines of the original garden are maintained, the effect is softened by the massed effect of planting for colour at various times of the year – rhododendrons, large drifts of snowdrops and daffodils, species roses, the formal bedding-out in the rose garden of some 400 Hybrid Tea and Floribunda roses and the long herbaceous border by the broad walk. Drifts of wild flowers carpet the edges of the avenues and quite recently a scheme for the planting of massed magnolias, cherries, Evergreen Oaks and more rose species has been drawn up.

It is of interest to note that the descendants of Robert Benson, first Lord Bingley, have always lived at Bramham, and that although the house was badly damaged by fire in 1828 so that the family had to live elsewhere on the estate while rebuilding took place, the gardens have always been maintained at a high standard and with every consideration for the original layout.

Canal Gardens, Roundhay Park

City of Leeds Council

Off A58 Roundhay Road from Leeds centre. Open at all times. Teas available at Park Mansion; dogs allowed. Part of larger 120 ha (300 acre) Roundhay Park, bought from the Nicholson family by Leeds Corporation in 1871 for £130,000. Well sheltered 1.6 ha (4 acres) of formal garden, mostly walled and sloping to the south. Large greenhouse and formal canal. Situated 120 m (400 ft) above sea level on heavy loam over millstone grit. Average annual rainfall 690 mm (27 in.). Staff of ten.

Formerly the kitchen, fruit and ornamental gardens of the Nicholson family, before the present road was built dividing it from the mansion grounds, Canal Gardens has long been a favourite haunt for garden lovers. Its name derives from the 91 m (300 ft) long formal canal, well stocked with water fowl, the sloping sides of which are always tastefully and colourfully bedded out for the summer. The charming little Victorian-type summerhouse on the bridge crossing the water at the far end of the canal adds to the visual quality of the garden.

On the lower side of the lawn, which in spring is covered with crocuses and daffodils, are plantings of *Magnolia stellata*, a small but beautifully shaped *Cedrus deodara* and a 12 m (40 ft) *Metasequoia glyptostroboides*, one of the tallest Dawn Redwoods in the area.

The wide herbaceous border under the wall is planted with perennials in traditional style, with large clumps of each plant. The old flued wall itself provides the setting for large, well grown, spreading climbers such as *Jasminum nudiflorum* and *J. revolutum, Kerria japonica, Forsythia suspensa, Ceanothus*, ivies, quince, clematis and vines, which fruited in 1976.

The gate in the centre of this wall leads into a walled rose garden sloping up to the Victorian turrets of the Coronation greenhouse. The roses have been planted out in a catholic range of Hybrid Teas and Floribundas in box edged compartments and the mellow brick walls around provide shelter and support for *Cytisus battandieri* and species and varieties of *Cotoneaster, Wisteria, Garrya, Forsythia, Hedera*, together with quince, *Magnolia grandiflora* and vanilla-scented *Azara microphylla*.

The Coronation house, a resort of plant lovers all the year round, boasts seasonal colour against the permanent plantings of the giant fronded palm *Phoenix canariensis*, the aromatic *Myrtus communis*, tree-height camellias, Kentia Palms, cherries and laburnums in pots to flower early in the year, the free-flowering Mimosa, *Acacia dealbata, Eucalyptus citriodora*, the Lemon-scented Gum, and *E. globulus*, the Blue Gum, the climbers *Cestrum* 'Newellii', orange flowered, the Spider Plant *Tibouchina urvilliana* (*semidecandra*), ivies in variety, *Jasminum officinale* and *J. polyanthum*, and *Bougainvillaea*.

Colour interest is continuous throughout the year, with successional massings of daffodils, hyacinths, *Clivia* and *Amaryllis*, the evergreen Kurume azaleas, *Acacia armata, Begonia manicata* and *B. haageana*, a fine collection of *B. rex* cultivars and other ornamental leaved begonias. This early interest is followed by cinerarias, *Streptocarpus, Calceolaria*, gloxinias, *Achimenes, Celosia, Hydrangea, Coleus, Fuchsia, Chrysanthemum* and, back to winter again, an extensive collection of winter flowering begonias.

By the main road outside the walls there is always an excellent example of carpet bedding, usually laid out to mark some anniversary or local event, and on the wall a large, spreading *Ceanothus dentatus*.

East Riddlesden Hall

National Trust

1.6 km (1 mile) NE of Keighley on A650 Bradford-Skipton road, signposted. Open March to end October, Tuesday to Sunday and Bank Holiday Mondays. For hours see current issue of National Trust *Properties Open*. Seventeenth-century manor house and magnificent tithe barn also open, period furniture and paintings in house. No dogs. Given to the Trust in 1954 by the brothers Mr J.J. and Mr W.A. Briggs. Formal, sheltered garden of about 0.4 ha (1 acre) in 5 ha (12 acres) of grounds, situated 90 m (300 ft) above sea level on alkaline soil over millstone grit. Average annual rainfall 860 mm (34 in.). Staff of one.

The manor house with 'Gothic' battlements and pinnacles is of 1648 while the façade to the west is all that remains of a 1692 addition. It is built on a high natural mound above the sinuous course of the River Aire with views down the Aire Valley to Bingley and up to Keighley hemmed in on both sides by high Pennine hills. A battlemented stable block in front of the house on the left is dated 1642. By the side of the west façade are four curious niches called 'peacock holes', but more probably built to provide shelter from rain for straw bee skips.

The entrance from the main road, through gate piers of *c.*1700, circles round the fish pond which, the antiquarians say, could well have been the Stagum de Riddlesden from which the canons of Bolton Abbey, over the hill in Wharfedale, bought fish for their stew ponds in 1320. On its way to the house the drive passes two barns of which the second is noted as the finest example of a medieval tithe barn in the north. Dated 1640–50 its interior presents the appearance of a cathedral nave with its massive oak pillars holding up the soaring arched timbers of the roof. Stands of old, high beeches circle the house and the pond.

The formal garden on the south front was designed in 1971 by Graham Thomas, then Gardens Adviser to the Trust, to catch the feeling of the Carolean period of English gardening. The garden is surrounded by stone walls behind which grow more tall beaches and only one tree, an old, high cherry, is featured on the house lawn. Leading from the south entrance is a newly planted avenue of the older named apples and pears on dwarfing stock. They include apples 'James Grieve', 'Egremont Russet', 'Laxton's Superb', 'Orleans Reinette', 'Charles Ross', 'Lane's

Prince Albert', and pears 'Doyenné du Comice', 'Winter Nelis', 'Conference', and 'Williams' Bon Chrétien'.

Bounding the lawn on the east and round to the long herbaceous border and a finely wrought cast iron seat curiously decorated with grapes and squirrels, is a hedge of holly *Ilex* × 'Hodginsii' with large, dark green, roundish oval leaves. The walls have been used for a variety of climbing plants, *Clematis macropetala, C. tangutica,* 'Lady Betty Balfour', 'Nelly Moser', *C. montana, C.m.* 'Elizabeth' and *C. rehderana,* the cowslip-scented primrose yellow one. Then there is *Chaenomeles* × *superba* 'Rowallane', *Hedera canariensis* 'Variegata', *Parthenocissus henryana, Lonicera* × *americana* (introduced 1750), opening white before turning to pale and finally to deep yellow, the fragrant rose 'Sanders' White Rambler', and *Schizophragma integrifolia.*

Both sides of the path round the walls have been skilfully and sympathetically planted with a mixture of shrubs and herbaceous material of both old and newer introduction to give an overall garden picture corresponding to the seventeenth-century blackened stone pile of the hall.

The small lawn to the west of the house is marked by a new planting of a short avenue of the mop-headed *Robinia pseudoacacia* 'Inermis' and behind them, with the façade screen of the burnt-out addition to the hall as a dramatic backdrop is a sunken paved corner surrounded by raised beds formed by paving stones on edge and hedged about with neat walls of box in which the Floribunda rose 'Marlena' has been planted exclusively.

The borders have obviously been planted with an eye to ground cover and labour saving. Among the shrubs are that old inhabitant of English gardens *Viburnum tinus* as well as *V. farreri* (*fragrans*) and *V.* × *burkwoodii* for early flowering. For evergreen year round interest there is the dark green, wavy foliaged *Mahonia* 'Undulata' and for a contrast in evergreen colouring *Phlomis fruticosa* of 1596 introduction. The planting continues with cultivars of *Potentilla, Hydrangea, Ceanothus* 'Gloire de Versailles', *Spiraea* × *bumalda, Kerria japonica,* the late flowering *Cytisus nigricans* (1730 introduction) and the white Spanish broom *C. multiflora* (1752). There is the cottage garden St John's Wort, *Cytisus* × *praecox* and *Tamarix gallica. Hibiscus* 'Blue Bird', probably the best of the single blues, finds its place here, as well as the fragrant *Clethra alnifolia* 'Paniculata' and *Deutzia* × *kalmiiflora.*

Among the roses the older shrub roses, chosen for their character and old world charm, predominate: 'Nevada', *R. rugosa* 'Frau Dagmar Hastrup', *R.r.* 'Alba', *R. rubrifolia,* 'Mme Grégoire Staechelin' mingle with the newer roses 'Constance Spry', *R. moyesii* 'Geranium', 'Fritz Nobis', 'Goldbusch' and 'Iceberg'.

The underplanting, designed to complement the period feel of the garden, includes masses of *Bergenia cordifolia*, London Pride, many geraniums among which are the bright red *G. macrorrhizum*, the magenta red *G. psilostemon* and 'Johnson's Blue', and for variety of foliage form there are clumps of *Iris pallida* 'Dalmatica', *Curtonus paniculata*, a montbretia type of flower with sword-like foliage, Lungwort (*Pulmonaria*), *Sedum spectabile* 'Autumn Joy'. *Spiraea* cultivars, *Hemerocallis* 'Marian Vaughan' and 'Kwanso Flore Pleno', Japanese Anemones, the graceful Solomon's Seal, *Polygonatum multiflorum*, *Euphorbia characias* (*wulfenii*), *Nepeta gigantea* ('Six Hills Giant'), *Yucca flaccida*, *Veronica gentianoides*, the hardy 'Headbourne Hybrid' *Agapanthus* all add their interest and flavour to the period picture. Lavender 'Hidcote' nestles in the narrow borders under the house walls.

Golden Acre Park

Leeds City Council

On A660 Leeds-Otley road. Open every day all the year round. Free car park; dogs allowed. Bought by Leeds Corporation in 1945 for £18,500. Before the war it was a privately owned public pleasure resort. Botanic and woodland garden of 34 ha (85 acres), situated 150 m (500 ft) above sea level on heavy acid loam on low lying ground and peat and bracken shallow soil on hillside. An exposed site with a sloping aspect to SW, liable to early and late frosts. Average annual rainfall 740 mm (29 in.). Staff of nine.

This West Yorkshire botanical garden rolls down a steeply wooded hillside to undulating 'levels' around a lake surrounded by natural woodland, mainly of birch. Since the purchase a wide variety of trees and shrubs has been got together, including many rhododendrons which now clothe the hillside under woodland shelter of Scots Pine and *Chamaecyparis lawsoniana* in variety.

Rhododendrons include *R. rex*, *R. williamsianum* seedlings, *R. wardii*, *R. smirnowii*, *R. calophytum*, many hybrids and an extensive collection of Exbury azaleas.

Among a varied collection of young specimen trees, giving the Yorkshire gardener some ideas of the possibilities of a cold site, are

Mountain Ashes including *Sorbus americana* with its striking ascending branches and red pointed sticky buds, *S. decora* with its orange fruit, *S. aucuparia* 'Fastigiata' (*scopulina*), of columnar growth and sealing wax red berries, *S. cashmiriana*, with white fruits, and *S. sargentiana*, which both berries well and gives good autumn foliage colour. One of the few specimens in the county of +*Laburnocytisus adamii* (the graft hybrid of *Laburnum anagyroides* and *Cytisus purpureus*) is planted here with the two parents nearby to show the contrast. A well grown specimen of the contorted form of the Pekin Willow, *Salix matsudana* 'Tortuosa', is on the lower slopes and among the selection of *Prunus* and *Malus* on the grass slopes skirting the woodland are *Prunus* 'Kursar', of Collingwood Ingram's raising, and *P. subhirtella* 'Autumnalis'. The ornamental barked maples are well represented, among them being *Acer pensylvanicum* (white and jade green striped), *A. henryi* (bluish striated), and *A. rubrum* 'Schlesingeri', of outstanding autumn colour. A planting of conifers still in a youthful state includes *Abies grandis, Pinus wallichiana, Cedrus deodara.* A single specimen of the Strawberry Tree *Arbutus unedo* is growing well at the foot of the rhododendron slope.

Among the shrubs, all fairly recently planted and doing well, are specimens of the Snowdrop Tree, *Halesia carolina* and *H. monticola*, hybrid camellias, *Pieris formosana forrestii* and *P. japonica*, which show by their wreaths of wax white flowers early in the year that they relish the acid soil, while *Hamamelis* in variety flower well in January and February. *Fothergilla monticola*, so beautiful in autumn colour, does well for this cold site. *Palirus spina-christi*, 'Christ's Thorn', whose curious fruits are reminiscent of cardinals' hats, is an unusual plant to come across, as is *Berberis hypokerina*, a Kingdon Ward introduction which he called Silver Holly because of the white underside of its holly-like leaves.

Golden Acre is well known to rockery enthusiasts for its extensive planting of named species and cultivars of *Sempervivum* and *Sedum* and its well planted heathers on tumuli-like mounds. It is good to see the ornamental onions, *Allium spp.*, making such an interesting show along with many *Primula* and *Meconopsis*, which revel in the moist conditions. At the time of writing a lily pond, recently constructed, is having its margins and surrounds laid out as a wild pondside, bog and woodland garden, adding interest and colour just above the lake with its natural edging of rushes and waterside plants.

Harewood House and Gardens

Earl of Harewood

In Harewood village on A61 Leeds-Harrogate road. House and gardens open from Easter to October every day, house open all year. For hours see current issue of *Historic Houses, Castles and Gardens.* Car park; refreshments available at stables restaurant. House by John Carr, 1759; a treasure store of art, china, Chippendale furniture, Robert Adam rooms and Kauffman decoration. Parkland and gardens of 120ha (300 acres), situated 90m (300ft) above sea level on medium light loam over millstone grit. Subject to frosts. Average annual rainfall 710mm (28in.). Staff of seven.

Harewood House, and the ruins of the earlier Harewood Castle, licensed in 1367, are surrounded by 'one of the most delectable landscapes', as Dorothy Stroud wrote in her biography of 'Capability' Brown. And from the Victorian terrace created (between 1843 and 1848) by Barry, the architect of the House of Commons, in the front of the house, the view is still one of the finest examples of Brown's genius and his way of turning farmland and rough, hilly countryside into a scene of 'natural' beauty.

When Brown came here in 1772 to landscape the grounds for Edwin Lascelles, the first Earl of Harewood, he dammed a small stream to make an extensive lake of 12ha (30 acres), hid the view of the water coming into the valley and its going out, planted clumps and circling belts of trees, saw to it that the land rolled away smoothly from the very walls of the house to the far distance and 'arranged' the pleasure garden well out of sight of the house vistas. From the front steps of the house there is a vista through a gap cut in the circling woodland to the dramatic mass of Almscliff Cragg. Brown worked for over eight years before his landscape was completed at a cost to the first Earl of £6,000 for Brown's work alone.

The Barry terrace itself has three ornamental fountain basins, balustraded walls and statuary. The centre fountain still sends up its *jet d'eau*; the others are filled with roses. The former complexity of the Victorian parterre and carpet bedding has gone, but roses still fill the ornamental beds and on the terrace wall are such old climbing roses as 'Chaplin's Pink', 'Paul's Scarlet', 'New Dawn' and 'Crimson Glory'.

To the west of the house and on a level with it is a small ornamental rose garden, box edged and with an old disused fountain basin to match the Victorian ornamentation of the terrace. On sloping lawns to the west of the house, leading to the gate into the parkland, are colourfully and artistically sited plantings of shrubs and trees – the white *Camellia* 'Pax', unnamed double pink ones, a clump of the fiery autumn colouring *Amelanchier laevis*, a giant old Cedar of Lebanon, ancient oaks, well grown *Acer griseum*, azaleas and a collection of rhododendrons including *R. mollyanum* with its long leaves and crimson bells, a good form of 'Jacksonii', one of the earliest hybrids, in bright rose pink, *R. uvariifolium* and *R. vernicosum*. In season daffodils bloom between the plantings.

The parkland walks are reached by the gate here or by going down the terrace steps and following on the top of the sloping bank beneath the terrace wall where the heather *Eric × darleyensis* makes large patches of colour between plantings of the smaller leafed rhododendrons 'Blue Tit', *R. racemosum* and *R. ciliatum*. In the shelter of the south-facing wall are a mixture of sun-loving subjects – the white bell-shaped flowering *Styrax japonica*, the exquisitively scented *Abelia triflora*, the Maidenhair Tree, *Ginkgo biloba*, surprisingly closely related to the conifers, the elegant foliage and striped bark of *Nothofagus antarctica*, *Cornus spp.*, a tall *Eucryphia, nymansensis* 'Nymansay' and a young Tulip Tree, *Liriodendron tulipifera*.

Going through the gate out of the terrace walk the path leads by the stables (Chambers, 1755–6, and said to be his first independent work before he went on to work at Kew and at building Somerset House) and by the exotic bird garden, then through a woodland path to the cascade bridge at the west end of the lake. From the bridge there is a view of the bog garden with its Japanese atmosphere. To our right is an Oriental looking green tiled summerhouse and below are stepping stones across the stream, bordered by massed *Gunnera manicata* and, at the right time of the year, the high colourings of *Astilbe* and *Primula* in variety, particularly a catholic selection of the Asiatic species. Enjoying

---

1. Lodge
2. Harewood Village
3. Harewood House
4. Harewood Church
5. Stables
6. Lake
7. North Park
8. Harewood Castle Ruins
9. Terraces
10. Rough Bridge
11. Wall Side Plantation
12. Parkland
13. Rose Garden
14. 'Japanese Garden'
15. Harewood Bridge

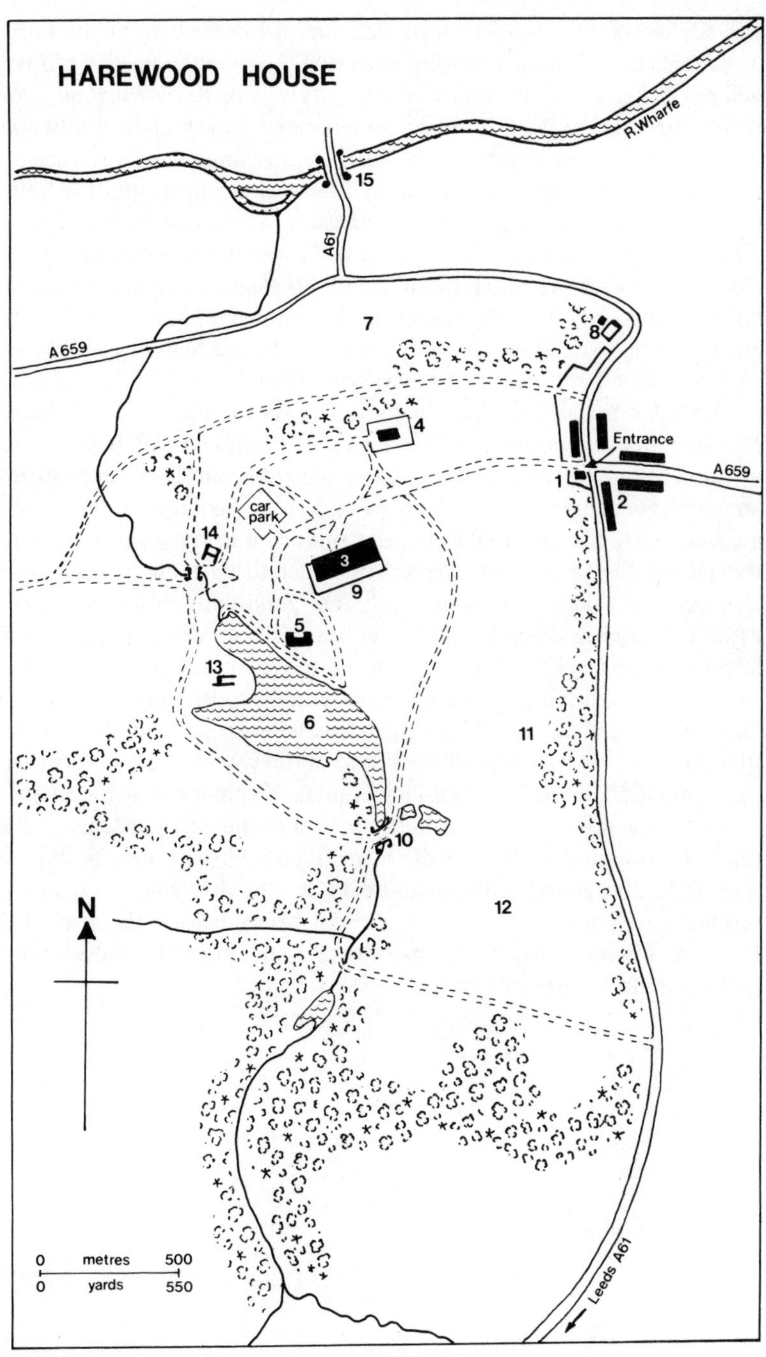
HAREWOOD HOUSE
R.Wharfe
15
A61
7
8
A659
4
Entrance
A659
1
2
car park
14
3
9
5
13
6
11
10
12
N
0 metres 500
0 yards 550
Leeds A61

the shelter of this bowl-shaped dell are *Rhododendron racemosum* in profusion, the brilliant crimson flowering *R. strigillosum*, the primrose yellow *R. lutescens*, the late flowering hybrid of *R. auriculatum* 'Polar Bear', then there are the suède undercoated leaves of *R. fictolacteum*, *R. rubiginosum* and *R. campanulatum* to admire among a large variety of azaleas. *Camellia* 'Donation' does well here in the open and the yellow flags of the Bog Lily *Lysichitum americanum*, stand out by the stream.

If you turn left after the bridge you will come to a wooded walk by the side of the lake. Here much planting of *Nothofagus antarctica*, one with a double trunk, has been done among the giant oaks and beeches; there are also maples, *Acer japonica* and *A. negundo*, the Scarlet Oak, *Quercus coccinea*, some hemlocks, *Chamaecyparis lawsoniana* in variety and a host of rhododendrons. Tall, thickly grown yews emphasize the colour of *Rhododendron auriculatum* in tree form, *R. schlippenbachii*, a spring and autumn colouring azalea, *R.* 'General Sir John du Cane', with funnel-shaped flowers, and a host of Harewood hybrid seedlings, so that, saving a severe early frost or a late one, the colouring in the glade is very fine indeed. By the lake is another autumn colouring subject, the Swamp Cypress, *Taxodium distichum*, and the pendulous branched *Cedrus deodara*. In spring there is a fine view from this woodland path, over the lake to the great drifts of daffodils in the woods on the opposite bank.

The path, winding upwards, ends in a wooden gate which leads directly to the pleasure and rose gardens where, against old flued walls (the flues can be seen behind the broken brickwork), are two terraces of roses, mainly Hybrid Teas and Floribundas. Virginia Creeper clothes the garden walls and those of the bothy where in the past gardeners on the estate lived communally. On the lawn overlooking an arm of the lake, seen from the period summerhouse built into the wall, is an ancient mulberry. A walk from the rose garden proper follows the wall of the extensive kitchen garden (not open) round and on to the lakeside where there are more roses in borders.

The Hollies

City of Leeds Council

Off A660 Leeds-Otley road turn into Weetwood Lane; entrance to The Hollies on the right. Open at all times. Free car park; dogs allowed. Given to Leeds Corporation in 1921 by the Brown family in memory of a relative killed in the First World War. A natural woodland garden of 36 ha (90 acres), situated 120 m (400 ft) above sea level on shallow, light, sandy, acid soil over millstone grit. On steep slope, falling some 45 m (150 ft) to Meanwood Beck, with an eastern aspect, but careful tree planting has given shelter and microclimates favourable to plants. Average annual rainfall 710 mm (28 in.). Staff of four.

This garden is a charming and tastefully landscaped Victorian heritage on a steeply sloping hillside down which run numerous streams and down which the visitor is led by natural stone steps set amidst large rock outcrops (part of the garden was once a quarry) amidst massed plantings of rhododendrons.

A level wild woodland walk on the ridge of the valley, both sides of which are planted with rhododendrons and azaleas, leads to the nearby Ring Road.

Because of the foresight of the original owners The Hollies can boast what is probably one of the tallest specimens of *Magnolia acuminata* in the country, some 15 m (50 ft) high with a girth at shoulder level of some 1,200 mm (48 in.), which flowers each year, and, unusual for the north, a 6 m (20 ft) high thick-boled *Rhododendron arboreum*, of the blood red flowers, as well as a mature specimen of the Umbrella Pine, *Sciadopitys verticillata*. Another old planting is a 6 m (20 ft) high thick trunked *Magnolia × soulangiana*. Planted among the outcrops for shelter are other magnolias, *M. denudata*, the Lily Tree, *M. kobus*, *M. liliiflora* and *M. sieboldii*. It is encouraging to see the beautiful *Mahonia* 'Charity' and the tender *M. lomariifolia* flourishing in a well sheltered spot.

Clothing the wooded slopes, planted to give a private woodland garden effect (indeed in its design The Hollies has many echoes of that famed Sussex rhododendron garden Leonardslee), is a quite extensive and varied collection of rhododendrons. Among species represented are *R. barbatum* which according to one specialist is the only one he has ever seen to flower in Yorkshire, *R. wightii*, *R. thomsonii*, *R. falconeri*,

R. floribundum, R. fictolacteum, R. fulvum, R. oreotrephes, R. ambiguum, R. insigne, R. aberconwayi, R. lutescens, R. sutchuenense, R. wardii, R. williamsianum, R. xanthocodon, with aromatic leaves, *R. strigillosum* and the small leaved *R. hippohaeoides.* Many of the large leaved species flourish here, showing on the underside of their leaves, throughout the year, the strikingly coloured suède-like indumentum. Among a representative collection of hybrids are 'Cornubia', 'Praecox', 'Valaspis', early and yellow flowered, the very early (or late – it flowered gloriously in November of 1976) 'Nobleanum Venustum', of 1829 vintage and a glistening pink. Also early flowering are 'Dr Stocker', 'Luscombei', an 1875 plant, rose pink with crimson ray markings, the Bodnant hybrid 'Cilpinense', white flushed with pink, 'Bo-peep', an Exbury hybrid of primrose yellow, 'Barclayi Robert Fox', a deep crimson, and 'Carita', an Exbury strain in palest lemon. Other interesting hybrids are 'Lady Chamberlain', with long narrow bell flowers; 'Lady Rosebery' of the same ilk, but with pink shades and selected clones of both; 'Naomi' and her fragrant clones; 'Carex White' another from the Rothschild stable; the popular 'Humming Bird'; the mid-season flowering 'Bibiani', crimson and maroon spotted, along with 'Bow Bells', and 'Ibex' whose leaves are brown felted beneath and whose flowers are rose-carmine with darker spots. To bring up the rear of The Hollies' magnificent display are such late bearers as 'Azor', salmon pink, and 'Polar Bear' of July and August flowering, its fragrant trumpet-shaped white blossoms looking like lilies.

As one might expect in such a damp woodland site, ferns grow well, with Royal Ferns flourishing in variety, *Osmunda regalis* and its cultivars *O.r.* 'Cristata' and *O.r.* 'Purpurascens', *O. cinnamomea* and *O. claytoniana.* In the beds opened out at intervals along the hillside walks the Moutan Paeony *Paeonia suffruticosa* does well in company with the herbaceous paeonies, including *P. lutea* and *P. delavayi,* and the Day Lilies. *Petasites japonicus giganteus,* a large leaved version of the Winter Heliotrope, is an unusual ground cover plant by the streamsides. On a naturally formed rockery heathers, *Cassiope* and *Bruckenthalia* give contrast to the dark green cover of the rhododendrons. Vistas to the valley below are through Silver Birch and other *Betula* species, planted for the colours of their bark. These include *B. ermanii,* with a bole of pinkish white, *B. papyrifera,* the Paper Birch, in white, *B. lutea,* with peeling golden brown bark, *B. platyphylla,* a larger white barked tree, and the common birch in its variety *B. pendula* 'Youngii', a lovely weeping form. *Nothofagus cliffortioides,* the Mountain Beech, is an unusual New Zealand species found here.

Two of the more tender shrubs which do well here, for a site so far north, are *Drimys winteri*, on the potting shed wall, and *Azara microphylla* on a nearby raised bed. Also nearby are three well grown *Eucryphia*, not really a tree for the north without good shelter, *E. glutinosa*, *E.* × *intermedia* and *E.* × *nymansensis* 'Nymansay'.

A good collection of 19 different named hydrangeas interspersed with the rhododendrons give summer colour; *H. quercifolia* gives autumn colour as well, *H. sargentiana* has the added attractions of large velvety leaves and mossy shoots and stems while *H. radiata* is notable for the white undersurfaces of its foliage.

On the lodge wall by the entrance gates there is the rare *Mahonia trifoliolata glauca* and opposite on the raised bed there are clumps of *Euphorbia characias* (*wulfenii*), a selection of *Meconopsis* species and the trailing *Penstemon scouleri*. On lawns nearby there is a flowering tree rarely seen in these parts, *Cercis siliquastrum*, the Judas Tree, and three *Embothrium coccineum lanceolatum*, the tender Chilean native, grown from seed. The evergreen *Photinia serrulata*, whose coppery red young leaves give interest to the spring garden, is grown here as well as the more common *P. villosa*.

30 Latchmere Road, Moor Grange Estate

Mr and Mrs J. Brown

This council house garden in NW Leeds has won first prizes in best council house garden competitions in both Leeds and Bradford and was judged the best of both council house and private house gardens in Leeds. Open occasionally for charity when light refreshments are served, or by appointment. No dogs. Created by Mr and Mrs Brown, the tenants, it is situated 160m (525ft) above sea level on good, friable loam. Average annual rainfall 690mm (27in.).

This narrow strip of garden, some 35m (120ft) long, with its pleasing corners, twists and turns has been so well 'landscaped' since the Browns came to the house just over 11 years ago, and planted with such catholicity of taste and choice that it surely earns a place in any selection of Yorkshire gardens.

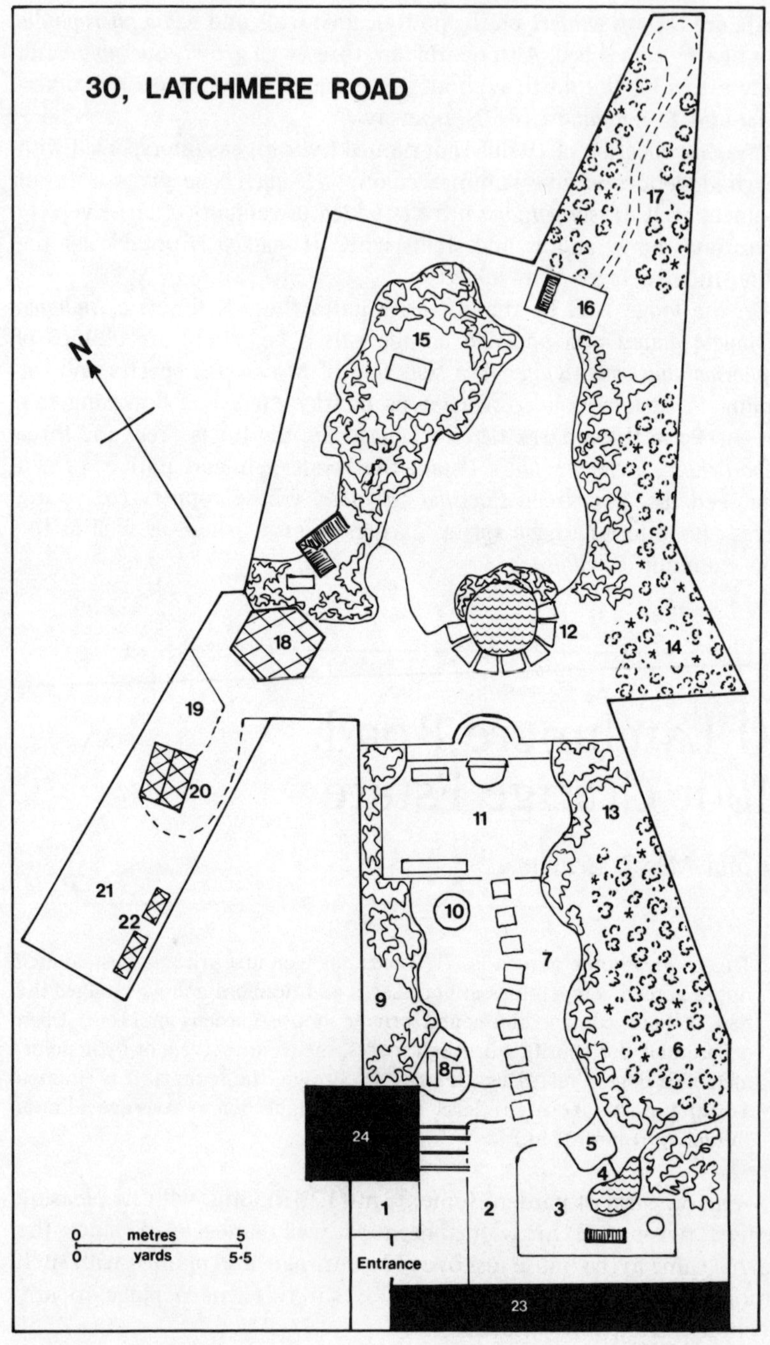
30, LATCHMERE ROAD
N
1
2
3
4
5
6
7
8
9
10
11
12
13
14
15
16
17
18
19
20
21
22
23
24
Entrance
0 metres 5
0 yards 5·5

The entry is through a rustic gate and fence over which the climbing rose 'Dr W. Van Fleet' clambers. To the left of the short L-shaped path is a small (910 mm × 1.5 m, 3 × 5 ft) cobbled area which gets late afternoon sun and is a home for ivies, ferns, sea lavender and white periwinkles. A Victorian gas lamp on a 910 mm (3 ft) pedestal is decorated in summer with a collar of fuchsias, begonias and annuals, transforming an otherwise dull corner. The path from the back door of the house continues for some 2.7 m (9 ft), with a rustic pergola on the right smothered in summer with the climbing roses 'Danse du Feu' and 'Golden Showers' and the clematis 'Hagley Hybrid' clambering through them.

A small circular raised bed terminates the path, dry-walled and planted with *Gentiana sino-ornata, Aquilegia alpina, Calceolaria falklandica, Polygonum vacciniifolium*, ferns and hardy fuchsias.

A small crazy-paved area has a step down to it to the right to the first sunken patio of which the rustic pergola forms one wall. Here is a sunken pool surrounded on three sides by narrow borders filled with more ferns and hardy fuchsias, lungworts, *Tiarella wherryi*, bergenias, the succulent *Cotyledon*, the Bleeding Heart, *Dicentra eximia* and *D. formosa*, astilbes and two more clematis trained up a wigwam, 'The President' and 'Jackmanii Superba'.

From this patio there is a step up on to a small lawn with a winding path of stone flowing through it between two borders, the left-hand one being shorter and narrower than the right, which is 2.4 m (8 ft) at its widest, but both are chock-full of variety. Beginning with a little terrace planted with *Euphorbia polychroma, Frankenia laevis, Scilla campanulata*, hyacinths and *Epilobium glabellum*, the right-hand border flows in gentle curves along the lawn edge. This is the stage for perennial *Eremurus*, the Foxtail Lily, *Libertia formosa*, with iris-like foliage, Globe Thistles, poppies, *Iris sibirica, Stachys lanata* for its lamb's ear foliage, *Monarda didyma*, the fiery red flowered tender *Lobelia cardinalis*,

---

1. Victorian Garden
2. Fern Border
3. Lower Patio
4. Sunken Pool
5. Waterside Planting
6. Herbaceous Border
7. Lawn
8. Sink Bed
9. Red Border
10. Ornamental Urn
11. Sun Patio
12. Raised Ornamental Pool
13. Lily Bed
14. New Garden
15. Alpine Garden
16. Manhole & Seat
17. Small Copse
18. 'Apollo' Greenhouse
19. Annual Bed
20. Tomato House
21. Vegetable Garden
22. Cold Frames
23. House
24. Outhouses

Helianthemum, Cistus, many species of the ornamental onions, *Allium,* pinks, the Obedient Plant, *Physostegia virginiana, Eryngium, Oenothera,* the Evening Primrose, and a collection of lilies embracing *L. speciosum, L. regale album, L.r.* 'Royal Gold', *L. davidii* 'Wilmottiae', *L. auratum* and 'Enchantment'.

The shorter and narrower left-hand border contains many of the Browns' climbing plants, giving much colour for little space – the clematis 'Proteus', 'Baroness de Veillard', 'Nelly Moser', the climbing Scotch Creeper, *Tropaeolum speciosum, Eccremocarpus scaber,* Early Dutch honeysuckle, rose 'Danse du Feu' – and in the border grow more lilies, *Lilium henryi* and *L. candidum, Lythrum* 'Canon West', *Linaria, Astrantia, Aruncus, Primula* in variety, *Gentiana asclepiadea* and *Phlox.*

The lawn path leads, past a large cast-iron urn having for its centre-piece *Cordyline australis* and in the summer filled with annuals, to the second sunken paved patio and then to a third, approached down semi-circular steps, with a raised ornamental pool and fountain only built in 1973, but looking an old-established feature. From the rear of the pool and blended into it with a skilful use of stonework and planting is the 38 sq m (45 sq yd), horseshoe-shaped alpine garden. This is filled with a variety of rock garden plants, some of the more choice of which are *Anthemis cupaniana,* the Prickly Thrift, *Acantholimon glumaceum,* the evergreen glaucous leafed *Aethionema* 'Warley Rose', *Lithospermum* 'Grace Ward', of the deepest blue, *Erodium corsicum, Sorbus reducta,* a rare dwarf, the dwarf lilac *Syringa microphylla,* the red flowered, low-growing *Delphinium nudicaule,* gentians *G. verna, G. sino-ornata, G. farreri, G. septemfida* and *G. acaulis,* stonecrops, saxifrages, *Campanula* and dwarf conifers.

Beyond the pool and to the right of the alpine beds is the new garden, so called because not so long ago it was a waste dump begged off the Corporation. A chamomile path, a new venture, leads windingly through two more borders, the curved-edge one on the right varying in width from 910 mm (3 ft) to 1.8 m (6 ft), the other quite narrow and straight-edged. Full use is made of this limited space for there are many herbs, miniature bulbs, *Iris danfordiae* and *I. reticulata,* the 'botanical' tulips, *Scilla sibirica,* the smaller *Allium* species, hyacinths, and the miniature *Narcissus, Mimulus, Osteospermum* (*Dimorphotheca*), that South African sun-lover, *Erigeron mucronatus* with its pink and white daisy flowers, hellebores, the graceful arching stemmed Wand Flower, *Dierama pulcherrimum, Androsace, Arisarum proboscideum,* the Mousetail Plant, *Lobularia maritima* and *Hypericum reptans.*

Under a half standard *Malus* 'Lemoinei' is a 'fairy ring' of *Cyclamen hederifolium* (*neapolitanum*), *C. repandum, C. coum* and *C. europaeum,* and to give height to the back of the border are rosemary, a white daphne, *Spiraea* and the variegated *Weigela florida* 'Variegata'. The path leads to the copse where three trees make a miniature 'woodland', *Betula pendula* 'Youngii', a Mountain Ash and *Acer platanoides*, the Norway Maple, underplanted with a carpet of more bulbs, *Anemone blanda* and *A. nemorosa*, tulips, daffodils, lilies and the low-growing shrubs *Lonicera nitida, Mahonia, Rhododendron* 'Praecox' as well as ornamental grasses, polyanthus, lungworts, auriculas, foxgloves, wild garlic, hostas, *Artemisia, Thalictrum*, and *Trollius*, the Globe Flower.

On a wire netting fence separating the garden from uncultivated ground at the back of old people's dwellings, Frieda, the plantswoman, and Joe, the 'architect' and builder, have made a flower fence for themselves and the old people with a tangled covering of *Clematis montana rubens* and the large flowered cultivars 'Mrs N. Thompson', waxy white 'Pennell's Purity', dark lavender double 'Countess of Lovelace', deep violet 'Xerxes', pure white 'Marie Boisselot', and 'Lady Betty Balfour', deep violet with prominent golden stamens. There are also, to extend the flowering season, *Eccremocarpus scaber, Hydrangea petiolaris* and *Jasminum* × *stephanense*, with fragrant pink flowers.

In another small (9 × 3.6 m, 30 × 12 ft) garden enough vegetables for the family's needs are grown and some room is given over to a small propagating greenhouse. There is also an ornamental miniature greenhouse nearby.

A particularly pleasant feature is the abundance of seating. There is a curved stone seat in the first patio, a wooden bench in the second, the stone surrounding the raised pool will seat eight, a stone lintel built into the alpine garden foot is another resting place, with a further wooden seat in the 'woodland'. Hanging baskets and wall baskets are used to break the monotony of the house wall, and urns, tubs, sinks and pans are filled with alpines, fuchsias, geraniums, petunias and other annuals to give yet another dimension to this attractive garden.

Ling Beeches

Mr and Mrs Arnold Rakusen

In Ling Lane off A58 Leeds-Wetherby road at Scarcroft. Open occasionally for charity. No dogs. A well planted woodland garden of 0.8 ha (2 acres) with a gentle slope to S, situated 150 m (480 ft) above sea level on well drained, thin, acid soil. Average annual rainfall 690 mm (27 in.).

The owners consider themselves fortunate to have lived in the house for over 30 years and to have been able to create a garden from a woodland site which formed part of old plantations of beech, oak, Scots Pine, larch, birch and rowan. When the house was built in 1938 a small clearing was made for it and no attempt made to provide for a garden beyond a path to the front door and a patch of 'lawn' approximately 18 m (60 ft) square. Beech trees met over the pantiled roof, little sun penetrated the woodland which was carpeted with bilberry, ferns and tall bracken in the summer months. The gentle slope to the south, away from the house, is a frost drain where grow low, dense, hardy hybrid rhododendrons. Species and more interesting varieties are planted on the west side but *R. ponticum* screens afford privacy in all parts of the garden. Although the sun is felt but little when it is low on the horizon this is an advantage as frost does not melt too quickly on early flowering plants.

The garden may be described as in the gardenesque style, informal and romantic, relying on contrasts of foliage and form, light and shade for a tranquil, harmonious and 'natural' effect, the owners aims being to 'marry' the house, a formal cottage, to the garden. Every season has been considered in planning the planting, winter especially, so that a continually changing picture is to be seen.

The first few years were spent in grubbing up tree trunks and roots, judiciously removing some trees to create space, not only for plants but for people to sit in, and also in making the soil. A certain amount of soil was imported but an efficient composting system has provided the bulk of the humus, much bracken having being composted, especially with sewage sludge, an ideal medium for azaleas. Peat dressings were, and are still, used liberally, all leaves are used for blanketing and most years at least some part of the garden receives either bonemeal or a general fertilizer to make up for the thin leached-out soil.

The garden supports a close-knit carpet of plants, often in two or even three layers; trees underplanted with shrubs which in turn are underplanted with bulbs and herbaceous material. It also provides something of a bird sanctuary, some 32 species having been sighted.

Some of the trees have been replaced by ornamentals. Several varieties of Sorbus are grown, including *S. reducta*, the fruits of which are mainly enjoyed by the birds. There are many maples – a young *Acer davidii*, *A. tetramerum* and various Japanese maples. There is *Piptanthus laburnifolius*, *Pittosporum tenuifolium*, *Osmaronia* (*Nuttallia*) *cerasiformis* with white currant-like flowers and several *Eucryphia*. Among broad leaved evergreens are several hollies, forms of *Ilex aquifolium* as well as *Ilex crenata* 'Aurea', *I. pernyi* with triangular foliage, the holly-like *Osmanthus heterophyllus* 'Variegatus', *Griselinia littoralis* 'Variegata' and the type form, several *Mahonia*, including the tiny *Mahonia nervosa* and a rather leggy *M.* × 'Charity', of the long yellow spikes, and the Benenden form of *Rubus* 'Tridel', whose arching stems have large white flowers with golden stamens.

Many New Zealand natives appear to be content with the conditions offered – *Olearia haastii*, *O. nummulariifolia*, *O. macrodonta* and *O. virgata lineata*, all grown from cuttings, *Hebe armstongii*, *H. hectori*, *H. propinqua*, with thread-like stems, *H. buchananii*, *H. rakaiensis* (*subalpina*) and several hybrids too. There are many *Euonymus* to bring their variegated greenery and light to the woodland all the year round, some camellias, *Enkianthus*, *Lonicera nitida* 'Baggessen's Gold', the variegated form of *Prunus lusitanica*, the Portugal Laurel, *Choisya ternata* and a few eucalypts.

There is a good collection of ferns enjoying the woodland shade and moisture, including the crested form of the Royal Fern, and a wide selection of ivies, some used as ground cover and some climbing and hiding the trunks of dead trees while others are to be found on the walls or in troughs. All these plants provide winter interest, as do the conifers, among which are to be found a young but already coning *Abies koreana*, *Picea breweriana*, the deciduous *Taxodium distichum* for autumn colour and *Metasequoia glyptostroboides*.

An attractive weeping Willow-leaved Pear is the only lawn specimen; it shows to advantage against the dark background of the wood and is underplanted with winter aconites on the longest vista from the house, east to west.

The house terrace is the most formally planted part of the garden, while walls are used to provide protection for tender plants such as the Sacred Bamboo, *Nandina domestica*, *Cytisus battandieri*, *Myrtus communis tarentina*, white berried, *Trachelospermum asiaticum*, with fragrant tubular flowers, and *Geranium maderense*.

The paving stones are interplanted with thymes and the low wall that separates the terrace from the lawn carries shade-loving plants on its northern side and sun-loving on the southern, as well as a wide variety in the wall itself.

Although many ericaceous plants are grown, especially in the three small peat beds in a clearing in the wood, few heathers are to be found; however, a 1.5 × 1.5 m (5 × 5 ft) specimen of *Erica mediterranea* 'W.T. Rackcliff' is a delight and loved by bees, and *Erica ciliaris* 'Aurea' makes pools of colour changing from gold to russet in the winter months.

Where space is at a premium much use is made of tree trunks to support climbers such as *Rosa filipes* 'Kiftsgate', now some 9 m (30 ft) high, *Vitis coignetiae*, probably the most spectacular of all vines, *Parthenocissus henryana*, with red autumn foliage, *Hydrangea petiolaris*, the golden hop *Humulus lupulus* 'Aureus' and an especially beautiful white *Clematis montana* that cascades from the top of a 15 m (50 ft) Scots Pine for all the world like a foaming waterfall when in full flower at the beginning of June. Other clematis in the garden are *C. chrysocoma*, soft pink, *C.c. sericea* (*spooneri*), *C. orientalis*, with 'orange peel' petals, and *C. tangutica* of the silky seed pods. *Muehlenbeckia complexa*, with foliage amusingly roundish, oblong or fiddle-shaped, rambles up a trellis on the house wall, while *Celastrus orbiculatus* displays its golden leaves and golden and scarlet spangled fruits on the loggia wall.

The dense shade on the east side of the house drive supports daffodils, then a carpet of bluebells followed by purple honesty and foxgloves, azaleas underplanted with *Claytonia sibirica*, rose pink flowered. Then, after various forms of elder have flowered and fruited, the autumn and winter months are lit by the silver honesty heads and the evergreen leaves of hellebores, of which this garden has a good collection. It will be noted that this is an all-year-round garden without bedding plants or bedding roses. Much of the material is propagated using a cold frame and every plant plays its part in the overall scheme and design.

Lister Park

City of Bradford Metropolitan Council

On Manningham Lane, Bradford, on A6037 Bradford-Shipley road. Open at all times. Bought for the city in 1870 for £40,000 from Samuel Cunliffe Lister, who was later created Baron Masham. A public park of some 22 ha (55 acres) of ornamental gardens, lake, rock gardens and woodland, situated 145 m (475 ft) above sea level on heavy loam over millstone grit. Average annual rainfall 830 mm (33 in.). Staff of 12.

During the summer months Lister Park is probably one of the finest examples in England of Victorian bedding-out at its best and most colourful, laid out like a great, many-tinted carpet in front of the Cartwright Memorial Hall (an art museum), itself a typical piece of Victorian architecture.

It is estimated that scores of thousands of plants are raised annually for use in this fine display which includes an intricate example (the pattern changes yearly) of carpet bedding into which the many low-growing plants of various coloured foliages are assembled to make a definite picture. There is also a floral clock.

Infinite patience is needed by the gardeners in planting out and every encouragement is provided for the display of their artistic temperaments, as for instance in the delicate and appealingly scalloped and 'embroidered' edging to the beds with such low-growing plants as the dwarf form of *Chrysanthemum parthenium aureum*.

Now in the process of being tidied up is the almost 100 year old 'Botanic Garden', which runs gently downhill, sheltered by edging woodland, from the top of the park for some 135 m (450 ft). A large heather bed features at the wicket gate entrance and the various beds and rockeries divided by intriguing pathways are further separated by specimen trees and shrubs including the tricoloured *+Laburnocytisus adamii, Cercis siliquastrum*, the Judas Tree, not really a tree for the north, *Robinia pseudoacacia*, the False Acacia, *Catalpa bignonioides*, the Indian Bean Tree, many variegated hollies, the Strawberry Tree *Arbutus unedo*, the feathery foliaged tamarisk, the Tulip Tree, *Liriodendron tulipifera*, maples in variety, a mulberry and one of the chestnuts, unnamed, which bears small, deeply dentated leaves and both flowers and small fruit at the same time. Fennel, *Heracleum, Ligularia, Echinops* and *Yucca* give height and foliage form to the beds while large plants of *Euphorbia characias* (*wulfenii*), dogwoods and shrub roses clothe the bareness of trunks.

A fast running stream provides a cool haunt for ferns, Asiatic *Primula* species and *Astilbe* and, at the lower end of the garden, falls sparkingly over giant rocks modelled to represent Thornton Force, one of the spectacular falls at Ingleton in Ribblesdale. In the mature tree walks opportunity is being taken to clear out much of the old Victorian shrubbery patterning of laurels and *Aucuba* to give sun-dappled vistas through the glades.

Lotherton Hall

City of Leeds Council

1.6 km (1 mile) E of A1 at Aberford on B1217 Towton road. Open all year daily 10.30 am–6.15 pm or dusk. Small admission charge. Free car park; teas available in summer; dogs allowed. Edwardian house, garden and art collection given to Leeds by Sir Alvary and Lady Gasgoine in 1968. House with Gasgoine collection of furniture, Chinese ceramics, paintings, silver and jewellery also open. Twelfth-century chapel in grounds. Intimate Edwardian garden of 4 ha (10 acres), situated 60 m (200 ft) above sea level on a medium alkaline soil (pH 7) over magnesium limestone. Average annual rainfall 610 mm (24 in.). Staff of six.

Lotherton Hall gardens, on land that once formed part of the Saxon kingdom of Elmet, are the loving creation of the late Mrs L.G.D. Gasgoine, the mother of Sir Alvary, most probably with the advice and encouragement of her friend Miss Ellen Willmott, of *Genus Rosa* fame. The layout is gently evocative of pre-1914 England at its country house best, and although the land is perfectly flat, compartmented gardens relieve any monotony. Sheltering woodland all around and the south-facing aspect of the garden coupled with two high-walled sun-trap gardens keep it comparatively free from severe frosts and high winds.

A perambulation is well started from the house front, effectively covered with shrubs and climbers, a large *Choisya ternata, Clematis montana rubens, Garrya elliptica*, a fine flourishing specimen of the large flowered *Magnolia grandiflora* and an extensive *Pyracantha*. In high summer the balustraded wall on the house lawn is a symphony in blue with a tangle of *Clematis viticella*, and *C. patens* 'Nelly Moser' and below a close planted border of *Agapanthus*. Also enjoying the warmth and shelter of this situation are the tender *Clematis armandii* and *Berberidopsis corallina*, a Chilean plant.

The large area directly in front of the hall is given over to a rose garden planted in pleasingly patterned box parterres and on the far side is a striking life-size bronze of the 'Paeony Priest', an Oriental figure riding on a flower bedecked bull and round him, appropriately, eastern paeonies and Japanese maples.

At right angles to the house facing east an avenue of veteran pyramidal yews by which are planted the Maidenhair Tree *Ginkgo biloba*, a Cut-leaved Beech and tamarisk leads the eye to a far vista point of a simple white summerhouse backed by forest trees.

Next go through the great battlemented yew hedge into the rose garden, walled on two sides and with a large recessed seat in the back wall, a veritable sun trap. Relishing this warmth and shelter, on the lawn grows a vigorous *Eucalyptus gunnii*, the Handkerchief Tree, *Davidia involucrata*, and *Magnolia denudata*. Enjoying even more shelter on the surrounding brickwork is as good a collection of wall plants as will be found in the county – *Hydrangea sargentiana*, with large, velvety leaves, *Xanthoceras sorbifolium*, with Horse Chestnut-like flowers, *Azara petiolaris*, fragrant and early flowering, the Mexican Orange, *Choisya ternata*, the New Zealander *Sophora tetraptera*, with curious beaded seed pods and drooping clusters of yellow flowers in May, the late flowering *Indigofera heterantha* (*gerardiana*) with racemes of rose coloured flowers and elegant foliage, the tender and normally southern grown *Lonicera splendida*, wisteria, a large tree of the Himalayan *Buddleia colvilei*, with large, tubular, rose coloured flowers, *B. globosa* of the miniature orange coloured and shaped blooms and a large *Drimys winteri*, fragrant ivory white flowered in May. *Mahonia lomariifolia*, with a tender reputation, has grown almost into a tree. In the borders in front are lilies including *Eremurus*, the Foxtail Lily and a collection of Day Lilies, heliotrope of the sweetest scent and the more interesting mints such as Eau de Cologne, the Ginger Mint, *Mentha × gentilis* 'Variegata' and the pungent purple leaved sage *Salvia officinalis* 'Purpurascens'. There is a row of cherry trees along the far side of this garden of sun, scent and rare wall plants.

Through a wrought iron gate in the far wall there is the William and Mary garden, created before the First World War, a gem of intimate garden layout with its spirally cut box, its sunken fish pond and its two small bronze statuettes with herbs and ground-smothering plants covering the paving. By the wide steps down to pool level there are beautifully carved Italian-style fruit baskets in stone. A border under another mellow brick wall here gives colour at two seasons with plantings of botanical tulips and large clumps of *Nerine bowdenii.* Through another decorative ironwork gate set in the dry limestone wall which bounds the garden on the east, the eye is led down a young lime tree avenue to a classical temple brought from nearby Parlington Hall. As a backdrop to this largely paved garden the walls are again notable for their rare climbers, unusual for the north. On the south-facing wall is a large *Clematis chrysocoma sericea* (*spooneri*), the side wall bearing such treasures as *Actinidia chinensis* as well as the tricolour leafed *A. kolomikta*; also *Akebia quinata* and *A. trifoliata,* the one with rosy and the other with dark purple racemes of flowers and both with curious violet coloured, sausage-shaped fruits. The genus *Clematis* is well represented here with winter flowering *C. balearica,* fern leafed and greenish flowered, the early flowering *C. tangutica,* with bearded seed pods, and the tender evergreen *C. armandii.* Not often seen hereabouts is the evergreen *Holboellia coriacea,* with flowers in terminal clusters of purple and, later, fruits in purplish pods, as well as *Ribes speciosum,* the flowering currant with fuchsia-like flowers, and the quite tender *Lardizabala biternata,* which bears chocolate-purple and white flowers very early in the year to be followed by edible sausage-shaped fruits. On the corner of the lawn here is a large specimen of *Viburnum rhytidophyllum,* its leaves dark green and corrugated on top, grey tomentosed beneath.

Leaving the formal gardens we come to the sunken rock garden, constructed in 1912 and now overgrown, and to get there the path leads by the graves of the family dogs under the trees. Winding paths sunk between rocky outcrops show the heathers and other acid-loving plants at eye level while ferns and *Peltandra alba,* the White Arrow Arum, fill the recessed spaces at path level. In the well defined ha-ha ditch, partly filled with peaty soil, are scores of the giant cow parsley *Heracleum mantegazzianum,* candelabra primulas, astilbes and the blue poppy *Meconopsis betonicifolia.* To the right of the rock garden is a brick floored tennis court, one of the first to be built, from the far side of which is a pastoral view over the Plain of York.

In the woodland planting at the rear of the rock garden, on the way back to the formal garden area, are the Mount Etna Broom *Genista aetnensis,* the pineapple-scented broom *Cytisus battandieri* and, planted appropriately in a thicket of bamboo, the Chusan Palm, *Trachycarpus fortunei.*

A most unusual feature in the greenhouses in the service area at the rear of the formal gardens, is a recently created Japanese temple where against an eye-jangling selection of reds and greens an eighteenth-century bronze Japanese figure stands on dragons overlooking water tanks in which lilies and aquatic plants grow. The sides of the tanks are paved and bordered with low stone tables on which stand enormous shallow dishes, the receptacles for erect growing rushes and other spiring plants. Next door a vivarium makes use of the old greenhouse range in a different way and outside aviaries built into the tree studded kitchen garden area contain a goodly collection of exotic birds.

Nostell Priory

National Trust

Some 10 km (6 miles) SE of Wakefield on A638. Open regularly during spring and summer: Easter Saturday to 10 October, Wednesdays, Saturdays and Sundays and Bank Holidays; from 1 August to second Sunday in September every day. For hours see current issue of National Trust *Properties Open*. The house, by James Paine (built 1745–50), the home of Lord St Oswald, who gave it and the gardens to the Trust in 1954, is also open and fine Adam state rooms, Chippendale furniture, Etruscan pottery and bronzes, tapestries and paintings can be seen. Ornamental gardens of 12 ha (30 acres) in parkland of 120 ha (300 acres), situated 60 m (200 ft) above sea level on poor, dry, light, acid soil over millstone grit. Only partly protected from strong winds by surrounding woodlands. Average annual rainfall 660 mm (26 in.). Staff of two and occasional help.

There are two separate plans for the layout of the Nostell landscape, one, dated 1731, by Joseph Perfect, almost certainly one of the family of Perfect who were well known nurserymen in Pontefract in the eighteenth century, and the other, of the early 1730s, by Stephen Switzer. The latter refers to an early ha-ha wall and a dam for the natural lake. Present research attributes the initial layout to Switzer.

Before one enters the pleasure gardens proper, from the east front of the Palladian house there is a vista up a grand avenue between elms backed with thick woodland underplanted with rhododendrons, as wide as the house and 1.6 km (1 mile) long. Cattle graze in the hazy distance and on the horizon a glimpse is caught of the surrounding, predominantly coal-mining, areas. It is almost unbelievable that so much greenery is here in this heavily built up West Riding conurbation of coal pits, pit townships and towns, and that the whole place except the house itself is undercut with active coal-mine workings.

South-east of the house is the tall clock turret and cupola of the Adam stable block and, passing by it on the path to the west, in front of the pillared and stepped terrace of Nostell we come by an ironwork gate to the way down to the 4.5 ha (11 acre) natural lake seen from the top of the steep wooded bank. On the windswept dry bank below the woodland which features some tall, splendid Copper Beeches, are planted *Ulex europaeus,* the Common Gorse, *Hippohae rhamnoides,* the Sea Buckthorn, and *Leycesteria formosa.* On the right of the steeply descending path in shrubbery bordering the woodland are *Skimmia japonica, Rhododendron ponticum* and *Viburnum.* As the path flattens out to go round the end of the lake the background is of lilacs, Mountain Ash, laburnums and sloes, *Prunus spinosa,* and a cascade spills the lake overflow into the lower lake, a favourite haunt of fishermen.

Looking up the broad expanse of the lake the eye is stopped by a three-arched bridge built by a neighbouring Yorkshire squire, Sir George Savile, in 1761. It is so romantically placed and screened by trees that it is hard to believe that this is the bridge which carries the main road traffic from Wakefield to Doncaster.

It also breaks the view of the lake, which continues at the far side.

The east side of the lake is carpeted with daffodils in the spring, under fine mature beeches, Sweet Chestnuts, Scots Pines and more *Rhododendron ponticum.* The path by the far, west side of the lake is bordered with new plantings of Mollis azaleas and *Hypericum calycinum,* backed by copses of old rhododendrons. By the pleasant lakeside path there are old cherries, *Gunnera manicata,* several fine Cedars of Lebanon and clumps of the pink flowering *Rhododendron* 'Pink Pearl' with blooms 'as big as a breadloaf' according to the head gardener, large bushes of *Skimmia,* full of shining red berries, *Cornus alba* 'Sibirica', the Westonbirt Dogwood, *Azaleodendron* 'Govenianum', underplanted with *Polygonum affine* 'Donald Lowndes', whose dark green leaves turn russet brown for winter. A newly planted bed quite near the bridge, on a slope, carries *Bergenia* in variety, *Rubus* 'Tridel', ferns and a collection of low-growing rhododendrons. A tall, mature Tulip Tree, *Liriodendron tulipifera,* Silver Birch, a fine cedar, a Cut-leaved Beech and a *Malus pumila* form the tree pattern round here.

To our right and at right angles to the lakeside walk the path climbs to a pedimented Gothic arch with two large recesses in its interior, probably for seats, which leads into a sunken glade, created many years ago out of a quarry, the rough face of which is the western boundary of this delightful spot. Almost immediately we come across a natural amphitheatre of grass, once the old cockpit. On the other side of the path is a giant, gnarled Holm Oak with a seat round its massive bole. This sequestered, almost secret garden is enclosed on the right by beech and oak. By the path is a very large *Pyrus salicifolia*, while *Magnolia* × *soulangiana* and its varieties light up the glade in spring along with the brighter colours of hybrid rhododendrons among which are the deep reds of 'Handsworth Scarlet' and 'Pink Pearl'.

The glade opens out now, after another ancient Holm Oak has been passed, into planted lawns dotted with more hybrid rhododendrons, maples planted to give colour both in spring and autumn, *Pieris japonica* and *Mahonia*. The tall quarry face to the left carries a screen of beeches, sycamore and yew on its top, rhododendrons clamber up the face and at its foot is a border of hostas, astilbes, mixed hybrid lilies, *Hemerocallis*, bamboos and the ornamental sea thistle, *Eryngium*.

Now a curving path leads through an avenue of magnolias, a delightful conceit, to a 'Gothic' Menagerie Garden House, certainly worked on by Robert Adam in 1776, for the menagerie keeper, the quarry walls around being at that time the back walls of the animal enclosures. What could well have been a Tudor mound, or the re-creation of one (Switzer did mention 'ye mount in ye Wildernesse' in his plan), is to the right of the Menagerie House. To the right also *Hydrangea petiolaris* is interestingly used to climb round a stone pedestal. Clambering over the now romantic 'ruin' are honeysuckles, climbing roses and in its shelter, *Magnolia grandiflora*. Behind the building is what appears to be a low entrance in a hillside. This was the entrance to an eighteenth-century ice house filled from the lake in winter through a trap door at the top of the artificial hill. Around on the lawns are Mollis azaleas and a particularly pleasing copse of rhododendrons with white flowering ones surrounding a deep red variety.

The path leads upwards and out of the cockpit and Menagerie Garden House garden by the white dell on the right, a natural depression, quite shaded and providing a genial home for the mock orange, the snow white blossoms of the blackthorn, white flowering hydrangeas, *Spiraea arguta*, white comfrey, snowdrops, white narcissi and ferns, all framed by a screen of ghostly Silver Birches at the top of the hollow.

We leave the dell to join the long path down to the lake, a massed rhododendron walk, where the plantings are old, massive and dense against a backdrop of shining large-boled beeches.

For the historically minded gardener the walled kitchen garden area to the south-east of the house is worth a visit to see its flued walls and the hooks and rails used to hang drapes as frost protection over early fruit. In what was once the vegetable garden are to be found growing the 'Nostell Priory Roses', a commercial venture of Lord St Oswald, who has won many top awards at northern shows. There is also an Adam-designed Needle's Eye gate, once an approach to the house from Pontefract, a huge pyramid with an arch pierced through it.

Oakworth Park

City of Bradford Metropolitan Council

On A629 Keighley-Stanbury road.

Oakworth Municipal Park was once the mansion and grounds of a notable West Riding textile magnate and pioneer, Sir Isaac Holden (1807–97). Only the pillared portico of the house is still standing, the site now a large bowling green, but around this are the remains of what was originally a quite remarkable Victorian fantasy garden.

Here are curious rock and stucco grotto walks, hanging gardens, caves and cave-like promenades all paved with Italian mosaic work. If the visitor passes the main entrance to the park he can enter the grounds by one of these grotto caves coming out at the side of the bowling green. The grotto work, still to be seen and marvelled at, was started in 1864; it took a band of French and Italian workmen ten years to complete.

At the rear of the lawn can be seen, now waterless but still impressive, the intricately worked stucco cascade complete with 'stalactites' and a summer retreat which once had as a window the film of water from the cascade. Following the grotto walk round under rock and stucco arches what appears to be a giant fossilized tree trunk is reached. This contains in its interior a spiral staircase leading to a raised walk, once the scene of hanging gardens and more water and cascades, which can still be walked on.

A summerhouse at the end of the walk has a stucco imitation timber-work façade and furniture. In one corner of the summerhouse is a small grotto open to the sky. The walls are cast in tree branches with footholes for ferns and other shade-loving plants. At one time skilfully arranged mirrors in both grotto walls and summerhouse gave strange optical effects.

In the heyday of the house a winter garden, domed and in glass, 0.2 ha ($\frac{1}{2}$ acre) in extent and costing £30,000 to build, was the pride of its owner with its waterfalls, palms and tropical plantings. Electricity, then in its early days, was used to light the grotto walks and winter garden at night.

As a local newspaper scribe wrote: 'The remains of this luxuriously elegant Victorian Garden are still sufficient to show the money, the endeavour, the artistry which wealthy owners would throw into the surroundings of their quite modest mansions.'

Temple Newsam

City of Leeds Council

---

8 km (5 miles) SE of centre of Leeds via York road (A64) on to Selby road (A63), fork right (signposted) at Irwin Arms on private road to house. Garden always open, house open all year round daily 10.30 am–6.15 pm or dusk. Free car park; meals in stables restaurant; dogs allowed. Historic Tudor-Jacobean house with collection of period furniture, fine art and one of the best collections of decorative art in the country. 'Capability' Brown landscape, parkland, woodland, rhododendron and walled gardens situated 76 m (250 ft) above sea level on heavy loam and woodland soils, land gently undulating on E slope. Average annual rainfall 690 mm (27 in.). Staff of 20.

Temple Newsam, the Hampton Court of the north, in its present form was the work of Sir Arthur Ingram in 1630. It took the place of the former manor of the Lennox family, built in the early sixteenth century and the birthplace in 1545 of Lord Darnley, who became the husband of Mary Queen of Scots and father of James I. In 1922 Temple Newsam together with its some 370 ha (920 acres) of land was sold to Leeds Corporation by the Hon. Edward Wood (later Lord Irwin) for the nominal sum of £35,000.

The first known reference to the gardens dates from 1535 when Sir George Darcy wrote to his father, 'The garthens at Temple Newsam could not be more out of frame. Pray send me some good garthener who has skill of the hop garth.'

Despite several large open-cast coal bites into this delightful and extensive landscape, Temple Newsam still undeniably bears the marks of Brown (his plans were dated 1762) in the undulating ground, the clumping and verging of trees and the open temple feature (*c*.1765). A long perfectly straight eastern avenue woodland walk – over a bridge and ponds by William Etty (1712–15) – is through masses of later planted rhododendrons to the village of Colton.

The surroundings of the great house with its inscription running round the three sides of the balustrading and reading 'All Glory and Praise be given to God the Father, the Son and Holy Ghost on High, Peace on Earth, Goodwill towards Men, Honour and true Allegiance to our gracious King, Loving Affection amongst his Subjects, Health and Plenty be within this House', are, at the moment of writing, being brought more into keeping with its period by the construction of an enclosing terrace walk, a Jacobean garden with box edge parterres, ponds, pleached lime walk, an Elizabethan knot garden and a brick surface maze in the great square forecourt. From the south-west corner of the house can be seen the remains of a Tudor mount.

Unusual breeds of cattle and sheep, including Highland and Long Horn cattle, Jacob's sheep and, it is hoped, deer, last shot at Temple Newsam in 1918, will be brought back into the parkland.

Walking eastward from the house down the long winding ha-ha walk to the small lake, notice the Sphinx gateway designed by Lord Burlington and erected by Brown *c*.1768. This walk is ablaze at rhododendron time with the massed colours of hardy hybrid varieties and with large drifts of Mollis and Ghent azaleas on the sloping parkland opposite. Tall laburnums at the rear of the rhododendrons give a beautiful effect. On the right of the walk is an unusual 'dwarf' Cedar of Lebanon. In the car park at the left, and by the top of the rhododendron walk, 50 or so different kinds of wild flowers have been sown.

The walk leads gently down to the small lake and the rustic bridge over it to the walled garden, but before crossing enjoy the colour of the far lakeside planting, a shining mass of Golden Laurel kaleidoscoped with the high colourings of Asiatic *Primula* species and other bog and moisture-loving plants.

The walled garden of 1.2 ha (3 acres), sloping southwards, is filled centrally with a large planting of roses, and the old brick path running down the middle between yew hedges is punctuated half-way by an Elizabethan-style pool with fish. Between two long brick walls, marking the entrance to the garden, are two long 73 m (240 ft) borders which herald the spring at Temple Newsam by the glory of a massive planting of vari-coloured polyanthus on the one side and, on the other, wallflowers and polyanthus. Both old and new roses fill the beds in the rose garden, among the old favourites being 'Etoile de Hollande' and 'Mrs G.A. Van Rossem', which rub shoulders with more modern Floribundas such as 'Mrs Sam McGredy' and 'Frensham'.

A year-round feature at Temple Newsam is the long lean-to greenhouse where 'climbing' pelargoniums completely cover the back wall with eye-stabbing bloom. A paved walk, the whole length of the greenhouse, has been tastefully planted with a great variety of plants, shrubs and climbers as well as pot plants in season, such as *Cineraria, Calceolaria,* daffodils, *Primula,* tulips, the long lasting *Begonia* species, among them *B. haageana, B. manicata* and the strikingly coloured leaves of *B. rex,* the Bottle Brush *Callistemon citrinus, Grevillea* species, camellias, Indica azaleas, ferns in variety and many ivies. The glass sides and roof are decorated with interesting climbers including *Jasminum officinale, Senecio speciosus,* the strange spidery looking *Passiflora quadrangularis,* the Cape Honeysuckle, *Tecomaria capensis,* and species and cultivars of the bell flowered *Abutilon.* At the entrance to the display is a natural cactus garden prominently planted with large specimens of *Aloe* and *Agave.*

The wide herbaceous borders round the walled garden are stocked with a fine assortment of old cottage garden perennials and annuals, while the walls provide colour and interest with their many climbing plants.

York Gate, Adel

Mrs S.B. Spencer and Robin Spencer Esq

On the outskirts of Leeds in Back Church Lane, Adel, behind Adel church and off A660 Leeds-Otley road. Open occasionally for charity or by appointment. Tea and biscuits served; no dogs. This most unusually designed plantsman's garden is situated 120m (400ft) above sea level on a gentle S slope on well drained, heavy to light, sandy loam over sand and sandstone. Average annual rainfall 710mm (28in.).

A most successful partnership between Mrs Spencer, the plantswoman, and her son Mr Robin Spencer, a surveyor by profession and the 'architect' of the garden design, has created over some 20 years, since the Spencers went to York Gate to an old orchard and a natural stream, one of the most attractive small gardens in the county.

In this just under 0.4 ha (1 acre) site, made to appear twice as big by use of skilful compartmenting, full of eye-catching features and interesting plants, there is something for everyone's taste. It is, as Mr Spencer says, on a scale almost minute, but so nicely judged that it could be a Hidcote divided by ten.

It contains, almost incredibly for its size, an orchard with a central stream from which you pass under an arbour to a miniature pinetum, a small pond with ducks, a folly, a nut walk, a raised canal, a fern border, one of the most outstandingly picturesque herb gardens you could find, a grass *allée*, a paved garden, a greenhouse, a kitchen garden and a grey and silver garden. The Spencers have an eclectic collection of antique stone, bronze and lead ornaments and statuary and each item is placed where it is most effective and appropriate. Such is the overall design of the garden that its differing aspects are come upon unexpectedly by cleverly contrived openings and walks.

The focal point for the front of the house is the raised drive edged by rounded yews above a ha-ha wall, the orchard pond and the tree and shrub studded lawn beyond it. In a sheltered corner by the entrance gate *Robinia pseudoacacia* 'Frisia' has shot away to a sizable tree in a short time. On the wall nearby a 'Conference' pear is espaliered and shares the space with the deep red rose 'Allen Chandler'. The pond is dominated by a huge nineteenth-century cast-iron jardinière filled with 400 crocus in four varieties which bloom from November to March, the whole carpeted and veiled with a drape of ivies.

A nineteenth-century barrow with a 'load' of pelargoniums and fibrous rooted begonias stands under the house terrace wall during the summer. Under the terrace wall, too, are to be found an uncommon young Weeping Wellingtonia, *Sequoiadendron giganteum* 'Pendulum', and the first of a quite extensive collection of *Phormium* species and

---

1. House
2. Garage
3. White & Silver Garden
4. Kitchen Garden
5. Barrow & Potting Shed
6. Summer House
7. Herb Garden
8. Fern Border
9. Paved Garden
10. Rose Beds
11. Old Orchard
12. Water Garden
13. Miniature Pinetum
14. Paving
15. Canal
16. Topiary
17. Iris Border
18. Kitchen Garden
19. Nut Walk
20. Folly
21. Duck Pond
22. Arbour
23. Pines
24. Allée
25. Field
26. Dell

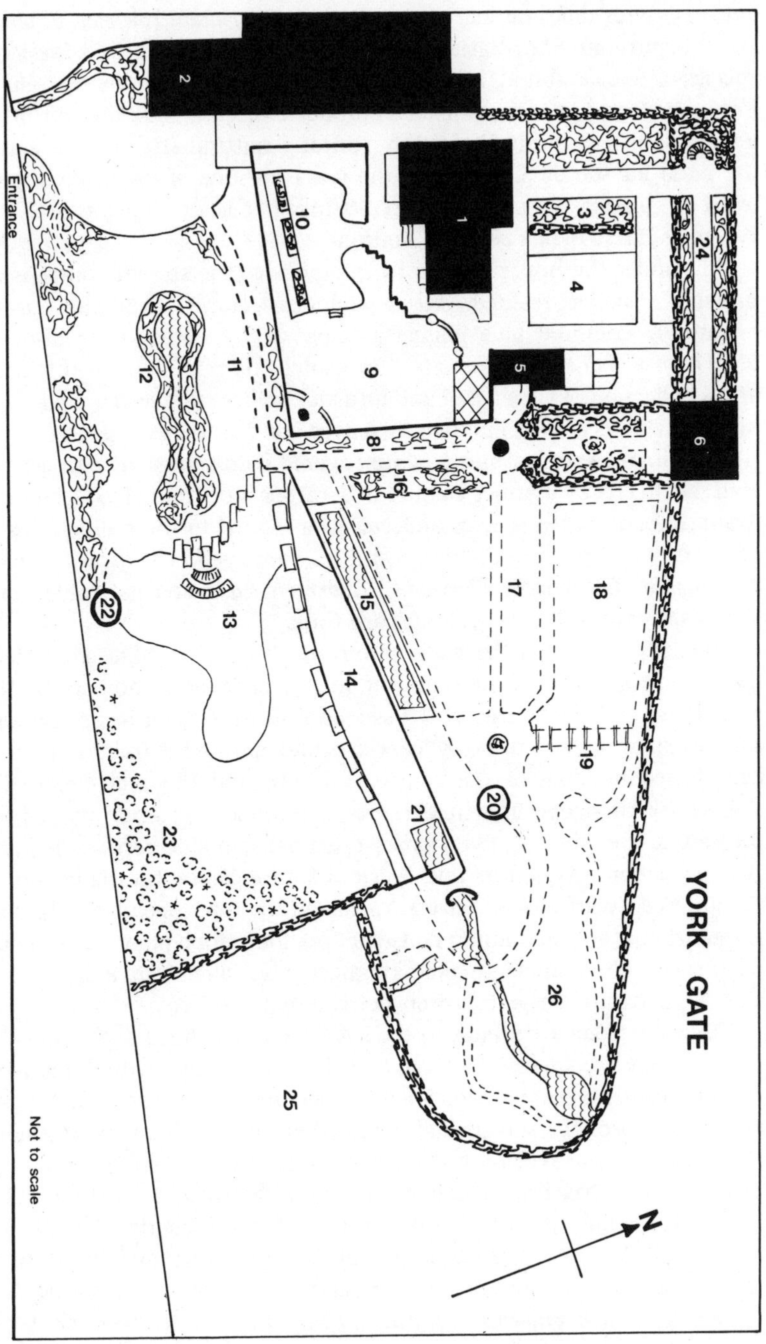
YORK GATE
Entrance
Not to scale
N
1
2
3
4
5
6
7
8
9
10
11
12
13
14
15
16
17
18
19
20
21
22
23
24
25
26

cultivars with differing leaf variegations – *Phormium colensoi, P. tenax, P.t.* 'Purpureum', *P.t.* 'Variegatum' and *P.t.* 'Veitchii'. Various *Rodgersia* species are also found here, as well as the moisture-loving Asiatic *Primula* species, a rare Chilean bamboo, *Chusquea couleou*, and other waterside plants lining the swiftly running natural stream as it leaves the pond for the duck pond. On the lawn are one of the original pear trees, a golden cypress, a three-trunked *Cedrus deodara* and the Weeping Birch *Betula pendula* 'Youngii'.

Still under the house terrace running above the stream course is an unusual espalier trained *Cedrus atlantica glauca*, throwing out its beautifully coloured blue foliage in long straight lines. Here also are *Viburnum × bodnantense*, precious for its delicate pink flowers in winter, and a collection of variegated and unusual hollies such as *Ilex aquifolium* 'Crispa' with its curved and twisted leaves and *I.a.* 'Ferox', the Hedgehog Holly, whose upper leaf surfaces are covered with spines. Also under the wall, sheltered by hardier plants, is a rather uncommon collection of *Arum*, the cultivated species and varieties related to the native Cuckoo Pint, *A. italicum, A.i.* 'Pictum', and a rare yellow flowering one, *A. creticum*. The winter flowering *Viburnum tinus* and its stable mate *V.t.* 'Variegatum' flower well at York Gate.

Towards the end of the walk here is an unusual sundial which tells the time in all parts of the world by means of several gnomen. By the duck pond and the runnel of the second natural stream is a stone font supported by three curiously carved stone gargoyles rescued from a demolished building in the centre of Leeds, and the half circle of a Copper Beech hedge in whose recess is a stone seat and, planted for interest in the shelter, two bonsai specimens in fine terracotta pots: *Acer palmatum* 'Dissectum' and *Cedrus atlantica glauca*. On the far side is the gnarled dwarf willow *Salix × boydii*. On the top slope above the seat is the arbour, an uncommon construction, four stone pillars holding an open roof of three ancient oaken kingposts also saved from a demolition site. A yucca in a large cast-iron pot is a feature here.

The view from the arbour to the left is to a path lined with conically cut flat-topped hollies and a large ball-shaped Portugal Laurel and over the miniature pinetum in which all the specimen trees have been planted in a 'floor' of cobbles screened at the northern end with an arrangement of 'driftwood', the skeletal roots of large trees from a Scottish bog now well above the tree line, which experts put at between 2,000 and 3,000 years old. While almost all the trees are fairly recently planted and mostly still low growing, their variety is surprising and interesting, with a specimen of *Pinus aristata*, the oldest living tree, heading the list. Others are *Picea omorika* 'Pendula', *Picea breweriana*, with 'skirts' of foliage, the Umbrella Pine, *Sciadopitys verticillata*, *Pinus strobus* 'Contorta', with twisted needles, *Pinus strobus* 'Nana', *Pinus sylvestris* 'Viridis Compacta', of vivid grass green foliage, *P. nigra* 'Pygmaea', the small blue foliaged forms of the Colorado Spruce *Picea pungens* 'Spekii' and *P.p.* 'Moorheimii', the upward cone bearing *Abies concolor* 'Wattezii' and *A. koreana*, with many dwarf conifers underplanted and, to add scale, taller specimens of *Pinus wallichiana*, the Bhutan Pine, and *P. monticola*, the Western White Pine. By the lower pond is the other Weeping Willow, the umbrella-like Kilmarnock Willow *Salix caprea* 'Pendula' and the *Cunninghamia lanceolata*, which looks like a Monkey Puzzle tree. Terminating the garden scene is the dell where under Silver Birch, bulbs riot in the spring. To the left of the dell is the folly, a shingle-roofed open structure at the intersection of several paths, and nearby are a *Taxodium distichum*, the Swamp Cypress, a Weeping Purple Beech, *Fagus sylvatica* 'Purpurea Pendula', and *Enkianthus campanulatus*, which blossoms well for this cold climate. From the folly a path leads to a triangular paeony bed heavily planted with daffodils, its central feature being a large mature Tree Paeony *P. lutea ludlowii*. Just before this is reached is the nut walk, a pleached alley of hazels underplanted with a thick carpet of the large flowering snowdrop 'Arnott's Seedling' and terminated by a wooden gate looking outwards over rolling countryside.

In the borders here is a collection of *Eryngium*, the Sea Thistles. Then the raised canal is reached, 18 × 1.8 m (60 × 6 ft), inhabited by carp and orf under the water lilies and terminated by a stone dolphin fountain with a screen behind of a large Corkscrew Hazel, *Corylus avellana* 'Contorta'. A right turn leads to the fern walk with a fine collection on the left and an attractively topiary yew hedge on the right with tall pyramids rising from its flat top. The fern walk leads straight into the herb garden with the kitchen garden to the left, the path between being stone-paved and bordered with an extensive collection of irises.

The herb garden, enclosed by tall yew hedges and terminated by a simple stone-built summerhouse, faintly classical in outline with its pillared portico, is a lesson in layout. Its spirally cut and rounded box in classical pots adds poise and dignity to the plantings, in box edged compartments, of the different coloured varieties of mint, marjoram, sage, the blue of rue, the greys of rosemary and the infinite variety of scents and foliage form. In the summerhouse are a few of the many bonsai which are a feature of the garden – one, a juniper, being at least 120 years old. In the side of the summerhouse another surprise awaits, for the door here leads into a narrow beech hedged grass *allée* up which the eye is drawn irresistibly to a stone ball perched on a pillar, which turns out to be another sundial.

But to return to the entrance to the herb garden, the path leads past the decorative potting shed and barrow store into another kitchen garden and, lined by a Copper Beech hedge on one side and a Common Beech one on the other, the white and silver garden with a millstone paved central path (only one of the many uses of millstones in the garden). Here clever planting really does give a 'lit up' effect, with white delphiniums, *Dianthus* 'White Ladies', *Senecio* 'Sunshine', the giant silver thistle *Onopordon acanthium*, pampas grass, *Artemisia, Helichrysum, Ballota pseudodictamnus*, variegated foliage irises and ornamental grasses. The raised walls Mr Spencer has built at the rear of the house are 'show benches' for many more bonsai.

Entered from the path by the potting shed is the delightful paved garden in which are displayed more specimen bonsai and many stone troughs and ornamental stone containers with *Sempervivum* in variety, the paved floor being filled with spreading, mounded plantings of ground-covering subjects. Under another old pear tree and near an *Abies koreana* is some decorative white garden furniture, elegant and somehow quite appropriate to this secluded corner. To the rear of this area is the lean-to greenhouse which houses a collection of *Echeveria*. It only remains to look at the house wall 'furnishings' and the small terrace filled with heathers and alpines. The wall on the eastern side is filled with a splendid espaliered *Pyracantha* and that on the front bears clematis and a *Magnolia grandiflora*, a bit shy in flowering, but flourishing all the same.

Index